Illegal Migration from Bangladesh

By the Same Author

- Naga Identity
- Small States Syndrome in India

About the Author

B.B. Kumar, M.A. (Hindi), M.Sc. (Chemistry), M.Sc., Ph.D. (Anthropology) is the Secretary, Astha Bharati, Delhi and the Editor of the quarterly journals, Dialogue and Chintan Srijan. He is Principal (Retd.) of Science College, Kohima and Sao Chang Government College, Tuensang. He was member of the Academic Council, Executive Council, University Court, College Development Council, Examination Committee, School Board of Physical Sciences, Board of Undergraduate Studies in Chemistry, Board of Pre-University Studies and more than a dozen committees of the North Eastern Hill University. He was Chairman of a Board of Studies and member of another one of Gandhigram Rural University.

Dr. Kumar remained associated with a large number of voluntary academic/ social service organizations as their founder President, Secretary and the member. He is founder member of India Central Asia Foundation, New Delhi. He has written/edited/co-authored 136 books and more than 100 papers/radio-talks.

Illegal Migration from Bangladesh

Editor

B.B. Kumar

ASTHA BHARATI, DELHI

CONCEPT PUBLISHING COMPANY, NEW DELHI-110059

Cataloging in Publication Data—DK
Courtesy: D.K. Agencies (P) Ltd. <docinfo@dkagencies.com>

National Seminar on Illegal Migration from Bangladesh (2001 : Delhi, India)
Illegal migration from Bangladesh / editor, B.B. Kumar.
p. cm.
Papers presented at the National Seminar on Illegal Migration from Bangladesh, held at Delhi during 21-22 February 2003.
Includes bibliographical references.
Includes index.
ISBN 8180692248

1. Illegal aliens—India—Congresses. 2. Illegal aliens—India, Northeastern—Congresses. 3. India—Emigration and immigration Congresses. 4. Bangladesh—Emigration and immigration—Congresses. 5. Bangladeshis—India—Congresses.
I. Kumar, B. B. (Braj Bihari), 1941- II. Title.

DDC 304.854 054 92 22

ISBN 81-8069-224-8

First Published 2006

Published and Printed by
Ashok Kumar Mittal
Concept Publishing Company
A/15-16, Commercial Block, Mohan Garden, New Delhi-110 059

Phones : 25351460, 25351794
Fax : 091-11-25357103
E-mail : publishing@conceptpub.com

for Astha Bharati, 26/501, East End Aptts.,
Mayur Vihar Phase I Extension, Delhi-110 096

Foreword

Insistence on excessive secrecy in all matters has been the hallmark of governance in India, irrespective of which political party is in power, whether at the centre or in the states. It may be pertinent to recall what Justice K.K. Mathew, quoting Justice Polak, stated in a Supreme Court case [1979 (3) SCC], "The secrecy system has become much less a means by which government protects national security than a means by which government safeguards its reputation, dissembles its purpose, buries its mistakes, manipulates its citizens, maximises its power and corrupts itself." The illegal migration from Bangladesh is one issue which brings out how true are these perceptive observations. Due to the conspiracy of silence of all political parties, in varying degrees, the issue, in spite of its serious social, political, economic, security, and law and order implications has not been permitted to come on the national agenda. If at all, it is viewed as a regional problem affecting the North-East and a few states. Against this background, the comprehensive discussion in this book of the various facets of this complex question needs to be widely and enthusiastically welcomed.

In analysing illegal migration from Bangladesh, it is necessary to take note of a few salient factors. The fact that there was considerable migration in Assam from erstwhile East Bengal, when it was a part of India, is important but cannot be a justification for the continuance of the same trend after independence. Illegal migration from East Pakistan and later Bangladesh, must be seen in the radically changed context of the partition of the country on the basis of the tenuous, totally mischievous and ill-conceived two-nation theory. Those in Bangladesh who are now advocating the spacious concept of *lebensraum* or living space ought to have paused and pondered on it before clamouring for creation of Pakistan. The fact that the Muslim League was making demands for other contiguous districts/parts of districts of Assam, Bengal and Bihar as a part of

East Pakistan can also hardly be lost sight of. The process of Islamisation being continued through illegal migration cannot be disassociated from this tragic history of the partition of the country. The mischievous ploy adopted by sham "secular" political parfies in India to give a communal colour to the question, therefore, needs to be exposed as nothing less than anti-national.

There have been repeated allegations over the years that successive Congress(I) governments in Assam had actively encouraged migration from Bangladesh. The record of CPI(M) government in West Bengal has been no better. Some political parties have unabashedly stood in the way of deletion of names of illegal migrants from the voters' list. Not too long ago, there was practically a revolt in the Assam Cabinet over the deletion of such names. Unfortunately even the BJP, the so-called fascist Hindu party, did not have the courage to take a principled stand on the concerned issues when it came to power at the centre. This reluctance was amply evident from a number of significant pointers. **First**, though the Working Group on Border Management appointed by the National Democratic Alliance (NDA) Government, of which I was the chairman, had made a recommendation that its report should be published to make the people aware of the critical issues pertaining to management of international borders, the report was not made public. **Second**, the government failed to issue an ordinance to repeal the Illegal Migrants (Determination by Tribunals) (IMDT) Act, which was yet another major recommendation of the Working Group. In fact, the BJP, which was the main constituent of the government, had itself repeatedly advocated the repeal of the Act when it was in opposition, presumably as only a political rhetoric. It is true that the NDA government did not have a majority in the Rajya Sabha. But, as was done in the case of enactment of the Prevention of Terrorism Act (POTA), a joint session of both the Houses could have been called to convert the Ordinance for repeal of the IMDT Act into an Act. The security implications of IMDT Act were no less significant than in the case of POTA. But, perhaps, the BJP too was worried about the combined impact on the Muslims of enactment of POTA and repeal of the IMDT Act. How is BJP different then than the Congress (I) and the other so-called sham "secular" political parties? **Third**, the concentration of *Madarsas* and mosques, set up with substantial foreign funding, in border areas whose demographic composition has undergone a radical change, is well documented. The NDA government failed to take any action to have this proliferation brought under close scrutiny of the concerned state and central agencies. No new law had to be passed for the purpose. The Foreign Contribution Regulation Act (FCRA), which has been rampantly misused by the government to harass non-governmental organisations (NGOs), has remained a dead letter so far as foreign contribution for spread of fundamentalist, religious and terrorist ideology is concerned. It is true that most of these foreign funds are received through *havala* transactions but a close watch on such transactions through various agencies could have curtailed the flow to some extent. As recommended by the Working Group, it could have been made mandatory that approval of district authorities would be necessary before establishing any places of worship or *Madarsas* in the border belt of about 10 kilometres. The mainstreaming of *Madarsas* and having state level boards to oversee their activities, at least in so far as border areas are concerned, is long over-due. But due to apprehension of inviting the ire of Muslims, political parties are reluctant to even talk of such matters, leave aside taking any action thereon. Needless to say, the process of Arabisation of Muslims is a factor which can be overlooked only at the peril of national security.

Major recommendations of the Working Group on management of the Bangladesh border, which were accepted by the Group of Ministers (GOM) of the NDA government, have remained without any energetic and time-bound actions though nearly five years have elapsed since then. The first was the adoption of the principle of one border one Force. This was meant to make the concerned Force, whether the Border Security Force (BSF), the Indo-Tibetan Border Police (ITBP) or the Assam Rifles, responsible and accountable squarely for their actions and inactions. Currently, since more than one Force is operating in the same area, there is often a tendency to pass the buck from one to the other. The second related recommendation, which too has been accepted by GOM, is to lay down clear and unambiguous criteria for judging the performance of each Force. This would enable, for example, making an assessment as to how effective has been the BSF in preventing illegal migration from across the border. The Working Group had recommended to distinguish between the Border Guarding Forces which are to be used exclusively for deployment on the border and the other paramilitary and police forces, such as the Central Reserve Police Force (CRPF), Railway Protection Force (RPF) and the Central Industrial Security Force (CISF), which are to be used for internal security duties. The Working Group had recommended a clear-cut policy announcement that Border Guarding Forces will not be withdrawn from the border, except in exceptional circumstances, and within a defined period, of say five years, steps will be taken to adequately augment the strength of the state and central police forces for internal security duties. There is no evidence to show that such time-bound action programme is being implemented by the centre with any firm public commitment. Yet another important recommendation was to have a no-man's land all along the border which can be fully sensitised. Currently, the most unnatural, man-made border between India and Bangladesh, drawn by Radcliff, sitting in his office, in just a few weeks, often runs through houses and divides them between the two countries. The cultivation of land is right upto the border with often neighbours tilling each other's land, whether he is a Bangladeshi or Indian. In such a situation, it is impossible to stop illegal migration and border-crossing in any sense of the term. Unfortunately, there is no political will to implement this recommendation. Yet another recommendation was that, due to the peculiar geographical features and reverine conditions, the border fencing in several stretches of Bangladesh border can hardly be effective to prevent illegal migration. While in some areas, border fencing would be effective, in some others it is a futile and wasteful expenditure and to rely on such fencing will be fool-hardy. It is not clear what steps are being taken to review the present policy and guard against such contingencies by other suitable measures. The Working Group had made a strong recommendation to substantially augment the water wing of the BSF to enable BSF to address the problem effectively. The GOM had concurred in it but there is no indication of the concrete steps taken so far. These are only a few illustrative examples of how the policies have continued to drift over the years, including during the NDA regime in Delhi. Looking to the pathological hatred of the constituents of the United Progressive Alliance (UPA) government for its predecessor, it will be a surprise if any of the major decisions of the NDA government on this subject are followed up vigorously.

A reference may be made to the efforts I made in my capacity as Union Home Secretary, way back in 1992, to bring this issue to the forefront and how they failed to make any headway. It was on 24 March 1992 that I convened the first ever meeting of the chief secretaries of the concerned states and the Union Territory of Delhi to discuss a package of measures which could be adopted on an all-India basis to deal with the frightening problem of illegal migration from Bangladesh. It came as a surprise to me that, even at the official level, there was reluctance on the part of some states, and particularly West Bengal and Bihar, to deal with the problem firmly. In spite of this, I pursued the matter further and persuaded the Union Home Minister to hold a meeting at his level. Accordingly, a meeting of the chief ministers was held on 28 September 1992 under the chairmanship of the Union Home Minister. The background note and the agenda prepared for the meeting were given wide publicity to create national awareness of the issues. The proposed programme of action included, among others, strengthening and modernisation of BSF, construction of border roads and fencing, strengthening of the Prevention of Infiltration of Foreigners (PIF) scheme and the Mobile Task Force (MTF) scheme, issue of identity cards to *bonafide* residents in border areas, organising a campaign from time to time for creating public awareness of the problem, keeping close watch on and plugging the avenues which provide protection to illegal migrants and ensuring punitive action thereon, safeguards against easy access to certain unintended benefits to illegal migrants, safeguards against the admission of illegal migrants or their wards into educational institutions, safeguards against their acquisition of immovable property, safeguards against inclusion of names in the voters' list, strict enforcement of protected area/restricted area orders, identifying villages prone to influx of illegal migrants, administrative and legal safeguards against employment of illegal migrants, and enactment of a central legislation for issue of identity cards. The major features of the proposed legislation were also circulated to the state governments for their comments. The background note had emphasised that "the threat posed by the illegal migrants to the economy and socio-cultural and political fabric of the country requires a "multi-pronged strategy". It is evident that "the problem of illegal migration needs to be tackled by formulating effective strategy jointly by the central and the state governments." It can be seen that the comprehensive proposals placed before the chief ministers' meeting were unexceptional and should have been readily endorsed by the chief ministers. But, I was in for another surprise. The chief ministers of West Bengal and Bihar were opposed to any such action plan being adopted at the meeting. The draft of the press note which was proposed to be issued did not meet with their approval. A great deal of persuasion was required on the part of the Union Home Minister to make them agree to the issue of the press note. He had to repeatedly urge that if a consensus on the subject was not arrived at, it will convey a very wrong message to the country on this very vital subject and weaken whatever efforts were being made at the time to contain the problem. Finally, reluctantly, the press communiqué was agreed upon for release but it was clear that the programme of action adopted at the meeting, for public consumption, would remain on paper. Nothing has changed over the last thirteen years since then and now the figure of illegal migrants from Bangladesh should be nearly 20 million.

As can be seen, the programme of action discussed as far back as 1992 included all the important elements that are crucial for tackling problem of illegal migration. They are being suggested all these years and also find a mention in the papers contained in this book. But, for want of political will, there has been no progress in respect of anyone of them so far. Neither has there been the pressure of public opinion which could have forced the governments to take the necessary steps. This is borne out by yet another significant pointer. The urgency of instituting a scheme for issue of identity cards to all *bonafide* residents is being talked about for years since independence. A pilot scheme for the issue of such cards was first sanctioned by the Central Government in 1986 for selected areas of the states of Gujarat and Rajasthan. Significantly, the North-Eastern states were not considered vulnerable enough to be covered in the pilot scheme. The objectives of the pilot scheme were to register *bonafide* residents, collect reliable information regarding the status of residents and to check the movement of visitors staying for over 30 days in the areas covered under the scheme. Subsequently, the states of Punjab and J & K also decided to implement the scheme in their border areas. The scheme was reviewed by the Committee of Secretaries in 1990 when it was decided to extend it to the border areas of all border states, in the first instance. Accordingly, the scheme was sanctioned for the border areas of Assam, Mizoram and Tripura in March 1991. The fact that illegal migration has continued unabated in spite of this scheme shows that it has remained on paper. The Ministry of Home Affairs (MHA) has got at least two comprehensive studies done, during the last decade, by reputed institutions to examine the feasibility and workability of the implementation of the scheme on an all India basis. In spite of this, the central legislation for issue of identity cards has not made any headway. Neither has any political party insisted on it being passed expeditiously. If such a legislation had been in force, infructuous expenditure on schemes initiated by various authorities for issue of identity cards such as the voter's identity card by the Election Commission of India, Permanent Account Number (PAN) by the income tax department, and Market Participant and Investor Identification Number (MAPIN) by SEBI (which has been held in abeyance pending further examination) could have been avoided.

Similar sad neglect is to be seen in respect of the preparation of the register of citizens. This scheme too has come up for discussion from time to time since independence but there has been no political will to implement it. If action had been taken on both these issues, India would not have found itself as helpless and vulnerable as at present. This shows the lack of foresight and resolve on the part of the political leadership of this country even in matters concerning national security.

The public interest litigation (PIL) praying for scrapping of the IMDT Act, which by any standard was a monstrosity and clearly undermined the interests of the country, could come up for final decision in the supreme court after a long delay of nearly five years. It is difficult to believe that such an ill-conceived and totally counter-productive legislation was a part of the Assam Accord which was supposed to address the problems faced by that state. This was yet another legislation which was passed by parliament without any scrutiny or application of mind on the basis of a brute majority of the ruling political party and is an eloquent commentary on the capability of that institution to function as the highest law-making forum in the country. The fact that this law could remain on the statute book for over two decades speaks volumes of the efficacy of the democratic processes and institutions in the country. The affidavits filed by the successive state and central governments too show how certain political parties have continued to woo the Muslims blatantly at the cost of national interest. The final decision of the apex court scrapping the IMDT Act is a matter of some satisfaction but, looking to the lack of commitment of the political parties to address the issue, one wonders whether this by itself will take us far. It would be recalled that the Shiv Sena-BJP coalition government in Maharashtra took up in about 1997-98 a programme to identify the Bangladeshi nationals in Mumbai and to have them deported. All necessary legal procedures under the Foreigners Act were followed, cases were instituted in courts and, thereafter, with the orders of the courts, action to proceed with the deportation of the illegal migrants was taken. When the Maharashtra police escorted the foreigners to Calcutta on way to the Bangladesh border, they were attacked by hooligans and had to face demonstrations by left-leaning and so-called "secular" political parties. The West Bengal police declined to give any help. There was a clamour in the "secular" media against the move of the Government of Maharashtra to identify and deport illegal migrants. Finally, the illegal migrants could not even be taken up to the Bangladesh border and eventually returned to Mumbai to live happily ever after! This clearly shows that unless there is public awareness of the gravity of the issue, there is hardly any possibility of change in the present stance of the political parties.

The over-all public apathy in matters pertaining to national security has been evident in other recent instances as well. The clamour for abolition of the Terrorist and Disruptive Activities Act (TADA) and later the Prevention of Terrorism Act (POTA) on the ground that these legislations were against the Muslims was ludicrous, to say the least. The mere fact that more Muslims were arrested and charged under these enactments than non-Muslims did not mean that the Acts discriminated against them. During the insurgency in Punjab, a number of Sikhs too were prosecuted under TADA. But, there was so much clamour by vested interests that the Congress (I) government led by P.V. Narasimha Rao permitted TADA to lapse. Immediately after coming to power, UPA government repealed the POTA, which was a much more toned down version of TADA, to prove its credentials to the Muslims. Another recent instance was of the circular re-issued by the MHA, a few years after it was originally issued, making it obligatory on a person, with whom a foreigner may be staying, to inform the police if the foreigner over-stayed beyond the visa period. These unexceptional instructions too had to be withdrawn due to clamour in the English media. And this is at the time when several other countries have passed draconian laws to meet the threats posed to their national security. It is amazing to see that though India has been a prime target of terrorist violence since 1990, there is total public apathy and disdain for matters concerning the security of the country.

It is a matter of regret that India has failed to raise the issue of illegal migration with the Government of Bangladesh in a serious and concerted manner over all these years. At one stage, it was believed that the settlement of *Tin Bigha* question will create the proper climate for finding a solution to this long standing issue. This has proved futile. Thereafter, it was believed that the settlement of sharing of Ganga waters will provide the opportunity to bring up this issue for an amicable bilateral resolution. This too has proved to be a non-starter. In fact, during his visit to Dacca for these negotiations, the then External Affairs Minister, I.K. Gujral, had stated that New Delhi had no plans to link water-sharing with any other outstanding issues between the two countries. On its part, the Government of Bangladesh has taken the extreme position that the problem of illegal migration is India's own creation and there is no migration from that country at all. The Bangladesh Rifles (BDR), which is a counter-part of BSF, has been most callous, unreasonable and unco-operative in its actions. There have been frequent instances of firing by BDR on the border. Against this background, it is difficult to believe that, soon after the creation of Bangladesh, an agreement was entered into by India and Bangladesh which envisaged close co-operation between the BSF and BDR, including joint operations by the two Forces, joint border posts and so on. These are the new realities of relationship between India and Bangladesh. But, it would be impossible to find any long term and lasting solution to the problem of illegal migration without active co-operation and help from the Bangladesh Government.

Illegal migration from Bangladesh is no longer a regional problem which can be pushed under the carpet. These migrants are now spread in several states and in distant places such as Rajasthan, Delhi, Madhya Pradesh, Maharashtra and so on. They have become so much a part of the citizenry of the country that one of them was, in fact, appointed as a special executive magistrate in Mumbai! They exert considerable influence on election results, not only in several constituencies in Assam, West Bengal and Bihar but also in Delhi and some other states.

How to deal with millions of these illegal migrants is a question to which there are no easy answers, particularly if political parties in India consider protection of Bangladeshi migrant Muslims imperative for nursing their Muslim vote-banks. Taking recourse to legal action under the Foreigners Act and to put up and pursue cases against millions of illegal migrants in courts will be next to impossible. The easy way out, which is effectively being advocated by a number of political parties, will be to regularise their stay. But, this will encourage more and more Bangladeshis to infiltrate in India. And there would be reception committees of "secular" political parties at the border to receive them with open arms! Sooner than later, pressures will build up to give them Indian citizenship. A reference may be made in this context to the proliferation of slums in metropolitan cities such as Delhi and Mumbai and other large urban conglomerations. Regularisation of hutments, time and again, has encouraged more people to flock to the cities and encroach on public and private lands with impunity. Since such slums are vote-banks, at the time of each election for the state legislature and parliament, the year for regularisation of hutments is brought forward. This whole process has given rise to a new Mafia which has made millions of rupees by encroaching on vacant lands and public places with active partnership of concerned public functionaries and selling the plots for construction of hutments. The same thing will happen once we publicly adopt the policy of regularisation of the stay of illegal migrants. There is, therefore, no alternative to reversing the flow of illegal migrants and sending them back. But the question is whether India is prepared to adopt such a firm policy. If the past experience is any guide, the unequivocal answer is No.

Illegal migration is due to both the pull and push factors. Foremost among these are the economic factors. Better employment opportunities in India act as a pull factor while the poverty, subsistence living, ravages caused by floods and other natural calamities in Bangladesh act as push factors. This has to be accepted as a ground reality. In the coming years, these factors will undoubtedly intensify. It must also be accepted that there are several menial, agricultural and other jobs which Indian citizens are reluctant to do. The emoluments on which Bangladeshi migrants (and illegal migrants in particular) are prepared to work are also much less than the Indians. Being unorganised, they can be exploited by their employers much more easily than the Indian labour. All these factors must not be lost sight of in evolving the future policy. One way to deal with these ground realities would be to institute a scheme of work permits by which Bangladeshi migrants can be permitted to work in India for a specified period. The Working Group had recommended adoption of such a policy. The other step, to which a reference was made earlier, would be to enact a law prohibiting employment of a Bangladeshi, other than one who has a work permit. Such laws are in operation in a number of Western countries and even in the Middle East. This suggestion was a part of the package proposed for the meeting of the chief ministers convened by the Union Home Minister way back in 1992. Unfortunately, as in the case of several other suggestions, this too has remained without any action.

Knowledgeable observers of the scene have expressed fears that it would not be surprising if the future chief minister of Assam is one of the illegal migrants. Constitution of India does not bar a person of foreign origin from holding even the highest constitutional position in the country once he acquires citizenship. As the things stand, anyone who enters India from Bangladesh, even illegally, becomes Indian citizen in no time. And with national leaders like Ramvilas Paswan who, after the elections to the Bihar Assembly in early 2005, was prepared for any compromise in the formation of a Ministry if the chief minister was to be a Muslim, this day will not be far off. In any case, most present incumbents of high political offices in the country are taking the same stand on illegal migration as a chief minister, or for that matter a prime minister drawn from the ranks of illegal migrants, would take!

The above discussion brings out that it would be impossible to find a lasting solution to this gigantic problem unless pressure of public opinion is built up to exert influence on the political parties to address the underlying issues with urgency and a firm commitment. This would call for concerted action by the civil society including various pressure groups, NGOs, print and electronic media, and intellectuals and influential persons who are fearless and committed enough to lend their names for this national cause. The present tendency to stigmatise anyone, who speaks on this subject with some fervour and earnestness, as communal and Hindu fascist has been largely responsible for the neglect of this subject. It is high time persons from all walks of life, and primarily the Indian Muslims, come forward to espouse this cause. This will make all the difference to the perceptions and the attitudes of political parties. The first step in this direction should be to insist on the Central Government bringing out a white paper on the subject for national debate and discussion. I trust this book, which provides deep insights in and highlights many facets of this complex question, would go a long way in strengthening these efforts.

5 August 2005. **Dr. Madhav Godbole**

Preface

Astha Bharati, Delhi organized a National Seminar on "Illegal Migration from Bangladesh" in Delhi on November 27-28, 2001 and a Repeat Seminar on the same topic in Guwahati on February 21-22, 2003. The first seminar was organised in association with the Centre for North East Studies and Policy Research (C-NES). The seminar was attended by senior scholars, members of Parliament, former senior officials, media specialists, non-government groups and others from the North East and other parts of the country. The opinions expressed are those of the eminent scholars who have deeply studied the problem or those who had the opportunity to handle it. This volume includes their papers and the writes-up based on the extempore deliberations. The reports of the seminars and their recommendations are included in the annexures of the book. The population data and other relevant information are also given in the annexures.

The illegal migration of the Bangladeshis is a serious problem the country is facing today. It is no more a regional problem, as they are spreading throughout the country now. Bangladesh is allowing its soil to be used by ISI against India and her citizens as ISI operatives and agents of fundamentalism. Their nexus with Indian terrorist groups is a well-known phenomenon. The aliens are posing grave problem for our internal and external security. The changing population texture is making Indo-Bangladesh border fluid. The aliens not only share the benefits of our development schemes, but also indulge in smuggling, drug trafficking, etc. A large number of Bangladeshis find place in the voters' lists and their grip over our electoral process is increasing day by day. Their growing hold in our national life is assuming worrisome proportion. Their nefarious design of greater Bangladesh and claim of *lebensraum* or living space in India adds new dimension to the problem. All this necessitates greater awareness among the Indian people about the gravity of the problem. We hope that this publication may serve the purpose to some extent.

The publication of this edited volume is delayed due to unavoidable reasons. At this juncture, I remember and thank the organizers, resource persons and the participants of the two seminars. I specially thank Shri J.N. Roy, Treasurer, Astha Bharati whose efforts made two seminars, whose proceedings find place in this volume, successful. I also thank Sarvashri Sanjoy Hazarika, Mrinal Miri, Jayanta Madhab, D.N. Bezboruah, Prakash Singh, Kamaleshwar Bora, Naresh Chandra, N.N. Vohra, Professor J.K. Roy, Professor Udayan Misra, K.P.S. Gill, Dr. Kumar Suresh Singh, R.P. Joshi and all others who helped us in various ways in getting our endeavour succeed. Shri Madhav Godbole, former Home Secretary, Government of India has kindly written scholarly foreword for the book. I thank him for the same. I also thank Shri Ashok Kumar Mittal of Concept Publishing Company for publication of the book.

B.B. Kumar

Contents

Annexures

1
Introduction

B.B. KUMAR

The migrants from Bangladesh may be broadly categorised into: (i) Hindu refugees and (ii) illegal Muslim immigrants. The Hindu population in Bangladesh has grown by a bare two million in 40 years, from 9.2 million in 1951 to 11.1 million in 1991. There are a large number of people who are missing. A Bangladesh scholar, based on the growth rate of the population of that country, found the missing Hindu population of that country to be approximately five million. And where have these people gone? These traumatised, frightened and brutalised lot have come to India. These Hindus are not migrants, they are true refugees.[1] It needs mention that the percentage of Hindus and Buddhists in Bangladesh was 33.93 per cent in 1901. It decreased from 29.61 per cent in 1941 to 11.37 per cent in 1991.[2] The minority population is less than ten per cent in that country today.

Illegal Muslim migration from Bangladesh to India became well-known phenomenon a decade after the partition of the country. Initially, it was mostly restricted to the North-East, West Bengal and the eastern fringe of Bihar. Now, practically every part of the country is within their reach. The population growth rates of Bangladesh and its neighbouring states of India provide abundant evidence of large-scale infiltration from that country to India. The Census report of Bangladesh of 1991 was not compatible with its fertility rate of 4.5 per cent. The said report placed the annual PGR of that country during 1981–91 at 2.1 per cent, whereas United Nations Population Fund estimated it at 2.7 per cent. This disparity was due to infiltration from Bangladesh to India.[3]

The Census report of Bangladesh of 1991 talked of the unique phenomenon of missing population, estimated initially at ten million, and subsequently at eight million, comprising of 1.73 million Hindus and 6.27 million Muslims. There were two million missing voters whose names have been deleted from the Voters' list of Bangladesh during 1991–95. These obviously point towards large-scale immigration from that country to India.[4]

The implecations of large-scale immigration from Bangladesh to this country are going to be very grave. It is adversely effecting our economy and social environment; creating law and order problem wherever they are present in sizeable number. The illegal immigrants have become bold enough to commit robbery even in Delhi.

Some of the serious implications of the influx of the aliens need special mention:

(i) The influx of the aliens is responsible for very high population growth in certain parts of the country, especially in the west Bengal, North-East, parts of Bihar and Jharkhand. Assam's population increased from 15 million to about 23 million during 1971–1991. The PGR of West Bengal during 1981–91 was as high as 24.55 per cent. It declined to 17.84 per cent during 1991–2001 but the PGR in the border districts of North 24-Pargana, Murshidabad and Malda was very high. It was 22.64 per cent, 23.7 per cent and 24.77 per cent respectively. The Growth of Muslim population in many districts of Assam and West Bengal during 1991–2001 was abnormally high. Karimganj and Nagaon districts became Muslim majority districts. Marigaon of Assam and Malda of West Bengal are just to follow. (See Annexure VIIIA).

(ii) Infiltration is disturbing the demographic texture of the population. The PGR for the Hindus and the Muslims in West Bengal during 1981–91 was 24.73 per cent and 36.89 per cent respectively. The disparity in the PGR of even the districts far away from the border was also very high. The PGR of Hindus and Muslims in Midnapur district was 19.74 and 53.80 per cent respectively; and that in Bankura district was 14.33 and 38.71 per cent respectively. The situation in the North-East was in no way different. The non-Muslim population in Assam increased at the rate of 45.39 per cent during 1971–91, whereas the Muslim population increased during the same period at the rate of 77.42 per cent. The three border districts of Assam—Dhubri, Cachar and Karimganj—registered very high Muslim population growth during that period.

(iii) Our border with Bangladesh has become fluid due to heavy influx and settlement of the aliens in the border areas. General (Retd.) Shankar Roy Chowdhury rightly told in the Rajya Sabha in April 2000 that on account of illegal migration, Bangladesh's demographic border intruded upon India's political border over a 10–20 km deep area.

(iv) Practically every country of the world receives immigrants from other countries. But this case differs from others. The number of immigrants in this case is very large. The Home Ministry's Working Group on Border Management estimated the total number of Bangladeshis in India to be about one crore some thirteen years back. Madhav Godbole Committee Report of the Task Force on Border Management submitted to the Government of India in August 2000, estimated the number to be 1.5 crore with about three lakhs Bangladeshi immigrants entering India illegally every year. According to Balajit Rai (in his 'Demographic Aggression Against India', 1993) the total number of illegal immigrants in west Bengal, Assam, Bihar, Delhi, Madhya Pradesh, Uttar Pradesh, Rajasthan and Bombay was 1,08,10,000.[5] Apart from the fact that the number of illegal immigrants from Bangladesh is very large, another disturbing fact that needs mention is that they are unskilled labourers and a drain for the economy of this country.

(v) Illegal immigration from Bangladesh is the greatest irritant in the relationship of India with that country. Unfortunately, the Bangladesh Government not only does not make any effort to stop it; it even denies their presence in this country. Some intellectuals of that country are even trying to legitimise the theory of 'lebensraum'—living space for the Bangladeshis in India. The views expressed by Sadeq Khan, a former diplomat of Bangladesh in early 1990s is worth quoting:

"All projections, however, clearly indicate that by the next decade, that is to say by the first decade of the 21st century, Bangladesh will face a serious crises of lebensraum…there is no reason why regional and international cooperation could not be worked out to plan and execute population movements and settlements to avoid critical demographic pressure in pockets of high concentration… The natural trend of population overflow from Bangladesh is towards the sparsely populated lands in the South-East, in the Arakan side and of the North-East in the Seven Sisters' side of the Indian sub-continent.[6]

Many leading thinkers, economists and former diplomats of Bangladesh are articulating the idea of free movement of people across the international borders. According to professor Amena Mohsin of Dhaka University, "migration is a normal and natural phenomenon and can not be stopped, the need today is to evolve ways to legalise it."[7]

Thus it is clear that Bangladesh has design to push more and more people to this country to realise its plan of Greater Bangladesh.

(vi) Illegal immigrants have become very powerful in India due to the competitive politics of vote bank. They have become voters and can "determines" the outcome of poll in 52 Assembly constituencies of West Bengal. The situation might have worsened further during the past few years as the above-mentioned findings are based on the study made a few years ago. The situation in the North-East, especially in Assam is no better. The aliens have become so powerful and our politicians so powerless and short-sighted that a chief Minister like Hiteshwar Saikia had to withdraw his statement about them. The recent controversy about the statement of a Minister of State in the. Ministry of Home Affaris of the Central Government points towards the same phenomena. The West Bengal Government stopped the trains carrying the aliens from Mumbai to the border some years ago. The controversial IMDT Act protects the infiltrators, is a well-known fact.

The danger due to on-going immigration is extensively known. Lt. Gen. (Retd.) S.K. Sinha, the then Governor of Assam, in a report submitted to the President of India in November 1998 wrote:

"As a result of population movement from Bangladesh, the spectre looms large of the indigenous people of Assam being reduced to a minority in their home state. Their cultural survival will be in jeopardy, their political control will be weakened and their employment opportunities will be undermined. This silent and invidious demographic invasion of Assam may result in loss of the geostrategically vital districts of Lower Assam (on the border with Bangladesh). The influx of these illegal migrants is turning these districts into a Muslim majority region. It will then only be a matter of time when a demand for their merger with Bangladesh may be made. The rapid growth of international Islamic fundamentalism may provide the driving force for this demand .... Loss of Lower Assam (the area close to the Bangladesh border) will severe the entire land mass of the North-East from the rest of India and the rich natural resources of the region will be lost to the Nation"[8]

T.V. Rajeswar, a former Director, Intelligence Bureau has also expressed similar opinion that "there is a distinct danger of another Muslim country, speaking Bengali predominantly, emerging in the eastern part of India in future."[9] It needs mention that the fundamentalist elements in Bangladesh have been propagating that the borders defined at the time of Partition are no longer relevant and need to be changed, taking into account the recent demographic changes. The Jamaat-e-Islami of Bangladesh has also been talking about 'Swadhin Muslim Bangabhumi' in India. These developments in Bangladesh and the continuous ethnic cleansing of the minorities in that country amply prove that the fears expressed by Lt. Gen. (Retd.) S.K. Sinha and T.V. Rajeswar are not without basis.[10]

The factors responsible for illegal immigration from Bangladesh are the following:

(i) Religious persecution of the Hindus and Buddhists forcing them to leave their homes.

(ii) Islamic interests encouraging uncontrolled population growth and migration keeping in view the future expansion of the territory,

(iii) Competitive politics of vote-bank and the patronage extended to them by political parties/vested political groups in India,

(iv) Help rendered by organised groups of touts/anti-social elements,

(v) Increasing pressure on land and mounting unemployment in Bangladesh due to uncontrolled steep rise in population,

(vi) Un-natural partition based on two nation theory; difficulties of Regional Planning,

(vii) Recurrent floods and cyclones uprooting large segments of population,
(viii) Better economic opportunities across the border,
(ix) Porous and easily negotiable Indo-Bangladesh border,
(x) Dominance of fundamentalist agenda and fundamentalist groups in Bangladesh, and
(xi) Presence of strong pro-Bangladesh lobby in India often creates myths and confuses Indians about the gravity of the problem.

Economic Factors

There are many in India who try to justify illegal migration on the plea that migration takes place due to economic crisis. Responsible news-papers, like *Times of India,* publish editorials like "The Bangla Bogey". Many suggest that India should help Bangladesh revive its economy. Some of the questions that arise and need to be answered are: (i) Is it India's responsibility to solve the problem created by demographic bomb explosion of irresponsible Bangladesh? (ii) Has India solved its own economic problems? (iii) Has India the capacity to develop neighbours like Bangladesh? (iv) Should India allow dilution of its electoral process by allowing the large scale voting by the aliens? (v) Should we allow undermining of our national security, cultural integrity and social harmony because the aliens' migration takes place due to economic reason also?

In a study made by National Council of Applied Economic Research (NCAER) in 1995 on smuggling across West Bengal's border with Bangladesh, it was pointed out that essential articles of everyday use such as cycles, machine parts, livestock, vegetable oils, spices, etc. are smuggled in huge quantities from West Bengal side to our neighbouring country. As the supply from that side is insignificant, they smuggle arms, gold and narcotics from that side to this country. This is obviously facilitated by the linkage between infiltrators, smugglers and the terrorists.[11] There are items that our neighbour can supply, and we need it also, such as the fuel gas. Bangladesh may get huge money by allowing transit facility to our North-East. Obviously Bangladesh is not interested in trade balance. It needs mention that smuggling helps Bangladesh economically and weakens India too.

Where is the Big Brother?

India is often accused as 'big brother' in the context of its small neighbours? In reality, India is the sufferer. Take the case of the Ganga Water sharing at Farakka point. Ganga is mainly an Indian river. Only 0.73 per cent of its catchment area is within Bangladesh. But the country receives far excess of the share of water than it should get as per the Helsinki regulations. Both the Water Sharing Agreements of 1977 and 1996 have converted Ganga, an Indian river, into a Bangladesh river. Both Bangladesh and its collaborators in India talked about imaginary desertification of Bangladesh due to Farakka barrage. But the Study by the Food Action Plan (FAP) shows otherwise. Actually, the food production and the land under cultivation increased during the dry season as the crop during the period mostly uses underground water.[12] Thus Bangladesh raises the bogey of 'big brother', terrorises India and gets far more concessions than it deserves.

Pro-Bangladesh Lobby and the Myth-making

A myth was created and highly publicised, especially in Indian media and among Indian intellectuals that the creation of Bangladesh disproved the 'Two Nation Theory'. In reality, when the Hindus returned to Bangladesh after its liberation, they found their houses and properties occupied by the Muslims. Sheikh Mujib retained 'Enemy property Act' in one form or the other. In reality, Mujib himself lacked conviction about transforming his country into a secular democracy. At the same time, he had consciously allowed re-induction of pro-Pakistani and anti-liberation elements into politics, civil services and armed forces of Bangladesh.[13] For Bangladesh, the 'Two Nation' theory never ceased to exist. The strong pro-Bangladesh lobby, directly or indirectly helps illegal immigrants hy assigning economic reasons and thereby justifying their migration in India. They act as the spokesmen of Bangladesh ignoring our national interests.

Bangladesh continues to be a haven for militants. Indian Ultras continue to get shelter and training in that country. BSF submitted list of 195 terrorists camps in that country some times back.[14] There is no let up in terrorist menace.[15] Bangla ultra's plot to train NE youths have been unearthed.[16] A terror friendly regime,[17] emerging Talibanization of that country,[18] Bangla Bhai Syndrome,[19] reported Al-Quaeda presence,[20] the largest arms seizure at Chittagong port[21] and many other similar reports do not assure us about our future good neighbourly relationship. Bangladesh is sheltering ISI.[22] Its minorities are constantly under attack.[23] After Taslima, now it is the turn of Salam Azad to pay the price for talking against the oppression of the minorities in that country. His book *'Bhanga Math'* has been banned.[24]

REFERENCES

1. Sanjoy Hazarika, Illegal Migration from Bangladesh: Problem and Long term Perspective,—Dialogue, 3:3; New Delhi, January–March 2002, pp. 23–32.
2. A.P. Joshi & others, Religious demography in India, Chennai, p. 49.
3. J.K. Ray, Migration from Bangladesh to India, Dialogue, 3:3, p. 39.
4. Ibid.
5. Baljit Rai, quoted in the referred book, p. 175.
6. Holiday, Dhaka, October 18, 1991.
7. Wasbir Hussain, Demographic Invasion, Anxiety and Anger in India's North-East, Faultline, Vol. 7, p. 128.
8. Faultline, Vol. 7 pp. 114–15.
9. Prakash Singh, Bangladesh' Immigration: Are We Heading for Another Partition, Dialogue, 3:3. p. 43.
10. Ibid, pp. 42–43.
11. J.K. Ray, op. cit., pp. 40–41.
12. Ibid, pp. 35–37.
13. Dixit, J.N., Liberation and Beyond, New Delhi, Konark Publishers, 1999, p.249.
14. *Dainik Jagaran,* (Hindi), 8 August, 2004.
15. *Statesman,* Kolkata, 15–16 July, 2004.
16. *Hindustan Times,* 22 July, 2004.
17. Fundamentalist groups are partners of the ruling combination.
18. http://www.saag.org/papers11/papers1058.html
19. Ibid, paper 1035: *The Hindu,* 11 May, 2004.
20. Ibid, paper 1031.
21. Anil Bhat, Eastern Gateway of Terror, The Pioneer, 14 July, 2004.
22. Asian Age, 27 July, 2003.
23. Ibid, 28 August, 2003: Faultline Vol. 14, pp. 2–3.
24. Jansatta (Hindi), 27 July, 2004.

2

Illegal Migration from Bangladesh

NARESH CHANDRA

This is a very complex subject and it has become terribly complicated over the years because it has all kinds of overtones. You referred to the national security considerations, the sensitivity involved because of the communal factors which come into play and the politics of it. If ever local problems due to neglect or worse become complicated, I think this will be a good or bad example of this.

I think if we address some simple but basic issues, it might help us to appreciate who are the people who are affected and start from that rather than bringing into a locally problematic issue the factors of national import all of a sudden. And I find that whenever a discussion of this nature takes place, we keep jumping from one to the other. What we are dealing here primarily are village communities, land and sources of living. In the debate, we often forget that the land belongs to the people of that area, it does not belong to Delhi or the national Parliament. So when we look at a local village and all that, we have to see that whatever is happening, whether it is legal migration or illegal migration, what is the impact on the people living in these villages who are going about their business and who want to improve their level of living. When people enter these villages, people in Delhi, Mumbai or Madhya Pradesh are not affected. The impact is very local on a very few hundred people in a village, or a thousand people in a block and so on. So in determining those issues, their views are paramount. If you don't keep that fix in mind, then what happens is that people at state headquarters, or at the national level, not only play politics, but they have the opportunity to be very liberal. And I think Indians are always very liberal at somebody else's expense! That is what seems to characterise much of the debate that takes place in Delhi or Calcutta or elsewhere. If we have a local fix on the problem, then in the economic situation of a village community, land is terribly important. While we should have gone about having special courts and identifying people and so on, we should have had an accurate description of village land and its disposition—who owns what land? What is village common land? And have regular authentic maps, and freeze them, because if you allow a whole lot of people to enter these areas, the first casualty is the pattern of land holdings, and because agriculture is the mainstay, the greatest amount of resentment is caused locally when they find that people from other villages, what to say of other States or other countries, come and start putting pressure on land which is the chief means of livelihood for the village community. I thought I should bring this up because this is very important.

The other thing is that communal issue or factor should be brought in last. I suggest if we can refine this recommendation a bit, it is not Hindu migrant or Muslim infiltrator. I think these words are not proper. They should be avoided in my view. It is for what consideration a person is coming. If there are people who are running to India as a result of persecution, whether Hindu or Muslim, we should have a liberal approach. It may be a novelist who is on the run, or a poet or a public activist, hounded by the government or some fundamentalist body or the other, he should be dealt with sympathetically irrespective of the religion to which he belongs. But when it comes to running to grab land or as part of concerted action to start changing the demographic pattern of neighbouring villages, then it is another matter altogether. I feel that having matters decided in Delhi has been a complicating factor. Even if decisions were to be taken here and federal laws were enacted and adopted, local consultation should have been much more meaningful than what has been in the past. We should have enabled some of the authority for managing this problem or bringing about an improvement in the situation delegated and decentralised so that the local people felt that they could do something. Today, in most States, particularly in the border villages of those States, the local people feel totally helpless. I don't think it is good administration that people in the border villages in Assam or West Bengal shout at Delhi. The very reason that they are criticising Delhi or the Central Government means that the administrative arrangement and the legal framework that has been provided is not correct. There is something wrong with decisions being taken far away from the field. The fact that these people have been criticising Delhi means that we have not provided them with the best possible administrative arrangements or reasonable recourse to appellate measures.

I think time has come today not to focus so much on things of the past, but to see what can be done now. Before we start to evolve any solution, we should have a set of recommendations which accurately describe the situation and what is happening. This is not only in terms of people. If I can reiterate, it is very important that maps are accurately made, land holdings in border villages are properly delineated and verified and put on public record. You can have these maps on computer. The software is available, anybody can access it. That, by itself, will help in stabilising the situation.

The second is the management of the border. Here, there are no half way measures. We have seen in Punjab and elsewhere where border fences had to be made—I think Mr. K.P.S. Gill and others must have covered it. In the terrain of Bangladesh, it is extremely difficult to have this kind of fencing. Even if you do it, what do you do at the time of floods or natural calamities? It is virtually impossible to manage inflow and outflow at the time when rivers are in spate in the monsoon season. I don't know how BSF manages the situation. So you may be very vigilant in good eight months in a year, but for four months you are totally helpless. There is no escape. As you have the Special Disturbed Areas Act and all that, we should have some kind of legal provision to identify and declare demographically disturbed areas. Here, one has to concentrate state's resources. Now, to have a register of citizens and to issue identity cards to everybody, the amount of resources involved is much too much and perhaps it is not very cost-effective because money is required elsewhere, you cannot spend it all on cards and registers and so on. But in the border villages, I see no reason why there cannot be a village register on a certain date, comprehensively determined in quasi-judicial proceedings and fixed, so that if there is accretion to it at any point of time, it could be easily assessed.

The same with regard to electoral registration rolls. We have the same set of rules, very easy procedures about putting oneself on the electoral roll. Now surely a time has come when we recognise the dimensions of the problem and see that evidence is not 'created.' The problem with these Tribunals was the evidence. Very often, the people who were clever and who were clearly illegal immigrants had the better records. The innocents had less, because they had no cause to prepare their case. So the fellows who operated as a group or with the help of a very clever operator, they would turn up with ration cards, voting register and so on and the Tribunal would have a devil of a problem. So whether it is 1976 or 1965 or whether it is 2001, the time has come when you must freeze this problem.

I saw some reference to 'living space" and all that. That Bangladesh is a very congested area and there are liberal people who say that everybody deserves living space. It is all right but if you see the density of population in India, I don't think we have hell of lot of space, and to be very easy about it, it is okay in places like Rajasthan, or Madhya Pradesh, or Maharashtra or Andhra Pradesh which are not afflicted, but you have to see that this grant of "lebensraum" or living space impacts in very few areas and it is in these areas that the problem arises. So we have to be very careful that we are not very large-hearted and liberal, as I said earlier, at somebody else's expense.

Now the question of law has been raised. I do not have much to say on it but I think the Foreigners' Act should be applicable. There is no reason why citizens of India in one area or the other should be made specially vulnerable and should not have the same guarantees or legal protection as are available to most foreigners in other parts of India. It is amazing that courts have not stepped in earlier. If there was a strong enough demand from the people of these areas against this measure, it has to be heard and I am sure Parliament sooner or later will come round to repealing the IMDT Act.

On the practical aspects of it, I am sure you have covered in great detail the issues of border management with Mr. Prakash Singh here and people from the IB who have spoken. I do not have much to say. But I feel that either you do something fully or it is not worth doing. If you have a fence and you aim and mobilise your resources for 80 per cent or 90 per cent it is no good. It is like having a huge dam with one block missing somewhere. All the water will come out. So the border management has to be near perfect in this area. The only way it can be done is by a judicious mixture of a kind of permanent fence where it is feasible, otherwise a tremendous upgrading of the Water Wing or Boat Wing, whatever it is called, of the BSF with facility to move fast, also to act to gather better intelligence and so on.

The other problem which remains is I think less severe. People who move into the neighbouring villages and stay there is in my view a more serious matter. But those who quickly move out and reach Delhi, at least the impact of that migration gets dispersed. I remember some work was going in my house at 1, Janpath and people were digging a trench for laying down some cable for lighting and so on. And I found that all of them were from Bangladesh. They could not speak a word of Urdu or Hindustani. And when I tried to talk to them, it was very clear. That was the house of the Home Secretary! Illegal migrants were working in that house! So I called a meeting and I called the Chief Secretaries of Bengal, Bihar, Assam, Tripura, Manipur etc. At least one Chief Secretary said that his government was not willing to do anything. He frankly admitted that before me. I won't name that State. But he said, "Look, it is very difficult to persuade the State Government to take effective measures." We have come a long way since then, but I remember in another meeting, there was this Teen Bigha thing and land to be leased and permission given. The question was as to who goes on land and who goes over the fly-over. The decision was that Bangladeshis will walk on the land and the Indians will use the fly-over. So one of the Ministers objected. He said, "Should it not be the other way round? We should go under the fly-over." I said, "Why are you objecting? Have you seen the fly-overs of Delhi? And under most of the fly-overs of Delhi, the people living are Bangladeshis. So if you can tolerate them under the fly-overs in Delhi, what is your problem at Teen Bigha." That broke the impasse and that agreement we had with Bangladesh could be implemented. But on a serious note, I think we have to take a stand, adopt measures which show that we are a serious government. It is all right to play politics, or be liberal or understand the problems of a group of people, but in the process we should not compromise the serious image that a self-respecting government must have. Today, many people from outside who come and study the easy manner in which we have dealt with this problem, would be a bit alarmed. It is not that the other countries don't have it. Look at the problem in the United States where they have got fences, they have got laws to deal with Mexican labour which comes. It is a judicial mix of seriousness, a pragmatic approach and a human approach—all three. But they have a very strong INS (Immigration and Naturalisation Service). The main purpose of INS is to stop illegal immigration. Although the service is called Immigration and Naturalization Service, they have very strict rules. If you observe the rules and all that, you can migrate to the United States because that is what has made that country. But if anybody breaks the rules or tries to do so, they have every trick in the book to find that fellow, put data on the computer, eject him or see to it that he never gets another visa to enter the United States. They have a large amount of staff for it, they have a large amount of resources committed to it, it is a whole service. We have I think a Foreigners' Division and if you compare, we are supposed to be a bloated bureaucracy, but the INS alone would be the strength of the Ministry of Home Affairs. So when you find that it is a national problem, please apply the resources to it. I think the problem has been addressed far too inadequately. Instead of taking steps on the ground and taking concrete administrative measures, we have indulged in political debate, laws which either cannot be implemented or have been partially implemented and the problem goes on as before.

So I am one with the speakers who have stressed the seriousness of the situation. And I support many of the recommendations, which have come out. But I would suggest some refinement in the wording not to raise hackles or give ammunition to people to attack the recommendations on a pseudo-liberal platform. It is a serious security problem, it is a serious economic problem, for a number of people settled in areas bordering Bangladesh and it has implications for our national security. These factors cannot be wished away.

3

Historical Aspect of the Illegal Migration from Bangladesh

UDAYAN MISHRA

Actually I must begin with an apology because the topic which was suggested to me was "Historical Aspect of Illegal Migration from Bangladesh." Now two things are important there. One is historical aspect and the other one is the word "illegal" which creates some problems for me because it brings in a lot of other questions. I will definitely take up a broad overview of policy matters since the British times very briefly so that we have a background, but my interest would be not just with illegal migration. When we say 'illegal' we fix up a particular date and method of coming in. But I am also interested in the fall out that has taken place in the demographic structure of the Assamese society and I think that also is a part of the historical process where there has been a major transformation in the concept of identity itself from the 19th century onwards till present times because of the assimilation or otherwise of large segments of immigrant population into what we broadly might call the Assamese nationality. So that part will constitute the second part of my arguments.

Now initially when we talk of the historical process, we are all acquainted with the British policy in the land system which was thought of in 1916 which was implemented in 1920 and then the consequent rise in numbers. But since I cannot take into my discussion all the different points, I would just like to take up the different positionings that were adopted as far as migration from East-Bengal, then East-Pakistan and then finally from Bangladesh, both illegal and refugee migration that took place. Ultimately what was the type of positioning that had taken place. This is very important for us just to have a very broad overview. For example, how did parties like the Congress react to it historically when the process of demographic change was taking place. So from the point, I think the main controversy that was always bogged us down has been on figures, on how many people have crossed over, what is the demographic change? There are basically two sets of scholars, one for and one against. And the position that is taken by those who are slightly apprehensive about what they consider the fanning up of communal frenzy, they would like to tell us that the observations of Mullan and others are not in line with facts. But basically if we take up even these scholars, and I would like to quote from them if time permits, I feel that it has been generally acknowledged that there has been a progressive denudation of tribal belts and blocks over the decades and much of what we term as the Bodo problem or the other plains tribals problem, I think they all boil down to the problem of land in Assam. The idea that there has always been plenty of cultivable land in Assam—and I am using the word "Assam" primarily with reference to the Brahmputra Valley, I am not using the word "North-East"—here there has been a lot of misconception because the land figures have not been properly utilised, we do not have a lot of land data to work on, and ultimately if we analyse most of these movements, we find that basically it is because of pressure on land. I would like to take up the land issue first and read out some of the figures about land. These are only indicate figures. There are more figures that would come up. If we start with what scholars like Prof. Amalendu Guha has been maintaining that the whole concept that was put forward by Mullan is wrong, that migration has not brought about a major change and so on, even if we take up Prof. Guha as a point of reference here, and if we take up phase-wise, period-wise, say from 1920 when the land system was introduced, till 1930–36 (I am giving a short overview), as many as 59 grazing reserves (forest and village reserves) were thrown open in the Nowgong district to the immigrants under the colonisation scheme which was introduced by the Britishers in the late 1920s where they grouped the migrants in particular areas. Out of the total district area of 5,41,000 acres in 1936, 2 lakh acres or 37.7 per cent were under the immigrants' occupation as against 62 per cent still in the hands of the indigenous people. The cultivable land other than fallow in the district accounted for more than 1.4 million acres. The land hungry Muslim immigrants—I am quoting Guha—segregated and pitted against all odds never appreciated the Assamese point of view and if all men were equal in the eyes of our law, why should thousands of acres of land remain waste particularly when men in search of a livelihood and lebensraum were available to turn them into smiling fields. Now that is one particular position, that they wanted the land system to go. This I am quoting from Prof. Guha throughout. Till March 1933, in Nowgong district, 47,637 acres of land had been given to 441 Hindus and 1619 immigrant Muslim families. Then of course we have the very famous and oft quoted statement from CS Mullan in 1931 census where he predicts that the Assamese would be a minority but for in one or two districts in Upper Assam in course of time. Now this trend has continued and even in the last 10–15–20 years, the researchers who have been working even in the Nowgong district would enlighten us how transfer of land has been taking place gradually and there has been pauperisation of both plains tribal peasantry as well as indigenous Assamese peasantry.

This takes us back to a much wider debate on the question of immigration where if we take up the debate finally between Sadullah and Maulana Bhashani historically, because I can't give all the details, Sadullah as the Prime Minister of Assam at that time is said to have been responsible for encouraging a lot of Muslims from East-Pakistan, basically Muslim migrants. We also have the famous Wavell's statement that "Grow More Food" was "Grow More Muslims." But even Sadullah went to the point of difference with Maulana Bhashani when we compare the migration in Assam to Jewish migration into Palestine. This is basically one historical point which repeatedly come up. I do not want to go into figures because others have done much better work on this. Even people like Sanjay have worked on figures and they have shown from Bangladesh statistics and we have Mr. Bezboruah here who has written extensively on the Bangladesh figures and how they have been displaced from there and how they have not been able to account for a large segments of people in the Census. But basically my contention is that what we are moving towards now in Assam is something much more complicated than what is commonly believed to be seen from Delhi because it is not just a question of demographic change. It is true that Mr. Bhuiyan yesterday presented his paper and acquainted the house with enough of figures about rise in the population of different segments of population. But basically my contention here is that this demographic change which has historically been taking place—you take the British period, then you take the land system, you take the system of grouping which ultimately came as far as these migrants are concerned, the debate in the Assembly where they wanted to open up—it is not just something that has happened overnight. It has been a very long process which has gone on for almost a century. But in that process, I have two points to say historically. One is that the Assamese middle class which has always been fighting for a linguistic identity, it has basically been a linguistic type of identity that they have been fighting for and that takes us much earlier, I don't want to go into that, the imposition of Bengali, the replacement of Assamese, that struggle I think everyone knows and I don't want to go into it, but basically the small point which I would like to make is that over the years ever since Anandram Phukan submitted his memo, the Assamese middle class was emerging and had become a very vocal middle class by the time the Congress came into being in Assam in the late twenties, and the preoccupation of this class which virtually had hegemony over Assamese opinion right upto the Assam movement. That is where it troubles me a lot and that is what I would like to throw open before the house today which we have been saying in every census.

Mullan has been contradicted by figures from the Governor which Amalendu Guha quotes. He says that Assamese speakers have not gone down, so Mullan is wrong. But I think Mullan has been proved right in a very different way. He has said, the Assamese are under a threat culturally. That is what basically he wanted to say. I feel that the transformation that has been taking place—I will come to that last point on illegal migration at the end—has led to a situation where the Assamese middle class, because of its preoccupation with linguistic nationalism, has totally bypassed the pressure on tribal land that took place in the Brahmputra Valley. Because if you go through all the Congress resolutions from the twenties upto the forties, and the resolution of 1945 where they talked of a linguistic Assamese State, where they said that if the Assamese culture and identity is to be saved, we have to separate Sylhet, we have to have a homogeneous Assamese homeland. Whether within that structure, the aspirations of the plains tribal people were accommodated or attempted to be accommodated, is a very important question. So I feel that this obsession, or whatever, with sustaining one's linguistic identity against grave odds led to pushing under the carpet the very large and important issue of land alienation that was taking place amongst the tribal communities. They were being pushed to the wall. There are a lot of figures available and if we go through all the figures how the tribal belts/blocks were successively taken over, grazing reserves were taken over, community lands were taken over, ultimately a stage was reached where these people were virtually pauperised. Just because certain figures are not available about the pauperisation of tribal peasantry, it does not mean that pauperisation had not taken place. So whether we talk of the Bodo movement or we talk of the aspirations of other plains tribals, the land factor is very central to our understanding.

Along with the land factor, since the peasants' culture and tradition are so tied up with the land, we move to another point. It is not only displacement of tribals from one area of Assam to another, it is not only pauperisation of a large segment of Assamese peasantry, but it also involves far-reaching cultural changes. This is where I come to my second point about the Assamese middle class. The first one was that it was not particularly concerned about the tribal aspirations for a variety of reasons. Here I could go on to quote most of the writers of the time beginning with Ambika Roy Chowdhary and all those people, their idea of tribal Assamese identity was very amorphous. When we come to the later phase when the legislations were introduced like Prevention of Infiltration from Pakistan scheme and later on different other legislations and how they failed, that is of course a different part of the seminar why they failed and where the forces did not work up, but the point that now comes up at this crucial juncture is the very definite formation of the identity of the Assamese people which is again related to the question of migration and also illegal migration because illegal migration has brought things to a point of saturation. That is why illegal migration has become a very important point.

Now when we talk of this transformation, it has long been said and maintained that the amalgam of folk tribal and so-called alien mix has been the cultural mix of the Assamese people. Whenever we talk of Assamese nationalism or Assamese national identity, we think of Shankar Dev as a very accommodative person who brought in a totally new trend of Vaishnavism which brought in thousands of tribals within the Assamese fold. Now that part is Okay. But when we come to the present situation, the long-standing position that the plains tribal element in the Assamese society or community has been very central, that is no longer true. The reality is very different. The reality is not that you have an amalgam, because the reality is that in the process of a very strong Assamese linguistic movement, when we made in 1960 the State language as point of exclusiveness and the general feeling that allegiance to the Assamese language is allegiance to the Assamese community, that is the type of exclusiveness that came in. That has driven away large segments of plains tribal people from within the broad connotative umbrella of Assamese nationality and we have moved to a different direction. People who were considered to be enemies or threats to the Assamese nationality till about fifty years back form one of the major planks of the Assamese nationality today because instead of the tribal segment, it is the immigrant Muslim segment that has come in as the most potent and most organised segment of the Assamese nationality, because even in the Sahitya Sabha, the President of the Sabha in his presidential address in 1996 made it very clear that it was not a question of there being neo-Assamese or neo-Ahomias, it is a question of being fully Assamese. If you go through the regional press, or books written by people like Dr. Monir-ul-Hussain, this idea has been promoted that actually these are better Assamese because they send their children to Assamese medium schools than the core Assamese. So they have come in and the whole irony of the situation in Assam today is that while alienating the tribals you have taken large segments of people whom you considered till the other day as threats to your identity. So that is the basic change without any other type of confusion that has taken place. How far and what type of fall out will take place, is not for me to decide here. That is a point which needs further clarification. But that process is on.

Now since that process is on, I would like to raise one or two related questions objectively. This is naturally a very important change. I am not saying this is good or bad. I do not want to take positions so far as quality or quantity is concerned here. It's what is actually happening. So in this transformation certain points do come up. I raised this point earlier also, say if we take up certain cultural icons, or even if we take up the role of Namazgarh in an average Assamese village, it has been said that there has been total assimilation, there has been total identification of the immigrants. Nothing could be more Utopian and ideal. But if you take up Namazghar as one of the central points of Assamese cohesiveness, because Namazghar is a symbol not only of religious place of workship, but it connotes much more as a social institution. My simple point is, would the Masjid be able to play the same role as Namazghar? These are just questions I am raising, and in the process what type of adjustment would be needed in the changing context of the Assamese identify formation that is going on today.

I would also like to raise another very interesting point, that is the question of the Assamese Muslims which is very closely linked to the question of migration. Now if you go through most of the earlier accounts, it is said that there is a lot of difference between Assamese Muslims and Muslims in the rest of the country because Assamese Muslims are fully "integrated" into the Assamese nationality. So we have religious songs known as Jhigis and Charis which are much more social in content, much more influenced by different strands of Hinduism than may be elsewhere. I do not know, I am not qualified to comment upon the other regions of the country. Definitely the type of amalgamation must be there in other parts of the country as well. But if one goes through the writings of Assamese Muslim intellectuals of the last five years, of which I have tried to make a survey, the main problem that has been focussed is what is the identity? Where do I actually stand? Where do I actually stand comes up because a particular segment of people who was considered to be an absolutely, inalienable part of the Assamese community today thinks that their identity is under some sort of a threat. This is partly because of the Assam movement and more because of the demographic change. So linking up with the broad community elsewhere, earlier Amalendu Guha has written extensively on this. He represents a particular view point where he says that Assamese Muslim has very little social intercourse with the immigrant Muslim and in the process of time because the numbers increased, they also encouraged the coming of Muslims from East-Bengal, East-Pakistan and Bangladesh. But when it comes to the question of identity, I would just like to read a little bit from a very interesting piece. I am not getting it, I will come to it just now. The point which was being made by two very prominent Muslim scholars, ANS Ahmad and Ahmed Yasin, both of whom happen to belong to my Dibrugarh University, was look because of the changes that were taking place in the 1970s, 1980s and 1990s, we are facing an identity crisis, where do we link up, how do we relate ourselves to the immigrant Muslim community? In the process where do we actually stand? Are we really Assamese? There he referred to a very important resolution taken in one of the meetings just before the 1991 census, where they said, "Some of us at least would like to return ourselves as Bengali-speaking." I am just referring to it because the debate still continues. Even in the last census many controversies came up particularly about whether immigrant Muslims would return their language as Assamese or Bengali. And if I remember aright, Hemantbar Guha wrote extensively on this subject in the regional press. Actually he wrote a special editorial, imploring upon the immigrant Muslims to return Assamese as their mother-tongue. That is an indication that things have not as yet settled down. So basically the debate still continues. On the one hand, people like Munir-ul-Hussain and others say that they are part of the Assamese community, they are more Assamese than us, they send their children to Assamese medium schools, and everything else. On the other hand, you find in the regional press a lot of letters written by immigrant Muslims saying that though they have returned Assamese as their mother-tongue, still they have the right to talk in Bengali at home, still Bengali remains their mother tongue in a different way. "Why should we give up our culture just because we want to amalgamate?"

So we are moving to a very interesting situation in Assam where through a political decision—and this is what I would like to repeat, that through a largely political decision—a large segment of people who have developed a culture and civilisation of their own have opted to merge with another community/nationality. That is where we come to the politics of the question, i.e., whether we want or not to accommodate. The situation in Assam has changed to such an extent that the people commanding the politics in the State would ultimately prevent any major measures to curb infiltration. That is one of the realities of the situation where the demographic change has already taken place, where identify transformation is also taking place.

Lastly, I would like to focus basically on the question of land. I feel that proper work has neither been taken up by Government, or the NGOs or academic institutions on ascertaining land position in Assam. This is where a lot of new statistics would come up and my friend has referred to different measures about how we should curb infiltration. One of the very commonly accepted position today is that if you want to stop illegal infiltration into Assam, then please develop Bangladesh. I remember there was an Indo-Bangla dialogue organised by the CPI some years ago, where some very senior politicians and ministers from Bangladesh had also come and this proposal to develop gas-based industries in Bangladesh as against Assam was mooted by very senior persons like Mr. Muchkund Dubey and I remember saying that so many million cubic metres of gas is being flared away in Assam, what about the development of Assam in that case? It is easier if gas is developed in Bangladesh because labour is cheap. I do not know how far that sort of an argument would help people like ours who we still feel are suffering from backwardness maybe because of the extraced nature of the British colonial policy which continued much longer after Independence. So the perspective if at all it is changing now in Delhi, I think the change must also ensure that here is a state where you have 15 lakh unemployed and here is a place where the entire demographic pattern has triggered off large-scale cultural changes as well. So how we tackle the question of further migration is very important not only for the indigence but also for the immigrants turned Assamese because everything has a saturation point. I think it is more for them that they have to support further measures to stop infiltration. I do not know what governmental measures have resulted till now, but our experience of the IMDT Act is very bad experience as far as Assam is concerned. We consider it to be a major hurdle as far as laws for detection of foreigners are concerned. And it is also the duty of the centre here to prevent the growth of a mindset which feels that we are different because even the laws for foreigners are different. Now you have one set of laws for you and you have a different set of laws for us as far as Assamese are concerned. So that type of dichotomy, first of all, needs to be changed.

I would like to end up with what these people had said. I am not talking of any other parties, but there is a coordination committee of the North-East Congress which three or four years back passed a resolution and in that resolution if you read the resolution, you will be surprised, it is not a resolution passed by an angry students body asking for something from the Centre, but they have not minced any words, and they have said, if the centre continues like this in its policy, then maybe things would be too late. They have referred to the migration, they have referred to the illegal immigrants pouting in and they have said that things might go beyond control. That is from the Congress itself which has long been accused of harbouring infiltrants and pursuing a policy of trying to help the infiltrants settle on land in Assam. So the situation has reached a point here, I know maybe my friend from Tripura will bear me out better, that we have indeed reached past the saturation point and it is time when we have to stop it somewhere. I don't know about the other States but I always feel that States like Nagaland and Mizoram have problem of infiltration though they are much better off than us. They have ensured their identity because they have their 'inner line' provisions and they have very strict regulations as far as transfer of land is concerned, though sometimes subterfuge is attempted and land is taken over but basically they have very strong 'inner line' provisions. Apart from that, I think Nagaland is the only State if the Indian Union which has one clause in its formation which says that land and all the resources belong to the people. In no other State you have a similar provision. That is one of the provisions of the constitution amendment which is being used by the Naga Students Federation and Naga bodies to say that you cannot pump out oil from our State because land and resources belong to us. That is way, I think it would be wrong to place North-East on a common platform because Nagaland, Mizoram, Arunachal have very strong entry laws, very strong laws protecting their land though we have the Chakma problem in Arunachal also. But Assam is now an open corridor. That is what needs to be remembered and for that reason, definitely we have to have more stringent laws, to protect the border. It is not just that we develop Bangladesh. It is okay, that is one point I fully agree, but it would never ensure the movement of people from there to Assam. So for that we need a different set of measures.

4

Illegal Migration from Bangladesh

Problem and Long-term Perspective

SANJOY HAZARIKA

I am happy to present some of my thoughts because it has been really a central focus of my work over the past years and I would like to put some of these issues in perspective, based on my own experiences and field work in Assam, Bangladesh and elsewhere.

I will begin with some basics and some of the things, which I may say, may provoke some disagreement. I think for too long those who speak on these issues speak merely in terms of law and order and security and forget the human and geographical realities as well as the political realities on the ground.

The history of the world is of migration. All of us and our ancestors and fore-bearers had come from somewhere and are now placed somewhere else and people, like water, tend to find their own levels. Sometimes you have governments, such as in Indonesia, which resort to demographic engineering, as in the case of Irian Jaya. The Government used financial and lands incentives to send people from the main island group of Java and Sumatra to assert majoritarian control over smaller rebellious groups. In the case of Assam there was organised settlement in the thirties and forties especially with the Muslim League in power. At that point it was one country, so it was not really illegal. But since then and post-partition the movement has been largely voluntary, apart from the initial year of partition. Why do people move and what are the factors, the push and pull, which are incentive to the outflow. In fact I am very grateful to Mr. Bhuyan who is here today because he is a demographer and specialises in this. When I first began my detailed fieldwork on Bangladesh, he was the first person I went to see in Guwahati.

There are many kinds of migration, not just Hindus coming across, or some Muslims coming across and what have you? In classical terms you have the acute onset movements with the possibility of return, which means migration forced by flash floods, or natural catastrophe like a disaster of large magnitude like an earthquake. You can have an acute onset movement without the possibility of return. Which means armed conflicts, man-made interventions leading to the flight of refugees. Until there is a solution of that problem, the resolution of that issue is not going to happen. You have a slow onset movement with the possibility of return, like in the case of Tripura, which Prof. Singh was talking about. Many people come for daily wage entry or for seasonal work and then they go back. And you have a slow onset movement with predictability but no possibility of return. This is really one of the most important factors relevant to our ongoing work because it covers issue such as lack of employment locally and better chances of livelihood away from home, better health care and economic benefits in the receiving country. The fifth is the slow onset movement without the possibility of return because of the conditions in the migrant-producing areas, whether it is the Sahal in the Horn of Africa or whether it is Bangladesh, or Myanmar or Latin America—natural environmental changes: you can have desertification, soil degradation/erosion, coastal flooding resulting from climatic changes and sea level changes etc.

Some of these problems are irreversible and cannot be prevented. This is a fact of geography, of history, of the contemporary world. They can be curbed or mitigated through international multilateral assistance for adjustment and permanent settlement. Some years ago at an international conference in Geneva which was organised by the UNHCR and the International Organisation for Migration, I had suggested that the international community should consider compensation for countries which are essentially receiving migrants—countries like India whose infrastructure and other facilities are basically under heavy strain anyway. It received some interest but nothing has happened. But we find across the world, concern is growing over the issues of migration, which is forced or created by economic pressures of landlessness, unemployment, of diminishing soil fertility as well as the failure of state in the migrant producing area to provide economic security to its people.

Myron Wiene, a truly great political science scholar in the US before his death, further categorised the movement of people into two groups; one was unwanted migrants and the other was rejected people. Under unwanted "migrants" you have the people who are not liked by the host community, they are disliked, they are unwanted, whether it is the Bangladeshis who come to Assam and Meghalaya, whether it is the Nepalese who go from southern Bhutan to eastern Nepal, the Chins of Myanmar who are now in Mizoram, the victims of food shortage and famine in Afghanistan who are fleeing to Iran and Pakistan. One is not certainly speaking in terms of refugee outflows here, we are talking of those who are forced to flee.

As far as the refugees are concerned, this group would come under the second category, which Weiner defined, which is rejected people. In this description, the classical refugees of our times are the Tibetans, the Kurds of Iraq and Turkey, the Tamils of Sri Lanka, the Afghans, including those who live in this country, the Chakmas of the Chittagong hill Tracts, the Rohingyas of the Arakan (Myanmar). These are people who have been rejected by their own governments, or who have fled due to oppression by brutal regimes as in the case of the Tibetans. In the seventies you had the case of the Vietnamese boat people who left their country for the South East Asian nations braving extreme misery and horrible conditions including rape by sea pirates. Most recently you had a ship load of Afghans floating around Australia and Papua New Guinea seeking asylum.

One thing needs to be made clear that a migrant is not necessarily a refugee. If one is speaking in economic or ecological terms, you have ecological and environmental migrants. 'Refugee' remains a political term. Yet a refugee can be a migrant. I find in many of the discussions that one participates in, there is really a lot of confusion on this issue because a migrant is not forcibly evicted or displaced. He/she chooses to move. It is a matter of personal choice and the attraction is better life in the new homeland. Take the case of India and Bangladesh. There is a four thousand-kilometre long border along West Bengal, Assam, Meghalaya and Tripura, of which about 800 km, 200 km in Assam and 600 km. in West Bengal, are fenced. A cursory look at the map of the region, and Bangladesh's own statistics, will tell only a part of the story, though it is surely one of the defining conditions behind the situation. In the area, which now constitutes Bangladesh the population doubled from 1961 to 1991 from 55 million to 111.4 million, the latest data indicates a population of about 120 million. Density is over 800 persons per sq.km. making Bangladesh the most densely populated country in the world. The pressure on land is acute and we are aware that substantial numbers are coming to India.

But why do people move? They don't pack their bags overnight and say that they will go to Dimapur, or Dispur or Sibsagar or Delhi. They move because of a situation of desperation. In fact, one of the Bangladesh academics said that it is really a strategy of survival. I don't think it is some great conspiracy. The Bangladesh Government continues to deny that there is any such movement, but from the work that some of us have been able to do with some Bangladesh academics and others including policy makers, then and now, there is an acknowledgement that this movement is taking place and they are beginning to speak quite openly about it. In fact they are beginning to study it as well. We are aware that since 1979 there has been this movement in Assam against illegal migration, which spread to other parts of the North East, including Manipur and Meghalaya. The reaction in Bengal has not been that acute to the problem although it exists. But it is in the heart of the North East, the Brahmaputra valley, that the issue has been most visible, in terms of confrontation and the scale of the problem.

The population in Bangladesh doubled in 30 years from 1961 to 1991, if the density of population is more than 800 per sq. km. for Bangladesh, in Assam it is about 285 per sq.km. Obviously the attractions of lower population density areas are evident. But there is another area, which we need to look at, which is the scale of flooding in Bangladesh itself. According to the Jehangir Nagar University, 18–20 million people every year are displaced internally by floods in Bangaldesh. There are floods and riverbank erosion. Now all of them are not coming to India, but it would be not implausible to believe that some of them would be. The inherent law of migration, as Dr. Bhuyan will tell you, is that people move not necessarily long distances, they move to areas close to themselves which are compatible, geographically and culturally. Over a period of time this outflow can cross international borders.

Now the issue that Prof. Kumar spoke of has not been of concern to the region just from the 1950s. There is the well-documented census report of 1921, which spoke of how an entire population from East Bengal has transplanted itself "in the last 25 years." The then Census Commissioner has said, "I can compare it only to the mass movement of a huge body of ants." Interestingly enough, although this was supported and organised by the Muslim League Government in Assam at the time, the party, which opposed it most strongly, was the Congress Party. The Assamese position in fact angered leaders like Jawaharlal Nehru and Vallabhbhai Patel because they felt it was holding up the process of independence. Ultimately Gandhiji took the side of Assam. The aim was essentially to hive off Assam from India and make it join East Pakistan. This concern continues to trouble people in Assam today. We are surely aware of the agitation of eighties, which resulted in the ethnic, linguistic and religious blood bath of 1983. As a reporter of the New York Times, I had the rather unfortunate task of covering this tragedy. In one area alone, which is Nellie, 1753 people were killed just because they happened to be Muslims. Some of them were new settlers but many of them were old ones and they were killed by their neighbours, by a fairly well organised group which had been planning it for weeks. But again, the core issue there was land. The immigrants there, who were almost hundred per cent Muslims, had basically taken over land belonging to the Tiwa tribals illegally by getting a 'chappa' (or thumb impression on pieces of paper and when they wanted the land back, the agitation and the elections of 1983 proved to be a good opportunity to settle scores.

It is interesting again what Prof. Kumar spoke about the Hindu population of Bangladesh. According to one Bangladeshi scholar, there are approximately 5 million missing Hindus in Bangladesh, if you look at the growth rate of the country. The Hindu population has grown by a bare 2 million in 40 years, from 9.2 million in 1951 to 11.1 in 1991 which is impossible. The Hindu rate of growth is pegged at 2.4 per cent and there are a large number of people who are missing. And where would they go? They have not become converts, nor they have just vanished. They have essentially moved to what would be regarded as the 'homeland' over there, which is West Bengal, Assam and Tripura.

Now it is not my argument that only one religious group is moving. The demographic changes in the border districts of West Bengal and Assam, and, to some extent, the changes in Meghalaya, is a clear indication of this.

As for the new exodus of Hindus from Bangladesh, they are true refugees, they are not migrants. They are as traumatised frightened and brutalised as refugees in any other part of the world and this has been seen especially since the new government in Bangladesh took over. The attacks have abated and the exodus has eased, but these incidents show the uncertainty and insecurity which remains a part of their lives, leading specially the rural middle class and the marginalised to leave. But most of the professionals in Bangladesh, who happen to be in what is the minority community, because of their privileges and position, continue to stay there. They remain economically and politically secure. Those who are the most vulnerable remain the small communities in small pockets surrounded by large majoritarian groups.

Now over today and tomorrow, many issues would be discussed which will bring into detail the conflict zones that are being created by illegal migration not just from Bangladesh and you will hear from the speakers their views on the problem and what is to be done. But let me set the ball rolling by talking about our failures. For 22 years we have spoken on the same issue in forum after forum, on the streets of Assam, in the newspapers of this country and still nothing has happened. What has happened is, there is national consciousness, the issue is seen as a problem, it may not be seen as a national problem, people are conscious of it and for that one thing we must pay tribute to the Assam agitation. But the problem has not gone away. In 22 years, neither the All Assam Students Union nor the Asom Gana Parishad or any other group for that matter has been able to develop a kind of calibrated response. We have still people talking in terms of what was talked about 22 years ago—detection and deportation. People still don't know how many people have crossed across. We are talking in terms of crores of people. I remember at the time of the Assam agitation, some were talking in terms of 2 crore or 4 crore of people in the North East. The entire population in the North East today is 35 million i.e. 3.5 crores! This kind of situation is really so full of rhetoric. We must guard against rhetoric because it always misleads; it is divorced from reality. The Asom Gana Parishad, the AASU and the BJP, to some extent, have been speaking about the issues of illegal migration and threats to national security, potential violence etc. and the local people being marginalised and outsiders taking political and economic control. We have been bathing in this kind of soap water for the last 20 years and we have swallowed the soap and the water without questioning anything. We should be very careful when we use the word 'Bangladeshi' because it is becoming a pejorative word. Anybody who has been here since 1971 is a Bangaldeshi. Those who have come before then are not Bangladeshi because there was no Bangladesh. He is an East Pakistani, which does not exist. I would suggest that we need to look at issues in very practical terms because we must stop talking in the same monologue, in the same fashion, in the same dialectic, with the same flourishes which have characterised the movement since its start. What is the result of it today? Look at Assam where the whole thing began. The Congress Party has come to power because this chant of 'illegal migration' fails to enthuse people any longer because in 22 years you have not been able to do anything about it. That is why we need to look at things with a very specific approach as well as a broad-brush approach. And we need to start thinking with our heads and stop thinking with our hearts because logic is always sacrificed at the altar of rhetoric. So, as I said, it is a **nationally recognised** issue or problem, but not a national issue or problem.

One of the first things that we must all fight for is for it to come on the political agenda of all parties. Whether they believe there is illegal migration or not, the issue is strong enough in order to be on the political agenda of all parties. Right now it is on the political agenda of only two—one the Asom Gana Parishad which has failed abysmally to deal with it and the other is the BJP. And I don't see why the CPI (M) and other parties like the Congress and the Samajvadi cannot include it on their own agendas. Recently, I think in Denmark they had a vote and the government changed on the simple issue of migration. Migration was the issue. That was the issue that brought a political party to power. And I think that is one thing we need to focus on.

The second thing which we need to look at is to strongly argue— and I hope we will have some discussion and support for this—for a National Immigration Council or a National Immigration Commission because we can talk about all sorts of solutions to this problem. We can talk about a law and order approach, a security approach, a legal approach, a NGO approach, a human right approach, but there is nothing in this country that empowers anybody to look at the whole picture in its true perspective. And if you have a National Immigration Commission, as they have in the United States for instance, you would be able to look at all the laws. Let us look at all the laws that exist—the Foreigners' Act, The Illegal Migration (Determination) Tribunal Act which has been a failure and has sent out only about 1500 people, most of whom have probably come back with their families since it was promulgated in 1983. It can look at the Foreigners' Act. It can evolve a National Migration Law, it can evolve a National Refugee Law. We don't even know how many refugees exist in this country? How many have come from Tibet, we may know, and from Sri Lanka to some extent we know, but do you know how many refugees there are from Bhutan who escaped the wrath of the Drukpa and have taken refuge in Kokrajhar and Darrang en route to Eastern Nepal?

Then we can also see how the security aspects tie in. We have in fact somebody from JNU, Prof. Chimni, who has done a compendium on national refugee law for India. We should not make the mistake of thinking that barbed wire fencings are going to protect our country. They cannot, they can be a facilitator in helping to guard the boundaries, but the boundaries are best guarded by communities which are acutely aware of the problem and by supporting the border security force with local police because it is the local police who know what the routes are and who is organising them. The BSF, good as it is, is stymied by the fact of either lack of intelligence or the problem of non-cooperation.

Again we should look at the facts and figures. Prof. Singh spoke about the growth rate and that illegal migrants are everywhere in the North East. You just look at the growth rates in all the States. They are all higher than the national average. The worst case is

Nagaland. Nagaland has a 67 per cent decadal growth rate. That means in 1991 there were 10 lakh people in Nagaland. Today there are 16.7 lakhs. That is incredible, I mean you cannot have population growth like that. The natural fertility cannot be so high. (Interruption: 34 per cent is the average now). Yes, but this is double of that. Where does the extra 34 per cent come from? That is the question. In the question answer session perhaps we can get into the whole concept of identity cards and work permits, because I do believe that the ID cards must be the basis for identifying who is an Indian and who is a resident and who is not. And work permits should enable people to come in legally, stay for a year or two and go back. But without the ID cards, you cannot have work permit scheme.

There is one area we haven't looked at and even those who have studied the issue of migration have not touched on it—the question of AIDs and migrant workers. This is becoming an increasing problem within the country and I see no reason why this will not be exacerbated by migration. Mr. Prakash Singh, former head of the BSF and the UP Police, is here, a very senior and respected law enforcement officer of this country. He will speak on national security. I believe that there are elements in the migrants which are used by different groups—whether it is the insurgent groups in the North East or outside of it, or their patrons from Pakistan or Bangladesh—but I do not see migrants per se as a threat to India.There may be an economic pressure but I do not see them as a security threat except for those elements that exist.

Finally, one of the things that we should consider is reservations— that is a horrible word—for the local communities in the State Assembly which could be perhaps there for the next 20 to 30 years. Whatever the shape or size of the population, not less than 60 per cent should be reserved for the local communities. We may have lot of problem in defining what local communities are, but there is enough work through your magnum opus, Prof. Singh, *The People of India Series* which can be a basis for this.

I believe regional cooperation with Bangladesh is important, economic growth is important, because without building the nuts and bolts of infrastructure, we will continue to have this outflow. The best thing is to develop not just the border regions but a bit insides as well so that roads, railways and waterways are used to transport goods and to develop infrastructure. You can have fruit processing, free trade zones on the border and this will strengthen the economies of both sides. Otherwise we will feel falling into this spiral of poverty chasing poverty and will never be able to come out of it.

I have talked to people in Bangladesh who have travelled to Assam, who have worked in Assam for 20–30 years, who have voted in elections in Assam and who have been patronised by Assamese, who work as fishermen near Jorhat, in Sadiya and other places. We need to be a bit more honest in the North East and other parts of this country as to why people come. They come because we also patronise them. We have patronised them. If you go across the Yamuna in Delhi, look at the fishing nets. The fishing nets on the Yamuna are by no stretch of imagination from UP or Bihar. You see those fishing nets much more in West Bengal and Bangladesh. So we need to embrace reality and shed rhetoric and be very wary of quick-fix answers.

Just one quote from Amartya Sen and I will end. He gave this remarkable lecture on inclusion and exclusion a few days ago, because he talked about Hutington's clash of civilisations. He stated clearly, and I agree, that a person can be of a particular faith but have other identities as well.

He says here that categorisation is both a serious epistemic mistake and potentially great ethical and political hazard with far reaching consequences on human rights. People do see themselves in many different ways. A Bangladeshi Muslim is not only a Muslim but also a Bengali and a Bangladeshi, not to mention the after identity that he/she may have, connected with class, gender, occupation, politics, taste and so on. A Nepalese Hindu is not only a Hindu but also had ethnic and physical and political characteristics that have their own relevance along with other identities that make him/her what he/she is.

5

Migration from (East Bengal/East Pakistan) Bangladesh to India

JAYANTA KUMAR RAY

The territory designated as Bangladesh since 1971 was known as East-Bengal till 1956, and as East-Pakistan from 1956 to 1971. Migration from Bangladesh to India cannot be totally segregated from that in earlier periods. To write this is not to suggest that such migration has gone on for such a long time that it should be treated as natural and acceptable. It is certainly not acceptable to those for whom India's national interest is far more important than academic verbiage on economic-geographical compulsions behind migration.

While discussing migration from Bangladesh to India, it is politically as well as ethically important to distinguish between refugees, i.e. Hindus, and infiltrators, i.e. Muslims. Circumstances of the 1947 Partition, assurances given by top-ranking political leaders of India to Hindus staying on in Pakistan (including East Bengal), and an uninterrupted squeezing out of Hindus from East Bengal/East Pakistan/Bangladesh since 1947—in contrast to the care with which interests of Muslims are safeguarded in the secular-democratic polity of India, a contrast that is even compatible with the appeasement of, or blackmail by, minorities (mainly Muslims) in India—sustain this categorisation of migrants from Bangladesh into refugees and infiltrators.

In the late 20th and early 21st centuries, this distinction between refugees and infiltrators derives additional justification from the employment of a number of infiltrators by Pakistan, especially its Inter Services Intelligence (ISI), for the promotion of Islamisation of South Asia as a component of the campaign for

Worldwide Islamic Terrorism (WIT). Consequently, various attempts at underplaying this distinction, and minimising the threat to India's national interest from infiltration, are akin to abdication (voluntary or involuntary, selfish or disinterested) in favour of the forces of WIT.

Not to speak of what has been uninterruptedly happening in the territory currently comprising Bangladesh since 1947, even in Assam or West Bengal, whenever Muslims form a majority in a specific area, they try to evict Hindus from that or a nearby area, and often succeed. For this purpose, infiltrators initially try to resort to thefts, dacoities, murder and molestation of women. But, eventually, they do not hesitate to stage large-scale riots. Ruling politicians turn a blind eye. They are too preoccupied with treating infiltrators as vote banks, and winning short-term political gains. They remain oblivious of the long-term cultural-economic-political impact.

Social scientists reinforce this tendency of shortsighted politicians by isolating the cause of infiltration from its consequences. The cause may be economic in most cases. This is true of Indians migrating to Britain or Mexicans migrating to the United States—to take a few examples. But, to treat infiltration from Bangladesh to India as a part of the worldwide phenomenon of economic migration is to miss the vital points that, for instance, Indians migrating to British or Mexicans moving to the United States do not upset the demographic/electoral balance in the host countries. Nor do they strengthen such forces as the forces of WIT masterminded by Pakistan. In Assam or West Bengal today, infiltrators (of course in collusion with the older generation of Muslims) can determine or influence the outcome of elections in such large number of constituencies that ruling politicians fail to summon courage to curb infiltration, and thereby play into the hands of the ISI backed WIT.

An overemphasis upon the economic compulsions behind infiltration is unrealistic. For, interested persons, including political aspirants and promoters of WIT, have utilised economic factors to organise large-scale infiltration. The spectre of the 1931 census report of Assam is now haunting the Assamese Hindus—their culture and history are about to be altered (if not distroyed) permanently. Prosperous Muslims (as assiduous fieldwork and direct observation can easily demonstrate) have been buying up lands of poor Hindus in villages, and setting up compact zones exclusively inhabited by Muslim infiltrators. Alternatively, Hindus are forced by various forms of visible and invisible pressures to part with lands/houses/shops, which fall into the hands of Muslims. This is happening in West Bengal too, and social scientists parading the economic cause of infiltration should be able to muster the courage to carry out a comparative analysis of Assam and West Bengal on this matter. In Assam, moreover, numerous infiltrators have availed of the services of powerful (though invisible) agencies preparing fake passports as also bogus voters lists (of other States) to baffle government functionaries trying to arrest infiltration.

Those who tend to underplay the adverse impact of infiltration upon India by overstressing the economic impetus behind infiltration go as far as to plead that India should provide large-scale assistance towards the economic development of Bangladesh, especially when the Farakka barrage and the division of Ganga waters between Bangladesh and India (West Bengal) have desertified a large part of Bangladesh, thereby creating environmental refugees who emerge as infiltrators in India. This plea suffers from a number of infirmities. First, we may refer to the agreements of 1977 and 1996 on the division of Ganga Waters at the Farakka point. The 1977 agreement has been grossly inequitable to India, converting as it were a predominantly Indian river into a Bangladesh river. To take one example of inequity, since Bangladesh contains 0.73 per cent of the Ganga's catchment area, according to the Helsinki regulations (which comprise the current international law on the subject), Bangladesh can claim only 375 cusecs of water if, for instance, 50,000 cusecs of water are totally available. Similarly, comparing other data for the two countries, e.g., length of the river passing through the two countries, population, etc. Bangladesh should obtain far below the 62.5 per cent share allocated to it by the India-Bangladesh agreement of 1977. Unfortunately, the Bangladesh media seldom publicise such data, which strike at the root of anti-Indian propaganda centring on the Farakka barrage. But why should Indian scholars fall a prey to such propaganda? As to the 1996 Ganga waters agreement, a revision in the schedule of division of waters during the dry season (January–May) conveys a greater impression of equity than that in the 1977 agreement. For instance, in terms of the 1977 agreement, the Calcutta port (whose preservation was the primary aim of the Farakka barrage) received the necessary minimum of 40,000 cusecs of water for only one ten-day cycle in the entire lean season from January to May. In the 1996 agreement, this anomaly has been partially rectified. Nevertheless, the availability of water for the Calcutta port, and the outburst of anti-India propaganda in Bangladesh, depend basically on the weather god. If, as in 1998, there is ample rainfall, Bangladeshis scale down anti-Indian propaganda on the Farakka issue. If rainfall is scanty, as in 1997, such propaganda shoots up.

Secondly, those who try to relate infiltration of an imaginary desertification in Bangladesh because of the Farakka barrage, may be advised to study the Flood Action Plan (FAP) prepared in 1989 by the Government of Bangladesh with substantial aid from France, Japan, the UNDP, the USAID, and the World Bank. This study will convince them of the hollowness of the Bangladeshi complaint about the adverse impact of the Farakka barrage on agricultural production in Bangladesh. On this point, some Bangladeshi analysts (and their absentminded Indian counterparts) appear to be trying to convert untruth into truth by sheer repetition of illogical monstrosities. According to such analysts, withdrawal of water by India through the Farakka barrage during the dry season has desertified a large area of Bangladesh. This contention is flatly contradicted by data available from the 1989 FAB and other relevant documents. Thus, the production/acreage/yield of rice and pulses registered a steady increase in Bangladesh from 1981 to 1991. Whereas most of the pulses are dry season crops, and there is no opportunity to bring any new area under wet season cultivation, the increase of agricultural production can only take place if an increasingly larger quantity of land is utilised during the dry season. This cannot but demonstrate the futility of the charge that the Farakka barrage has had a disastrous impact upon Bangladesh agriculture. In fact, in 1992–93, Bangladesh produced 19 million tons of rice, and thereby did away with the necessity to import it. Moreover, interestingly, whatever smuggling of rice from West Bengal to Bangladesh took place previously, came to a stop by 2000. Obviously, dry season crops depend heavily on ground water for irrigation. Inadequacy of surface run of the Ganga-Padma, supposedly due to India's unilateral withdrawal of Ganga water, cannot, therefore, be regarded as the cause of shortfall in such water necessary for irrigation in the Ganga-Padma basin in the dry season. The argument that lifting of groundwater, on which agriculture in the region depends, is suffering because the water table is going down due to inadequate recharge in the monsoon season is not borne out by the facts. Normal rainfall, that is average rainfall, in a heavy rainfall region (i.e., the region under consideration) is good enough for replenishment of groundwater discharged during the preceding dry season.

Thirdly, those who advocate accelerating the economic development of Bangladesh by substantial Indian aid in order to curb infiltration, fail to take not of ground realities. It is not for lack of resources, including foreign aid (which is at least 2 billion United States dollars a year), that Bangladesh remains a low income country. It is because of utter mismanagement of available resources by ruling politicians, administrators, businessmen and criminals. It is, therefore, idle to expect that a huge infusion of aid by India can cause a dramatic rise in Bangladesh's economic fortunes. In this context, one can refer to the deplorably low impact of massive economic assistance supplied by New Delhi to Jammu and Kashmir, as also to some States in northeast India (which is several times larger than the assistance provided to other States in the Indian Union). It is, therefore, advisable to avoid being misled by the emphasis on the economic causes of migration, and devise realistic measures to cope with the evil consequences of infiltration for India (whatever the cause).

Those who overplay the economic origins of infiltration are probably less guilty of undermining India's national security, cultural integrity and social harmony than those who try to deny the fact of infiltration and/or its impact. The *Statesman* of Kolkata published in 1981 a series of articles on infiltration from Bangladesh to West Bengal. They analysed the seriousness of the impact of such infiltration upon the State. At that time, Jyoti Basu was the Chief Minister of West Bengal. He dismissed the *Statesman* report as wild speculation. Assam's Hiteswar Saikia, however, went much ahead of Jyoti Basu in ignoring infiltration. Before he occupied the post of Chief Minister, he promised to drive out Bangladeshi infiltrators from Assam. Subsequently, when he became the Chief Minister, he displayed an expertise in adopting those political postures which amounted to a virtual denial of the dangers of infiltration.

Another tactic of those who intend to deny or underemphasise the menace of infiltration is to complain of lack of absolutely accurate statistics. They easily forget that there are vital socio-economic matters on which it is not possible to collect absolutely accurate statistics, e.g., on the rate of interest charged by village money-lenders, the amount of black money circulating in India, the rate of inflation, or even the number of murders in a city. What is important is to collect approximately accurate and plausible statistics. Even more important, one should not use the pretext of lack of totally accurate estimates for stalling public response. On infiltration, one can prepare valid estimates by comparing, for example, the census data of Bangladesh and West Bengal.

But, the, strength of the coalition of national/international lobbies operating in India to conceal the data on infiltration—probably, partially aligned with the forces of WIT—is enormous. That may explain why the 1991 census report of Bangladesh could provide fairly accurate data about migration of Hindus/Muslims from Bangladesh to India, whereas the 1991 census report of India created confusion by withholding data about the number of Hindus and Muslims in various States. Although it published the number of Indians belonging to the Scheduled Castes and Scheduled Tribes. Nevertheless, this confusion could be removed, and the plausibility of Bangladesh census data on infiltration could be confirmed, on 17 August 1995, when P.M. Syed, India's Minister of State for Home, revealed in parliament the rate of growth of Hindus and Muslims in various States during 1981–91. Syed responded to a question by a Congress Member of Parliament.

A few example from Syed's statement may be cited here to underline the menace of infiltration from Bangladesh. The total Population Growth Rate (PGR) in Mizoram during 1981–91 stood at 39.70 per cent. But the PGR for Muslims was 105.80 per cent. In Arunachal Pradesh, again, the PGR for Muslims stood at 135.01 per cent, whereas the total PGR was 36.83 per cent. Immediately upon reading these figures, however, apologists of infiltration may point out that the population of Mizoram or Arunachal is so small that the total number of Muslims—in spite of the PGR being as high as noted above—is not large. This is, however, small consolation to those who are alarmed over the probable repetition of the Assam/West Bengal phenomenon in Mizoram or Arunachal in the coming decades.

A comparative study of the 1991 census reports of Bangladesh and West Bengal throws up abundant evidence of large-scale infiltration into West Bengal. The 1991 census report of Bangladesh placed the annual PGR during 1981–91 at 2.1 per cent, whereas the United Nations Population Fund estimated it at 2.7 per cent. Moreover, the 1991 census report Bangladesh was not compatible with the fertility rate of 4.5. Consequently, the Bangladesh census report of 1991 talks of a unique phenomenon, viz., the missing population, estimated initially at 10 million, and subsequently at 8 million, of whom 1.73 million are Hindus, and 6.27 million are Muslims. In contrast, in West Bengal, the actual PGR during the 1981–91 decade was 24.55 per cent, whereas the forecast of the demographic experts of the Government of India put it at 20.7 per cent. This disparity could be explained by infiltration from Bangladesh.

Remarkably, even the Election Commission of Bangladesh lends support to such infiltration by the deletion of 2 million missing voters during 1991–95. These voters (along with non-voter family members in many cases) could not have moved to advanced countries like Australia, Britain, Canada or the United States, or to oil-rich West Asian countries. Assuming that 1 million of these absentees left Bangladesh without family members, and another million left along with four family members on an average, the annual number of infiltrators to India can be estimated at 1 million as the minimum. It may be added that, on account of the massacre of a large number of infiltrators in Assam in 1983, West Bengal remains a preferred destination of most of these infiltrators.

Infiltrators have not only settled in West's Bengal's border districts, but also spread to interior areas. West Bengal's PGR during 1981–91 was 24.73 per cent, whereas the PGR for Muslims stood at 36.89 pert cent. Not to speak of border areas, even the interior districts of Midnapore and Bankura witnessed a huge disparity in the PGRs of Hindus and Muslims during 1981–91. In Midnapore, the

PGR of Hindus was 19.74 per cent. Of Muslims 53.80 per cent. For Bankura, the respective figures were 14.33 per cent and 38.71 per cent. Such disparities in the PGRs of Hindus and Muslims can be explained by infiltration only.

The Government of West Bengal did not exhibit any concern for the above noted data revealed in Parliament on 17 August 1995 by the Union Minister of State for Home, P.M. Syed, Newspapers in Calcutta behaved in a similar way, none of them bothering to print or comment on these data. At least two important assertions by Syed could not have escaped the attention of Calcutta's mediapersons, unless they decided deliberately to ignore them. In one of these assertions Syed even deviated from the classic secularist discourse as he admitted that infiltration from Bangladesh accounted for the growth of Muslims in West Bengal's border areas. Syed, however, struck to the secularist idiom in his second important utterance as he spoke of "locals moving into the interior" of West Bengal from the border areas. He camouflaged the truth: the collusion of infiltrators and other Muslims made Hindus the targets of ethnic explusion from border areas.

In 1995, the National Council of Applied Economic Research (NCAER) brought out an important study on smuggling across West Bengal's border with Bangladesh. Essential articles of everyday use like cycles, livestock, parts of various machines, spices, vegetable oil, etc., are regularly smuggled from West Bengal to Bangladesh in huge quantities. The number and volume of such essential commodities smuggled from Bangladesh to India are hardly significant. The question then arises as to how smugglers on both sides settle their accounts. **The NCAER study points to the smuggling of arms, gold and narcotics from Bangladesh to India as an answer to this question.** The significance of this finding was farreaching, but newspapers in Calcutta failed to pay much attention to the NCAER study. Nor was there any evidence that the Government of West Bengal was interested in this study. **The evident linkage between infiltrators, smugglers and terrorists (especially those in northeast India) was not duly explored. All infiltrators are not smugglers, and all smugglers are not terrorists. But, on account obvious socio-economic reasons, powerful syndicates, engaged in cross-border smuggling of arms, gold and narcotics, find it relatively convenient to recruit infiltrators for their deadly ventures.**

Such inaction or despondency on the part of Union/State Governments in dealing with infiltrators—presumably in pursuit of a peculiar brand of politics of vote banks in which a minority community is appeased, whereas the majority community is taken for granted—is nothing new. In the 1960s, it was possible for an alert and energetic Superintendent of Police in Assam to catch infiltrators and deport them. Gradually, these powers were taken away from the Police Superintendents, and infiltrators made the maximum possible use of a porous border. The Illegal Migration Determination by Tribunal (IMDT) Act of 1983 institutionalised the chronic inaction/ despondency of Union/State Governments in coping with infiltration. It is a sort of record in contemporary world history that the IMDT Act not only perpetuates infiltration but protects infiltrators by placing the onus of proof on government functionaries who do not have the minimum of resources (in terms of money, equipment and manpower) to generate this proof. Less than 1500 persons could be deported over a period of 16 years under the IMDT Act.

In 1993, Congress party leaders of seven northeastern States of India sent a detailed report to their party headquarters in New Delhi. This report linked infiltration to the ISI-funded campaign of subversion in India, as also to collusion between Pakistan and Bangladesh on this issue. In 1994, Prakash Singh, the retiring Director General of the Border Security Force, warned the Union Home Ministry of the grim possibility that, on a account of infiltration and terrorism, the situation in northeast India would degenerate into that in Jammu and Kashmir. In 1998, Lt. Gen. (Retd.) S.K. Sinha, the Governor of Assam, sent a 42-page report to the President of India. This report cautioned that the northeast region could eventually slip out of India's political control, because massive infiltration upset the demographic balance and diluted the identity of the people, whereas the ISI used bases in Bangladesh to carry on terrorist activities in northeast India.

All these reports/reminders/warnings, however, proved to be powerless before the continuing sway of the politics of vote banks. No decisive action was taken by Union/State Governments to evict infiltrators and stop further infiltration. Nevertheless, in the late 1990s, some State Governments, which were previously reluctant to acknowledge the importance of the problem of infiltration, were compelled to recognise it publicly. Presumably, the linkage between infiltration and terrorism became too glaring to be ignored. Thus, in early 1999, Manik Sarkar, the Chief Minister of Tripura, affirmed publicly that there were 24 main camps in Bangladesh which provided operational bases to terrorists in northeast India. In the same year, in an affidavit before the Supreme Court of India, required in a public interest litigation on infiltration, the Government of West Bengal tendered an unqualified admission about infiltration. It stated that detection and deportation of infiltrators remained an insuperable problem, because the patronage of local politicians, touts and government functionaries enabled numerous infiltrators to procure ration cards for themselves, and/or enlist themselves as voters. In March 1999, West Bengal's Director General of Police even affirmed that terrorists (including those accused of causing serial blasts in Mumbai and New Delhi) chose some educational and religious institutions (euphemisms or secularised terms for madrasahs and mosques in West Bengal as their hideaways. A number of newspapers in Calcutta, however, did not consider it fit to publish this important news. In June 1999, the ISI must have shocked West Bengal's decision-makers when an explosion at the New Jalpaiguri railway station killed and injured a large number of Indian soldiers moving to Kargil.

There was, however, little evidence that the Government of West Bengal was taking or planning determined steps to curb infiltration and terrorism. Necessary steps were not taken even in the Siliguri corridor forming a strategic link between the rest of India and the northeast region, as also between India, Nepal, Bhutan and Bangladesh. The Government of Nepal appears to be incapable of exercising any effective control over a large number of madrasahs and mosques at the India-Nepal border, which promote WIT. But the West Bengal Government, too, does not appear to be successful in restraining the growth of such madrasahs and mosques in West Bengal's border areas, including the Siliguri corridor. The politics of minority vote banks casts sometimes such an insidious influence on the Union and State Governments of India that the Madhab Godbole Committee Report of 2000 on infiltration remains unpublished. Among other things, the subversive role of madrasahs receives due attention in this report. In the late 1990s only 40 out of 900 madrasahs set up in West Bengal's border areas cared to secure government approval. One thousand mosques were illegally constructed in these areas during 1994–99. There is a reasonable suspicion that many mosques in West Bengal (including Calcutta) have set up armouries. Otherwise, there is no explanation as to why the Calcutta police had to call in the army on 7 December 1992, when, in a Muslim-majority area of the city, Hindu houses/shops became targets of arson and loot.

Insurgency/terrorism/unrest in India's northeast has its roots in massive infiltration from Bangladesh. In one sense, the problems of terrorism in northeast India have the potentialities of becoming much more complicated than those in Jammu and Kashmir. For, in Jammu and Kashmir, India has to deal mainly with one foreign country, viz. Pakistan. But, in the northeast, India has to deal with five foreign countries, i.e. Bangladesh, Myanmar, China, Nepal and Bhutan. In fact, northeast India has already exported its unrest to Bhutan. The people of West Bengal are, indeed, fortunate that as yet no northeast India-type infiltration-related eruption has occurred in West Bengal. But this is no ground for complacency. For as General (Retd.) Shankar Roy Chowdhury, a Rajya Sabha member from West Bengal, told the Rajya Sabha in April 2000, **on account of illegal migration, Bangladesh's demographic border intruded upon India's political border over a 10–20 km deep area. He also remained the Rajya Sabha that Bangladesh remained a base of ISI operations.** All this was a euphemistic (or secularist) way of underlining the menace of infiltration. **But newspapers in Calcutta failed to convey this message to their readers.**

There may be a tendency to draw comfort from the 2001 census report which puts the average population rise in West Bengal during 1991–2001 at 17.84 per cent. This is a decline from the PGR of 24.55 per cent in West Bengal during 1981–91. But there is no cause for complacency about the continuing danger of infiltration. For, according to the 2001 census, population rise in the border districts of North 24 Parganas, Mushidabad and Malda has been, respectively, 22.64 per cent, 23.7 per cent and 24.77 per cent. In the second place, the burden of past infiltration is too heavy to be shrugged off. In the third place, the 2000 general election in

Bangladesh has brought to power a political party, the Bangladesh Nationalist Party (BNP), which was born in the cantonment, and has close ties with Pakistan's ISI through the Bangladesh Government's Defence Forces Intelligence (DFI) and National Security Intelligence (NSI). In fact, over the past decades, the DFI and NSI have accumulated so much of clout, and have such organic relationship with the ISI, that even if the civilian government, led by the BNP, tries to tame the ISI, it is not likely to succeed. Moreover, the Jamaat-e-islami, the ally of the BNP, will not endorse any attempt to curb ISI operations. In the foreseeable future, therefore, the eastern and northeastern region of India has to be alert in breaking the terrorist-infiltrator linkage, especially in the aftermath of the anti-Taliban war in Afghanistan. For, many agents of WIT may be forced to switch over from northwest to eastern and northeastern India.

6

Illegal Migration from Bangladesh

D.N. Bezboruah

I would like to begin my presentation with two very important news items which appeared in the newspapers of the North-east yesterday. On Monday, the Khaplang faction of the NSCN accused the Isaac-Muivah faction of the NSCN (Nationalist Socialist Council of Nagaland) of encouraging large-scale and unabated influx of Bangladeshis into Nagaland mainly for the safety of its bases and camps in Bangladesh. The NSCN (Khaplang) says that the NSCN (Isaac-Muivah) faction "has been undermining the threat posed by the infiltrators to the cultural and linguistic identity of the Nagas." This warning came far too late in the day, because the Nagaland population increased from 12 million in 1991 to just under 20 million in 2001—in one decade an increase of 64.41 per cent. I am certainly not saying that this is entirely due to illegal migration from Bangladesh, but there is a certain component which is undeniable.

On the same day, the Vishwa Hindu Parishad took a vow to evict all Bangladeshi infiltrators from India if the Bangladesh Government did not stop harassing the minority Hindus from the country within fifteen days. Again, a vow which has come far too late in the day considering that the number of illegal Bangladeshi infiltrators into India exceed 1 crore, according to some very reliable estimates, and this is an estimate that even the Home Ministry concurs with.

To get an idea of how serious the problem of illegal infiltration from Bangaldesh is, it is useful to look at the population increase in the North-Eastern States of India between 1991 and 2001.

Arunachal Pradesh had a population of 864,558 in 1991. It has gone up to 1,091,117 by 2001, the increase is 26.20 per cent.

Assam had a population of 22,414,322 in 1991 and the population has gone up to 26 million 638 odd thousand. The growth rate is 18.84 per cent, lowest in the North-east and even lower than the national average, which leads me to have a very strong suspicion that the 2001 census might have suffered from certain infirmities because it is my firm conviction that the 1991 census in Assam was doctored. I will come to that a little later.

Manipur's population was 1 million 837 thousand odd in 1991, it has gone up to 2 million 338 thousand-odd in 2001, an increase of 30 per cent.

Meghalaya's population has gone up from 1,774,778 to 2,306,069, an increase of 29.92 per cent.

Mizoram's population has gone up from 689,756 to 891,058, an increase of 29.18 per cent.

Nagaland's increase is most shocking. From 1,209,546 it has gone up to almost 2 million, an increase of 64.41 per cent.

In Sikkim likewise, the increase is 32 per cent, in Tripura it is the lowest, 15.73 per cent.

But that apart, it is interesting to see what has happened to the decadal increase of population in Assam. Between 1951 and 1961, the Assam's decadal increase was 34.98 per cent, between 1961 and 1971, Assam's decadal increase was 34.95 per cent, close to 35 per cent, in 1981 we did not have a census, but the significant thing was that in 1981 the Census of India carried out a projection which put the population of Assam at 19 million 900-odd thousand. This would have put the decadal increase at 36.04 per cent. Interestingly, the Statesman Year Book published by Macmillan from London, which we consider to be a very reliable book on Statistics, also made a projection which strangely differed from the Census of India projection by a mere 6,000 which, in my opinion, is very close. I made my own projection which was a little more conservative, and therefore, it was lower. The point I am trying to make is that it was more or less uniform: 1951–61, 34.98 per cent, 1961–71 34.95 per cent, then 1971 to 1981, the projected 36.04 per cent, and then suddenly when we had the 1991 census there was interpolation and as a result of this, the 1981 projection came down drastically. **I have openly expressed the view that I do**

not accept the 1991 census figure for Assam because I have information that there were verbal instructions sent out that in the immigrant dominated areas, that only the first wife of the immigrant and her children were to be enumerated and not the subsequent wives and their children. The other thing that happened is that I know for a fact that in places like Guwahati and Tinsukhia, there were high density pockets of population where no enumeration took place. So the combined effect was that it did bring down the population. This was something on which Mr. Sanjoy Hazarika challenged the late Hiteswar Saikia and he, of course, denied it, but anyone who watched him on TV must have realised that the denial was not quite convincing. I won't go into that.

There are three important factors to be borne in mind when we talk of large-scale illegal migration from Bangladesh into India: (1) Immigration is a Central subject under the Constitution. We keep forgetting that. At the same time, I will say that the whole process of making immigration—cross-border immigration—easy or difficult is in the hands of the State. I am not denying that, but the subject under the Constitution, which takes care of immigration, the laws and all that, is a Union subject. (2) The large-scale migration from East Pakistan was encouraged by the Congress mainly to be able to win elections without any sweat. It started around 1962. I can tell you about the bygone leaders of the Congress who did not have to go out in the sun to canvass for the elections. They sat in their verandahs, called in the *matabbars* and leaders of the immigrant communities and said, "Look, I am standing for the elections, you know what you have to do. You do that. They said, "We will do that, but then what about the voting rights for these fellows?" "Don't worry, we will take care of that." "What about some land for these fellows?" "Don't worry, it will be taken care of." This is how the trend started. Today, every Congressman that I speak to personally admits that the problem was created largely by the party, but they cannot afford to confess it publicly. So what they do is to pretend that these fellows are, in fact, Indian minorities. So this is the problem. The Congress has been in power for the longest in Assam, they have had the time to do the mischief, and now because they have got used to the power that the vote-bank brings, others have also put on the same shoes and benefited from this. There is a saying in Assamese, whoever goes to

Lanka becomes a Ravana. It has happened to other political parties in the State as well.

That apart, my third point is that large-scale illegal infiltration from Bangladesh has not taken place only for economic reasons. I am not denying the economic reasons part, but it is not only for economic reasons. Most of it is being orchestrated. And this is evident from the fact that the ISI is today playing a very large role. And where is the base of the ISI operations in the North-east? It is in Bangladesh. We can have all kinds of friendship treaties between India and Bangladesh, but when you actually come down to brass tacks, I don't know whether there is something wrong with our foreign policy, but India has not been able to find one single neighbour that is genuinely friendly. Every neighbour, including Bhutan, has begun to be unfriendly towards India. They call it the "Big Brother syndrome," that is another issue altogether, but I don't think it is just a "Big Brother syndrome." (Interruption: Even the States are not friendly). It is planned and orchestrated by people within the country. Look at what happened to the immigration law. There is in the case of Assam a terrible double standard not only in respect of the immigration law, but also in respect of the cut-off date for migrants from erstwhile Pakistan. For the rest of the country, if I am not mistaken, it is 18th July 1948, but for Assam it is 25th March 1971. For the rest of the country, you still have the Foreigners Act of 1946 enforced, whereas for Assam you have the IM(DT) Act about which I will talk a little later. And who drafted the IM(DT) Act? Mr. Abdul Mohin Mazumdar, who was Law Minister in Hiteshwar Saikia's time. And when was the IM(DT) Act pushed through? In 1983 when even Assam had boycotted the elections and therefore did not have any representatives in Parliament. So it was an Act brought *against* the people of Assam behind the backs of the people of Assam.

Now there is also a strong demand within Bangladesh on the basis of what the Bangladeshi intellectuals call "*lebensraum*" or living space and they seem to put it across as if they have a right to the living space that is available around Bangladesh and I will quote excerpts from what people like Sadiq Khan and Abdul Momin, both Foreign Secretaries of Bangladesh and considered to be intellectuals, have said. I will read from an Article I wrote long ago—"Our Land, their Living Space." "A few articles in the Bangladesh press by some responsible and eminent Bangladeshi thinkers should throw light on the Bangladeshi perception on the question of the country's unbearable population growth and its large-scale illegal immigration to other countries. On the question of "*lebensraum*" by Sadiq Khan, in the Weekly *Holiday* of October 18, 1991, the writer, a former diplomat and intellectual, puts forth a strong defence of the large-scale Bangladeshi immigration." Incidentally the name of the newspaper *Holiday* is most misleading. It is a bit of a digression, but it is an interesting bit digression. Far from having anything to do much with holidays, the paper is about the most highly political publication of Bangladesh. The innocuous-sounding name had to be chosen because it commenced publication during the early years of martial law, and a newspaper with a less innocuous-sounding name would not have had any chance of securing permission to publish. This was revealed to the writer by the editor of the *Holiday* himself, who also owns the paper. This is how Mr. Sadiq Khan's article on Lebensraum, a German word meaning 'living space,' begins. I quote:

"The question of '*lebensraum*' or living space for the people of Bangladesh has not yet been raised as a moot point. All projections however clearly indicate that by the next decade, that is to say by the first decade of the 21st century, Bangladesh will face a serious crisis of *lebensraum*. No possible performance of population planning, actual or hypothetical, significantly alters that prediction."

And then come two crucial paragraphs that leave no one in any doubt about the Bangladeshi intentions. I quote:

"It is said that a borderless world has become the prime requisite for economic growth under the new world order. In fairness, if consumer benefit is considered to be better served by borderless competitive trade of commodities, why not borderless competitive trade of labour? There is no reason why Bangladesh should not insist on a globalised manpower market as consumer markets of nation states are being progressively globalised under the dictates of monetarists. There is no reason why regional and international cooperation could not be worked out to plan and execute population movements and settlements to avoid critical demographic pressures in pockets of high concentration. There is no reason why under-populated regions in the developed world cannot make room for planned colonies to relieve build up of demographic disasters in countries like Bangladesh."

Then I will just add one more sentence from the next paragraph. I won't bother you with the rest of it. It says: "The natural trend of population overflow from Bangladesh is towards sparsely populated lands of the South East on the Arakan side and of the North East in the Seven Sisters side of the Indian continent."

Now obviously the whole Indo-Bangladeshi equation is not as simple, or as friendly, or as innocuous as our treaties would make it seem. And then came the mischief by our own law-makers in the year 1983. As I said earlier, we did not have our MPs in Parliament because we had boycotted the elections. In retrospect, boycotting the elections was a major mistake at that time. The IM(DT) Act was touted and pushed through on the specious plea that the minorities in Assam—and the Bangladeshis are generally referred to as the minorities, and were always referred to as such by the Congress at that time—were being harassed by the authorities in the matter of detection and deportation of foreigners. Now the question is, were there no minorities in the other States of India also? And did they not also need to be protected if we want to be democratic and fair about it? If so, why not have a separate law for the protection of minorities? That is the obvious thing to do. And if as Mr. Kapil Sibal says, the minorities will have to be protected and so we have brought in the IM(DT) Act, well, in para 2 of the IM(DT) Act there is a provision for the Act being accepted all over the country through a gazette notification. If the Act is all that good, why do you not find one single Chief Minister of any State in the country who is willing to accept it? And even if the Centre were to try to enforce it, they will not accept it. And which country in the world sabotages its immigration law in order to provide protection for the minorities? This is unheard of, because after all if you sabotage your immigration law, you are in fact sabotaging the integrity and security of the country. And this is precisely what we have done—we have sabotaged our immigration law.

I call the IM(DT) Act a 'black law' for at least four or five reasons:

(1) It discriminates strongly against Assam since Assam is the only State which has this law, whereas the rest of the country still follows the Foreigners Act of 1946.

(2) It makes the detection and deportation of illegal migrants virtually impossible. This is because the tribunals that we have constituted are not in place in many parts of the State, and even where they are there, they comprise retired judges who have all had their innings and are not looking forward to anything more than sinecures of a cushy salary every month. I can assure you that there is nothing happening in the tribunals. No cases are being processed as speedily as one would expect.

(3) It places the onus of proving nationality not on the illegal migrant, but on the individual citizen who must even pay a fee to make a complaint. And the best part of it is this: that he can complain only about somebody–originally it was a radius of three kilometers, it was later amended to someone within the jurisdiction of the police station. Now if I know that there is an illegal migrant in Mangaldoi, I cannot make a complaint.

(4) It ensures that all illegal migrants in other States will move to Assam because it is the only State from where they cannot be deported. I have my own explanation as to why the population increase in the neighbouring States of Assam is so high and it is not so much in Assam. As Udayan rightly pointed out, there is a saturation point and we may have reached that. Possibly what is happening is, now that they know, they can quickly return to Assam in the event of anything happening, in the event of any crack-down in the other States, they are moving on towards the greener pastures in the neighbouring States. The moment there is a crack-down and the deportation move starts, they will all come to Assam from where they cannot be deported.

(5) This is a law designed to protect the illegal migrants by pretending that they are minority citizens.

Now I am not a lawyer. I have no legal background, but I did a little bit of home-work. What I did was to get the immigration laws of 40 civilized democracies from the Internet and I studied the immigration laws just for three little things:

(1) Is there any country in the world which has two immigration laws? I found none. I am not taking into consideration the banana republics.
(2) Is there any country in the world which has an immigration law that is kind to the illegal migrants? I found none. In fact, the British law stipulates that any illegal migrant detected has to be deported within ten days.
(3) There is no country in the world where the onus of proving nationality is not on the illegal immigrant but on somebody else. And there is no second example in the world that I can think of where the nation has sabotaged its immigration law in order to provide protection to certain minorities. I don't know. You have more experience on this. But I did my little bit of homework and from the study of immigration laws of about 40 countries, that is what I find.

So there is proof of very large-scale migration from Bangladesh. There is one other proof. The figures that I gave you speak for themselves. There is something else. The 1991 Census Report of Bangladesh talks about six million missing citizens. I do not know, I cannot think of any parallel of any census report anywhere in the world which talks about six million people becoming "*gayab*". So how would you explain this six million missing population? (Interruption: It is eight million. Initially it was 10 million. It was revised to eight million.) Anyway, I am not aware of that. I am aware of only six million.

People are talking rather loosely about a demographic change in the North-east, particularly a demographic change in Assam. Honestly, between all of you and me, I would put it like this. If the demographic change in Assam was brought about by the indigenous Muslims of Assam becoming suddenly very fertile, I would have had no complaints. We already have one Muslim State in the Union; there would have been another Muslim State in the Union. We already have three Christian States in the Union, so what? This is a secular country. But I am talking about a demographic change which is being engineered by importing foreigners from another country. And the people who are engineering it are not just ISI agents, there are people also within the country who want it. That is frightening, this is not on, this is not cricket.

Now I spoke of double standards, or let us say discrimination in respect of Assam on two counts. One count was, the cut off date for migrants from erstwhile Pakistan. For the rest of the country I think it is 18th July 1948, and for Assam it is 25th March 1971. So all those who have come upto 1971 are to be accepted as citizens of the State. The second count is the IM(DT) Act which I always call the 'black law.' I hope and am keenly looking forward to what our law-makers have undone, to be set right by the Supreme Court in some way by the middle of next month when the final hearing takes place on the PIL that has been filed. But there is one other double standard which worries me. In the election manifestos of the BJP it was clearly stated, not once but twice, two manifestos have clearly stated that they will get the IM(DT) Act repealed. Every time I meet the political leaders here, I have talked with Mr. Advani. He says, "We are keen to do it, but we do not have the parliamentary arithmetic." So in between the two phases of the BJP-led government, there was a time when the BJP thought about bringing in an Ordinance. I do not know why they did not do it. But the feedback that I got was that they thought, "We will come back with a much bigger majority. So why spoil things? Why earn a bad name? When we come back with a bigger majority; we will get it passed in Parliament." But it did not happen.

Now look at the double standard in respect of the IM(DT) Act. If you can push through the POTO as an Ordinance, this was something on the cards much earlier, why could you not, in the case of IM(DT) Act, push it through as an Ordinance? It is something which is not fair. That is what I have to say about the present state of immigration. And as Dr.Udayan Mishra rightly pointed out, the equations are not going to remain very simple in the coming years. There are going to be manifold ramifications which some of us may not even conceive of. As you rightly pointed out, Dr. Singh, one safeguard that is needed is a law against alienation of land. And this is nothing new. It is there in Jharkhand, it is there I think even in Himachal Pradesh. It is there in Kashmir and it is there for the Coorgs in Karnataka. So what is wrong with this? That is one.

The other is that there has to be some kind of legislative safeguard by assuring a certain minimum number of seats to the indigenous people. Above all, I hold our people responsible. It is all right to say this is largely economic, you get a large number of migrant workers moving to another place where the wages are higher only if there is a vacuum for them, only if there is need for them. If we had not created that vacuum, this problem would not have arisen. I mean people don't go to another place, leaving their homes and hearths and start there afresh on a whim. Obviously they are looking for better opportunities. If the better opportunities had been utilised, the people had done their work, it would have been fine. Now there is a way out, but this is again asking for the moon. If our boys, as they have begun to do with mini green revolution, if they continue this momentum of doing their work, doing hard labour in some cases, then I am not suggesting that the trend will be reversed, I am not suggesting that Bangladeshis will go back, but I am certainly saying that the continuous, unabated flow of Bangladeshis into the North-east will probably stop, it will be arrested i.e., that we will still have some hope of retaining political power in our hands and making sure that political power through illegal vote banks does not go to Bangladesh and to that extent, I have said in the last part of my three-part article "Our Land, their Living Space" that there is scope if you have character for economic boycott. Every contractor must be told that if you are going to employ Bangladeshi labour, you are going to be blacklisted. You can stop buying goods from them, stop taking services from them. There is no law in the country that says you cannot boycott the economic activity of a foreigner. But this calls for character. Now if we can change from within and bring in that kind of work culture where the imported labour is redundant, then I think a quarter of the battle may have been won.

The second point is, there is all this talk about work permits. BJP thinks that issuing work permits will solve the problem. There will be nothing of the sort. Do you think that those who have been there illegally after 1971 (for thirty years now) are going to come and say, "Look, I have lived in your land

illegally for 30 years, now give me a work permit?" Nothing like this is going to happen. What is going to happen is that they will go on trying to get citizenship rights by dubious ways as they have done all along, and this will lead to a fresh lot of immigrants coming in and asking for work permits which, in the ultimate analysis, will probably turn into citizenship rights. So this is something you need to think about. **And where do you provide them work? If the unemployment rate in Assam is 10 per cent, where do you provide them work?**

7

Governance and The Illegal Migration in The North-East

N.N. Vohra

Friends, first of all, let me apologise I had explained to Dr. Kumar a few days ago that I would not be able to be present here this morning because of some other commitment away from the Centre. I had also explained to him in all humility that I am no expert on the immigration issue except to the extent that I had dealt with this problem when I was in service. I find in this room we have valuable personalities who have spent their entire life in the security management of the country. Mr. Kalyan Mitra, Mr. Joshi, my friend Mr. Prakash Singh and other colleagues who have very intense experiences of these various problems. But as the essential subject which Dr. Kumar mentioned to me is related to immigration, I would briefly say that while others would have explained this problem at some length in the forenoon session, by all governmental accounts and statements in the Parliament, we have had continued immigration into the North-East over the last thirty years and before the 1971 war. That part of the problem was dealt with under the Mujib-ur-Rehman—Indira Gandhi Accord and some understandings were arrived at as to how the illegal immigrants would be dealt with in the post-1971 period. But I am sorry to say that there is no evidence on the ground of any of the commitments of the Federal Government/Central Government in regard to this important issue having been seen through. The .administrative and legal arrangements which were made in the post-1971 period in regard to identification of citizenship and related issues have been non-starter. It has been a non-starter for two simple reasons. One, quite obvious lack of concern by the States and the Central Government combined. And the second which is again a combination of interests is the likely electoral gains from groups of these migrants who have settled in large numbers in several parts of the North-East and travelled upto the North to Delhi and beyond. Even Delhi has a very large pocket of immigrants.

If you look upon the illegal migration issue from the electoral gain point of view, then obviously there is no answer and my very humble perception is that that had happened over the years. There had been total unconcern. *The demographic profile of the North-Eastern States has changed. It has changed even in certain parts of Northern Bengal. It has changed in Binar and it has changed elsewhere.* And one of the consequences of this continued inflow is the impact it has had on the tribal communities, their sensitivities, their aspirations, their desire to govern their own States. In a State like Tripura for instance, you see a very sharp reflection of the inherent conflicts which permeate the entire governmental structure. The local tribal population had a given percentage in 1947, a given percentage when Tripura became free, and you see their percentage today, they are reduced to a minority. Obviously they cannot digest the situation, much more so when the politics of the day highlights these aspects and these issues to create further dissatisfaction and confrontation and violence.

So I do not know where the remedy lies except to reiterate their very simple and brief view that there has been total lack of will and total unconcern. And one of the consequences of this lack of concern and lack of any regimented action plan to deal with the problem over the last three decades has been the emergence of turmoil in the North-Eastern States which has arisen, or which was already in existence in some States even before 1947 but which has got more complicated and more complex. So when you look at the North-Eastern map, or when you discuss in a room like this the North-Eastern picture, you hear many observations about insurgency, militancy, you even hear the word "terrorism," and yet, I am afraid, none of us who use these words has the interest or the patience to go deeper into the malaise and find out where it all began from.

The situation in the North-East, from my limited experience over the years is that while on the one side we have this enormous problem of which we are focussing today, which is only one of the problems, i.e., illegal migration from Bangladesh, the ground situation, to say the least, is very worrying. And this also arises from the fact that the governance of the States has been neglected.

Now in our democracy, when you have a representative system, you can well get away by saying that those who govern the State are thrown up by an electoral process and in a democracy you cannot foist any other structure or pattern of governance in any state which is autonomous and under the Constitution which is a sovereign state. But if you look a little deeper, you look at the recent histories of Manipur, Nagaland and Assam, to mention three States which have endemic insurgencies which have virtually throttled the developmental process, which have ensured against any investments being made in these States and delayed whatever was possible to be done even within the resources available, then you find that the problems are diverse and as worrying if not more worrying than the illegal migration.

The bureaucracy is tainted. In many States bureaucracy is also subverted. It is not as if bureaucracy alone is subverted. Alongside the political parties represented are subverted. And with the combination of subversion in the ranks of senior bureaucracy, the police and the civil services and other departments have joined hands with the leaders of certain political factions which have sympathies with one or the other group of insurgents. Then over the years all that we have done is to impose spells of Governor's rule from time to time and think that that is the answer.

The other alternative has been to rush battalions from the Centre and declare certain areas as disturbed. And worst still is to involve the army. We have seen the manifestation of these moves over the last several decades. But all that we find on the ground in several States is that it is now growing and the malaise has now even travelled upto Arunachal Pradesh, into Meghalaya which were otherwise peaceful States some ten-fifteen years ago. Is this the nature and quality of governance? Lack of development, corruption, extortion and variety of other disadvantages to which the ordinary persons are subjected to have led to progressive alienation or a feeling of alienation. When you go to any part of the North-East today, and you talk to somebody who is reasonably sensible and you refer to Delhi or the Government of India, the immediate response is as if you have come from another country. They refer to Delhi with that kind of disregard. And if you consider such responses a little closely, I am afraid you will be compelled to accept such responses, because the ordinary persons anywhere in this country are not compelled to look into all the intricate reasons for and against, the do's and don'ts that we talk about in the so-called educated societies. They are concerned more with the pattern of their daily lives, their vocations, their livelihood, the education of their children, the future of the families and they are little bothered with the more complicated arguments that you raise about the nature of the politics and the feddenal structure and the Centre-State relationship.

Even in regard to taking positive steps to manage the borders, Prakash Singh is here, so it seems ridiculous for me to say anything in his presence, I am afraid we have failed quite miserably. A few battalions scattered here and there in the terrain that obtains on the ground in the North-East is ridiculous. North-East has borders with several countries. Besides the coastal border, it has borders with Myanmar, with China, Bangladesh and Bhutan. And worst of all, some of the States like Tripura are surrounded. 90 per cent of their boundaries are in another country. There are pockets of subversion all along the borders. People come in and go out with immunity and impunity. Clashes take place, killings take place, the disturbance of law and order takes place and in most cases, if not all, the answer is to increase the strength of the police or to rush in more para-military or involve the army. I am afraid—I hope I am not misunderstood when I say—that one of the facets which reflect on the Central Government's approach to dealing with the North-East has been manifested in the last 10 or 15 years in appointing ex-military or ex-police officers as Governors. Except in one State, all the six States now, have Governors who come earlier from the army or the police. That is quite understandable when you are dealing with frontier areas and if you appoint governors who come from that kind of experience, it is very beneficial. That is my personal view. But I am afraid what I do not relish very much is that the reason why these select people have been sent there is not because they have vast and valuable experience of secuirty management, but it is because it is felt that that is the only problem in the North-East and that appointment of a military or police personnel as a governor would resolve most of the problems. I would disagree entirely with such an approach. I am not suggesting that a person from military or police background cannot be able development administrator. He can be, but what authority have you given to the governor in the North-East to do that? They are governors under the constitution and governors under the constitution have not much role to play during democratic rule. So where does this take us? The entire developmental process is in the hands of the elected representatives of the States and the civil services. And I am very sorry to say, that even in the civil services at the all-India level the civil servants who get deployed or are appointed to the State cadres or to the joint cadres are unwilling to work there. Or they are appointed there and they spend most of their time here and there, mostly in touring to Delhi. If it is a day's work, they will spend a week here and they come several times a month. At one point of time, I had taken the extreme step of saying that no North-East officer of a certain rank will come to Delhi without the prior written approval of the Chief Secretary who will send me a list of such officers coming on tour for what purpose they were coming and for what period they were coming to Delhi. Some of these officers who were close to the political masters got this interpreted as interference and I was questioned. So I stopped there, I said, "Fine, that is the wish of the Chief Minister, who am I to interfere?" But it is my very sad conclusion that the quality of attention that we devote to the day to day problems of the people in the North-East is minimal, to say the least. Even the vast funds that are made available by the Government of India are not spent fruitfully, not spent for the purpose for which they are meant, or are frittered away or looted at the source and the net result is that the pace of socio-economic development and growth in the North-East is far behind that of the rest of the country.

We have vast potential and resources in each State in the North-East. It is another tragedy that the North-East Council which has been revamped from time to time and more so in the recent years has so far failed to deliver.

So one does not know where the answer lies. Maybe the discussions in this seminar would throw up some ideas. But my own perception is that while dealing with illegal migration, side by side you have to devote very high attention to the developmental process to satisfy the urges, needs, aspirations and demands of the local people such as they may be from state to state and it will not be the answer to merely suspend the legislatures from time to time, which fortunately has become more difficult than in the years past because of the rulings of the Supreme Court and the role of the Parliament. But nonetheless it so happens that Manipur is at present under the spell of President's rule and it is said that it will lead on to the next elections. I am not sure whether the next election will generate an outcome which is better and superior to what one has seen in the years past because the same personalities get rotated, the same personalities tie up with other groups/caucuses and come back to power and they deliver the same kind of governance as they had delivered in the past.

Now another facet which I think should worry this seminar is that if you take all these various things together and other factors which must have been discussed in the forenoon session, we have a very severe and very worrying internal security situation and what with this current talk of fighting terrorism and dealing with various external enemies, how do we look at North-East today after September 11 attacks in the USA? Do we have a change of heart? How urgently to deal with the problems of the North-East? And is the problem still only relating to border management or illegal migration, or does it also relates to doing many other things which are of concrete, positive, developmental nature?

Funds, I have always believed, are not a problem in this country. It is misuse, misapplication of available resources or poor utilisation with the net outcome to the ordinary man being very minimal. So who is going to attend to that? Is the North-East Council competent to look into these problems? Are the individual governors and individual chief ministers and their cabinets responsible? Are they willing to do these things? Are they willing to go in this direction? And if not, what is the future of the North-Eastern States. If, God forbid, the situation gets more out of hand than it has been in the last 25–30 years, my own perception is that the situation would be far worse than what we have seen in J&K. J&K is a defined area with one international boundary fortunately and the other boundary is rather limited and that boundary has been handed over by Pakistan to China. For all that it matters, we have a limited boundary on that front which is high, difficult mountainous area. So essentially we are dealing with one international border. In the North-East we are dealing with several international borders of vastly varying nature and terrain and varying problems which emanate from across the borders—the transportation of subversion, insurgency of terrorist groups operating there. It is not as if only we have suffered and the North-East has suffered. I may mention for your consideration if it is a matter worth discussing that we also transported some of our problems to Bhutan. Southern Bhutan is now infested for the last several years with ULFA Bodo groups and there was a point of time in 1997 when we had almost brought rounds His Majesty the King that our forces would go and do what is required to be done. Somehow or other, thanks to our usual dithering, that opportunity was lost. The King got worried, the King got frightened, the King was given different versions of the problem and naturally he also has to run his country, so he felt that he needed to take Parliament into confidence, he needed to orient his Cabinet Ministers and so on. All that has taken time, he has introduced an element of democracy in the system of governance in that State. But meanwhile the problem has become very complicated. At this stage, even if the Government of India and the concerned State Governments were to join hands and send uniformed forces, commando forces to deal with the problem, I am not sure what the outcome is going to be, whether the outcome is going to be any better than military intervention in our country, in our own states, in our own territory. And operating in a foreign territory is always more difficult as our experience in Sri Lanka has shown. People who know the ground situation, who know the ground well, are always able to launch attacks with limited force, with limited weaponary and cause much larger destruction.

So, Gentlemen, all in all, all I have to say is, as I submitted to you right in the beginning, I have no expertise, I have no specialised knowledge of these problems except to the extent that I have had the occasion to deal with them and it is my continued concern and worry. I had said some of these things in the report that I submitted to the government last year. It was a Task Force Report on internal security that we need to wake up in so far as the North-East is concerned. We need to wake up on all fronts where we have failed. We have a Task

Force approach for each State, you strengthen the intelligence apparatus in each State, have the Central Intelligence Bureau set up its own small cell in each State's Crime Bureau, State's Intelligence Bureau. They are not functional. Get the information that is required, then deal with the problem as is required to be dealt with. But perhaps it is equally unfortunate that in our federal system, even the State Governments are not altogether happy in a high profile role of the Centre, or any kind of excessive role by the Centre. But I do feel that it is not merely the deployment of battalions or declaring areas "disturbed" which has to be done from time to time in any case but the organised strengthening of the State Police, State Civil and Armed Police forces, the strengthening of the Intelligence apparatus, very effective strengthening of the border management system in the entire North-East and above all, a very, very planned approach to the developmental process and ruthless and efficient execution of the various development schemes which are targeted to certain areas and to certain tribal populations which are far flung and neglected and which are more alienated than others. Even the capital towns' population is alienated.

So all these are, if I may say so, stray thoughts and structures because Dr. Kumar desired that I should come here and speak anyhow. So I have not better answer or better wisdom to suggest or offer except to join with you in saying that we need to raise voice and further stress and highlight the enormous dangers which lie in the North-East if we continue with our indifferent and unconcerned approach.

8

Management of India's North-Eastern Borders

PRAKASH SINGH

At the outset, I would like to say that the most comprehensive study on border management since Independence was probably done by Mr. Madhav Godbole, former Home Secretary, who headed one of the Task Forces on the subject. There were four of them, Mr. Vohra headed the one on internal security. Unfortunately it has been treated as a confidential document and has not been made public. I had occasion only to run my eyes through the report and I must say it is a very comprehensive document, and it is a great pity that it has not been made public and the issues raised by Mr. Godbole have not been thrown open for discussions. I also have an uncomfortable feeling (though I cannot really substantiate it) that some of the very important observations which he made on problems confronting us in regard to border management have been rather suppressed because the facts were inconvenient, particularly those relating to migration from Bangladesh, the issue which we are discussing here today. What he has written, what he has recorded is a very scathing indictment of government's handling of the problem and I suppose that is the reason why it has not been made public. In the context of border management again, it has a very revealing chapter on the madrassas which have come up in the border areas. There again, I am sorry to say, it has been suppressed for obvious reasons because the facts were inconvenient to the government and it would have necessarily generated a controversy to the embarrassment of the government. But the fact remains that one of the very important issues that Mr. Godbole has highlighted and in respect of which he has written very comprehensively, very incisively and come out with a devastating indictment of the government is precisely the subject-matter of our discussion here today—the migration of people from Bangladesh.

Having said that by way of preamble, the concept of border management is undergoing a transformation with the increasing acceptance of the concept of globalisation for the simple reason that nations are coming closer, trade barriers are getting lowered and people are moving across international frontiers for a variety of reasons. There are normal reasons, there are reasons forced by political circumstances, and there are economic reasons. In any case, there is a lot of movement of people across the borders. There was one school of thought which sometime back gave a projection that this process may gradually lead to the disappearance of the nation states. But that has not happened and the nation state, as Peter Drucker has observed, have shown resilience and the nation state is going to survive. Of course, it will be a different kind of nation state with a different financial management, with a different concept of international relations, etc. But the exact nature of cross border management would depend upon the kind of political relationship which we have with our neighbours, the economic relations that we have with the neighbouring country and the religious or ethnic ties between the people across the borders. There are areas where no arrangements are required like the US-Canada border for example. It is called the longest undefended border in the world. You do not require any arrangement except the routine customs and immigration arrangements. Then there are borders where intensive vigilance is required as we have along the Pakistan border because of cross border terrorism or across the Bangladesh border because of the human waves that keep on trying to cross the borders for better opportunities here, something similar to what the Mexicans try to do across the American border. But border management, as I have said in my note, is broadly a comprehensive package which involves defending the border in times of war, securing the borders in times of peace, ensuring that there are no unauthorised movements of men, taking steps against smuggling of arms, explosives, narcotics and any other kind of contraband items, using sophisticated technological devices to supplement the human effort, coordinating the intelligence inputs from various agencies and ensuring that the socio-economic development of the border population takes place.

Now we have very long borders. Our total borders run into about 15318 km, that is the total international border that we have. I mean these are borders with China, Pakistan, Bangladesh, Myanmar, Nepal and Bhutan. We are here concerned mainly with the borders with Bangladesh. The borders with Bangladesh have a length of 4095.70 km, to be precise, or approximately 4000 km. This border runs along the States of West Bengal, Assam, Meghalaya, Mizoram and Tripura and it is generally a peaceful border except that now and then there are incidents of firing and, of course, we had a very unfortunate incident last year.

A peculiar problem along the borders is the problem of enclaves. We have 111 Indian enclaves in Bangladesh and the other country, Bangladesh, has 51 enclaves within India. It is very strange that even during the period of last 30 years which we had ever since Bangladesh was created, there was enough time to sort out this problem but for inexplicable reasons this problem has been allowed to fester.

Now the main problems which we have along the Bangladesh border, in fact along the North-Eastern borders, broadly come under three headings. One, cross-border movement of terrorists and insurgents. Two, trafficking in drugs and other contraband items. Three, massive infiltration from across the eastern borders. I will take up all these items one by one and very briefly refer to them.

The first is the problem of cross-border movement of terrorists and insurgents. Now this has been taking place from the very early fifties, in fact from 1954 when Phizo raised the banner of revolt in Nagaland. Since then, this cross-border movement of insurgent groups has been taking place. Mr. R.P. Joshi is here, he would recall that the first gang of Nagas which went across to the then East Pakistan was led by Kaito Sema. He took the easy route through the North Cachar hills. But subsequently when the security forces got wiser about this, then they started taking a longer route. They would cross from Pochouri area across to Somra tract, skirt all along the Indian border through Burmese territory and then traverse to East Pakistan. That was the route that the Naga gangs used to take. Later on, of course, when this route also became difficult, they tried the Chinese route also and the gang of Muivah (who is the chief negotiator from the Naga side) and Thinuselie took the first gang to the Yunnan province of China. So this cross-border movement has been taking place. The Nagas took the largest number of gangs. Subsequently, when there was insurgency in Mizo hills the Mizos had no problem because they had a contiguous border with East Pakistan. All that they had to do was to cross into the Chittagong hill tracts and enter East Pakistan. They had no problem in sustaining their insurgency from East Pakistan.

The ULFA rebels have gone to Burma, they have gone to Bangladesh, they have gone to Bhutan, all over wherever they found an opportunity they have made a foray into the adjoining territories.

Now one conspicuous result of these insurgent and terrorist movements in the north-east has been that the authority of the State has been undermined and this is a phenomenon which is broadly prevalent all over the North-East. **Mr. Vohra made a reference to it in his talk and he gave a lurid picture of, as he said, subversion of the bureaucracy, subversion of the police services, subversion of the politicians.** So that is exactly what has happened and the State authority being undermined has broadly reflected itself in four areas:

(1) People are not sure about the competence of the State to be able to protect the life and property of the citizens. They know that it is the writ of the underground or the writ of the terrorist outfit which runs and if they decide to strike at you, then probably the State would not be able to protect you.

(2) The levying of taxes is another area where we find that the insurgents have scored over us in the sense that they make their own demands and of course their demands are always met. We have reached a stage where probably in Nagaland one could say that all the civil servants are paying taxes to the authority of the Naga Federal Government. On the other hand, any demand made by the State in the form of taxes may be met, may not be met, but any demand coming from the Naga rebels has to be complied with. The same applies now to most of the North Eastern States and, as Mr. Vohra said, even Arunachal is getting affected and the two sub-divisions of Arunachal, Changlang and Tirap, are particularly affected today.

(3) The third area where this facet of the undermining of the State authority is being manifest is in regard to the enforcement of normal laws. The normal laws are there but whether the State would be able to enforce them, there is always a question mark about it.

(4) And the fourth area where this weakness is being manifest is ensuring the loyalties of its own employees. The employees may be drawing their sustenance/salaries from the government treasury but their loyalties are generally divided. You could say that they are running with the hare and hunting with the hound. Maybe they are forced to lead that kind of life, or maybe they choose to lead that kind of life because their real loyalties are elsewhere. Whichever way it is, the fact remains that the government is not able to ensure the loyalties of its own employees.

Apart from the **State authority being undermined in the North Eastern region,** some other features which are noticeable and which would apply to most of the North Eastern States would be— **the corruption level is very very high.** In fact I remember having read an article where the writer mentions that if all the money that has been allocated to Nagaland since Independence were to be totalled up, and if it were only to be divided by the then population of Nagaland, each Naga would be richer by 2.5 lakhs. This is the amount of money which has been spent or allocated by the Government of India to Nagaland. And where Nagaland is, one can very easily see — **except for the bureaucracy, the contractors, the politicians — otherwise at the ground level, things are still the same.** I would not say that there are conditions of acute poverty became their concept of life is different, their standard of living is different, but certainly the kind of improvement that you have a right to expect with such heavy financial subventions, that is not to be seen.

Then, as a corollary to this, **the development funds are siphoned off by the terrorist outfits.** In fact I have all along held that the **greatest financial support to the terrorist outfits comes from the Government of India itself** and the government is the greatest financier of these terrorist movements which are there all over the North East for the simple reason that the funds earmarked for development somehow or other find their way to fill the coffers of the terrorist groups.

The other point is that **there is no coordinated policy to tackle the insurgent and terrorist movements in the North-east.** I mean what we are witnessing today are ad hoc responses by different State Governments according to their own perceptions. And their perceptions are not very profound. Their perception generally, as was mentioned, is, well, there is a law and order problem, so we need more forces, more police, more para-military, and now and then induction of army. That is their perception. The long-term way to tackle this problem, how to go about it in a systematic and methodical way and with the total spectrum of North-East being kept in view, that unfortunately is not there even today.

There have been peace initiatives in the North Eastern region. You would be aware that there was the Shillong agreement with the Nagas in 1975, there was an Assam Accord in 1985, there was a Mizoram accord in 1986, there was a Tripura accord in 1988 and Bodo Accord in 1994. Out of all these accords, the only accord which has really worked satisfactorily and which has justified itself has been the Mizoram accord. All other accords have had problems in their implementation. With Nagas, the problem continues to this day. We saw the faux pas over the extension of the cease-fire to the contiguous Naga-inhabited areas and the alienation it caused in Manipur. In Assam, the ULFA continues to perpetrate violent incidents. The Bodos continue to be unhappy over the implementation of the Accord.

Tripura is on the boil today. So the only accord which has worked really is the Mizoram Accord. In this context, I would like to make a brief reference to a statement made by the Chief Minister of Assam on April 6, 2000. At the government level, Government of India has been talking ad nauseum about preparing a white paper on ISI and releasing that to the public to educate them about how this intelligence agency has been engaged in subversive activities in the country. But somehow for political reasons or just because they do not have the courage to call a spade a spade, they have not been able to bring out that white paper. The Chief Minister of Assam, Profulla Mohanta, may have had other weaknesses, but the fact remains that even if it is very short and cryptic, they brought out a small booklet on ISI activities on Assam. This was placed on the floor of the Assembly on April 6, 2000. In that he has mentioned that the ISI was engaged in different kinds of activities which included supporting the local militant outfits, creating new militant outfits along ethnic and communal lines, supplying explosives and sophisticated arms to various terrorist groups, sabotaging oil pipelines, communications, railways, roads and vital installations, promoting fundamentalism among the local Muslim youth and generating communal tensions. All this is mentioned, although briefly, but even then it is mentioned in the White Paper brought out by the Chief Minister of Assam. This is what I had to say about the cross-border movement of terrorists and insurgents.

The other point I made mention of was trafficking in drugs and other contraband items with reference to the North-East in general. Now India has the unfortunate distinction of being sandwiched between the two large drug producing regions—the Golden Crescent and the Golden Triangle countries. That makes India very susceptible and vulnerable to trafficking in drugs. Some of the trends noticed in the recent years are—India has become a transit point for illicit heroin, hashish from Mynmar and Nepal; also smuggling of heroin from Myanmar has increased considerably; some opium based products are sent from India to Bangladesh and Nepal; there is also movement of brown sugar from India to Bangladesh and Sri Lanka.

Now an interesting feature of drug trafficking is that **insurgent groups in the North-East are fully involved in this drug trafficking.** I suppose it is a global phenomenon. We have seen how the Afghan terrorist groups were deriving their sustenance from drug trafficking and the revenues accruing as a result therefrom. Similarly we have enough evidence that ULFA and the NSCN (both the Muivah group and Khaplang group) have been engaged in drug trafficking. These groups have maintained nexus with the rebel groups across the border, with the Kachin Independent Army, with the Burmese Communist Party and with the Arakan Liberation Party. The modus operandi has been that the rebels from across the border from Myanmar side would bring drugs right up to Tamu, from Tamu the drugs would be taken over by the local syndicates and brought to Manipur or any other region of the North-East (but generally Manipur) and from there spread over different areas of the North-East and further on to the hinterland of India. That has been the modus operandi and **in fact a lot of clashes which we witnessed between the two tribal groups—the Nagas and the Kukis—were mainly over control of this drug route from Tamu to Imphal.**

Now I come to the more sensitive part of the problem—the infiltration or movements from across the border, and the large-scale entry of immigrants from the East. Much has been said on the subject. I will not go into the historical background, that has already been covered. Of course, I would very briefly refer to some of the factors, which are contributing to these human wave movements.

One has, of course, been the steep rise in the population of Bangladesh which has also been referred to in the morning. Then the frequency of disasters, the floods and the cyclones. Very staggering figures were mentioned in the morning of number of people who get displaced; something like 18 million people get displaced every year as a result of floods. Then there are better economic opportunities in India compared to Bangladesh. Then there are some vested political groups which have been extending their patronage. This point was also mentioned in the morning that they have been extending their patronage to Bangladeshis to come over to India. And of course the borders are very porous and therefore easily negotiable.

One factor which I would like to mention specially which is rather disturbing, is the encouragement being given by Islamic fundamentalist elements to people to move across the border because they have been propagating the theory of "*lebensraum,*" search for living space. I have several quotations from scholars of Bangladesh who have supported this theory. I will not take your time on that. Suffice it to say that different scholars in Bangladesh have supported the concept of "lebensraum," that they need to spill over, and that one of the areas where the expansion can legitimately take place is the Seven Sister States of the North-Eastern India. All these factors have contributed to large-scale human wave movements from Bangladesh to India.

Now some of the disturbing features which have become evident as a result of this movement, I will very briefly refer to that. Number one, the population of Hindus in Bangladesh has registered a sharp fall from 29 per cent to 10 per cent. After all, where have all these Hindus gone? From 20 per cent they are now reduced to just 10 per cent of the population.

Then, looking at Assam, if you look at the demographic figures for the years 1971 to 1991, we find that population in general has increased, but while the population of non-Muslims increased by 45 per cent, the population of Muslims increased by 77 per cent. So this large scale increase in the population of Muslims should be an eye opener, although people here refuse to open their eyes, I mean the people who matter in the government.

Then I could give you some figures of the border districts also. During 1981–1991, the percentage increase in the population of Muslims in three border districts was—Dhubri registered a percentage increase of 71 per cent, Cachar 56 per cent, Karimganj

58 per cent. This is the increase not in total population but the increase in Muslim population in these districts between the year 1981 and 1991.

Reference was also made to the IM(DT) Act. It has proved to be a toothless piece of legislation. To date just about 1494 persons could be declared illegal migrants by the Tribunals. That means less than 15 hundred. This shows how ineffective the Act has been in detection and deportation of illegal Bangladeshi immigrants. Of course, Mr. Hazarika had the last word on the subject. He says that even these people, after deportation, have probably come back to India. So the net result becomes zero.

It is amazing, the former Government of Profulla Mohanta—mind you I hold no brief for Profulla Mohanta but they did take some laudable steps against this Act—was very vociferous and they demanded from the housetops that this act should be repealed and, like other States of the country, the Foreigners' Act should apply to Assam also. It was a correct demand and the matter had gone up to the Supreme Court and the Supreme Court in one of its judgments called upon the Union Government to make "honest and serious" attempts to stop the influx. A Division Bench comprising Justice AS Anand, Justice Srinivasan and Justice Lahoti said that the influx of Bangladeshis was posing a "danger to the region's demography." That was the state of the case until there was a change in the complexion of government in Assam. Now with Tarun Gagoi's government coming in, they have done a 180 degree turn and, in a complete volte face, they say, "No, IM(DT) Act is the ideal thing to detect and deport and nothing more is required and the Act should not be repealed as it protects the interests of India." Now this is something which is beyond my comprehension and all I can say is that this is purely motivated by narrow political considerations, that they have done a complete volte face on the stand which Profulla Mohanta's Government had taken on the subject. It is disgraceful and shameful and with this kind of attitude on the part of State Governments, we can forget about any effective steps being taken to detect or deport the illegal immigrants.

A few words about West Bengal. According to a study, out of the 292 Assembly constituencies of West Bengal, the Bangladeshi immigrants can determine—I repeat the word "determine"–the outcome of poll in 52 Assembly constituencies. The word is "determine"; I am not saying "influence," mind you. This is where West Bengal has landed itself in. (Interruption: Now this number may have gone up because this study was a few years back). Yes, it may have gone up. That will make the situation even worse. And in another 100 assembly constituencies, they can significantly "influence" the poll outcome. So this is about West Bengal. (Interruption—That is majority in the polls) Yes, you don't need 50 per cent majority for winning an election. 30 per cent is good enough for sweeping any election.

About Tripura, a reference was made in the morning. What has happened there is some kind of a demographic topsy-turvy; tribals who were in a majority of 54 per cent in 1941, they have now been reduced to a minority of 30 per cent in 1991. In fact this is one of the main reasons for tribal unrest, disaffection and for the insurgency that we are witnessing in Tripura. In fact, this is a factor which is spreading all over. The other day I read in the papers there some tribal group in Orissa was fired upon by the police because they tried to recover the land which had been grabbed, or allotted to or taken over by Bangladeshis. I don't know, the exact details are not known to me, but going by the newspaper reports, the tribals were fired upon because they were trying to regain the land which was being occupied by Bangladeshis. In the morning a reference was made by Mr. Sanjay Hazarika to the Nellie massacre. And he also said why the Nellie massacre took place. Because the dispossessed tribals wanted to regain their land and when they were not able to regain it, they said, "Alright, we will settle it ourselves. And nearly two thousand Bangladeshis were massacred. I have no hesitation in making this observation that the seeds of Nellie have been sown all over the North-East. It is only a question of time when the tribals run out of their patience and decide to take to arms and come down heavily on any pocket of Bangladeshis, it could happen just anywhere.

About 10 thousand Bangladeshis are estimated to be in Nagaland and there is a fair sprinkling of them in Manipur, Mizoram, Meghalaya and Arunachal; in fact in the entire North-Eastern states there are Bangladeshis. Of course, the largest pockets, as I said, are in Assam, West Bengal and Tripura. Nagaland is witnessing the heaviest decadal growth of population as was mentioned in the morning. But Nagas generally—having served in that area I know how rigid and inflexible they can be—if at any stage they find these

10 thousand Bangladeshis unwelcome, they will have no compunction in slitting their throats. This is something they have specialised down the history, land of head hunters as it is known.

Now talking about this problem of Bangladeshis, the narrative would be incomplete without a brief reference to what Lt. General (Retd.) S.K. Sinha said in his report to the President of India. Mind you, this is not an observation by a Hindu fanatic or a police officer, but this is an observation by a very sober and I think one of the most competent Governors that we have in the country today—Lt. General S.K. Sinha. It is a longish quotation but I will just read some sentences out of that:

> "As a result of population movement from Bangladesh, the spectre looms large of the indigenous people of Assam being reduced to a minority in their home state. Their cultural survival will be in jeopardy, their political control will be weakened and their employment opportunities will be undermined. This silent and invidious demographic invasion of Assam may result in the loss of the geostrategically vital districts of Lower Assam. The influx of these illegal migrants is turning these districts into a Muslim majority region. It will then only be a matter of time when a demand for their merger with Bangladesh may be made. The rapid growth of international Islamic fundamentalism may provide the driving force for this demand."

A former Director, Intelligence Bureau, Mr. T.V. Rajeshwar, has also expressed his misgivings precisely on these very lines:

Now a number of suggestions have been made to deal with this problem. Mr. Hazarika mentioned about them very cryptically but his suggestion about the work permit is quite pragmatic and it deserves a fair trial. I know it is difficult to think in terms of throwing back the Bangladeshis. I was not present in the morning session when there was a discussion on the total number of Bangladeshis in India. I have no authoritative figures on the subject but let me quote from the Task Force Report which is the first comprehensive report on the border in the last fifty years since Independence. That report has placed the figure at 1.5 crores. There has to be some reference point and of course when they have come to this assessment, they have given this tally, they have met a whole lot of people all over the

North East, they have met a whole lot of people who are border experts. (Interruption: When was this Godbole report suppressed?) It was submitted to the Government last April. (Interruption: It was not published, so it was suppressed. There was a report of the Group of Ministers) I will come to that also. Godbole report was submitted in April 2000. Now I know that these one and a half crore people, you cannot throw them back, but there has to be an attempt to stem further infiltration and then somehow give them work permits, regularise their presence here and once we decide on a particular scheme, what I have suggested in my paper, that there should be compulsory registration of anyone living in India and this anyone would be—(1) citizens, (2) non-citizens, that would include the Bangladeshis and (3) the foreigners who come with valid documents. But everyone should have a registration. To these non-citizens who are Bangladeshis, we should give them an identify card of different colour. So that if it is blue, you show it, you know he is an Indian, but if it is yellow you know he is a Bangladeshi, or yellow or green or whatever colour you choose. This scheme must be implemented. I do not know why we have been dragging our feet on this. We have lost thousands of crores in scams and embezzlements, but we cannot find money for I-cards, this is beyond my comprehension. My point is that Mr. Hazarika's suggestion about work permits deserves a fair trial.

Apart from that, some of the other measures that I have suggested in my note are—one is, as I said, compulsory registration, and this is a scheme which I feel should be immediately implemented and we could do that in three phases. First let us take all the areas, say, upto a depth of 25 km from the border. Let us take that. That should not be such a stupendous exercise. Having done that, let us take, in the second phase, the border States. Having completed that, then let us go to the other States which are in the interior and cover the rest of the country. Over a period of 10–15 years, I think it is an easily achievable target provided we have the political will and we are prepared to identify the Bangladeshis as such. Why Bangladeshis, there are a whole of Pakistanis in this country who become untraced after entry. About them, there is no trace, there is no account.

Then the IMDT Act should be repealed, I have already said that. Then the BSF strength along the border. There is a general impression the BSF is deployed in full strength along the Bangladesh border. That impression needs to be corrected. I do not know what is the present stage, but let me tell you that maybe it is half its sanctioned strength which is deployed on the Bangladesh border, or maybe it is even less. Because a large part of the force has been withdrawn for counter-insurgency operations, particularly in Kashmir and other insurgency-affected areas. For that there is no separate sanction with the BSF. Whatever sanction BSF has is only for the border. So from the border, the forces are pulled out. My point is that whatever is the sanctioned strength for the border, let it be there at the border. And whatever is your requirement for counter-insurgency operations, you raise the force, you expand it, but don't thin out your forces along the border.

Then about the Water Wing. The suggestion may appear very trivial to you, but while glancing through Godbole's report, I found that he has devoted a whole chapter to water wing. He has underlined the great importance of BSF Water Wing because he says that a large part of the border is riverine and unless you have a strong BSF Water Wing, there are several routes which he has indicated in the report, from where infiltration can't be checked by land forces. There are rivers running from Bangladesh side to India. All you have to do is to get into a boat at night time and by next morning you are automatically in India. You don't require any effort and no land forces can intercept you. So he has recommended very strongly the strengthening of the BSF Water Wing also.

These are some of the points. I would like to conclude by saying that there was a mention by one of my colleagues to the Group of Ministers report. The Godbole report was not published, but I have seen the Group of Ministers report, it is a public document. I am sorry to say it is a very excised, castrated version of what is mentioned in Godbole's report. It is a very disappointing report, it is a very slipshod treatment of the Godbole's report. But talking about the problem of infiltration of Bangladeshis into India, even this Group of Ministers have said—and I quote: "The massive illegal immigration poses a grave danger to our security, social harmony and economic well-being." I underline the word "security" because the learned speaker had some reservations on that subject in the morning. So even the conservative Group of Ministers who were not prepared to take the unpleasant extracts from the original report have at least admitted this much that this illegal immigration poses a grave danger to our security, social harmony and economic well-being.

9

Illegal Migration from Bangladesh and the Demographic Change in the North-East Region

JOGESH CH. BHUYAN

Migration to the north-eastern region has a long history. In various reports, the migration was vividly described. In the 1891 census report of Assam, Shri E.A. Gait of Indian Civil Service (ICS), who was the Superintendent of Census Operations in Assam described about migration as such: There has been an enormous influx of foreigners into Assam, but the corresponding exodus is comparatively small (Foreigners mean those who came to Assam from other parts). This result is what would naturally be expected as Assam is a fertile but of sparsely peopled country with large demand for labour.

The immigrants consisted of two types: those who came from the neighbouring districts of Bengal to take up land for cultivation. The second types were those who came from distant places to work in tea-gardens and elsewhere. This flow of migration continued from the later part of nineteenth century till independence. The labourers recruited to work in the tea-gardens were mostly from far-away states of Madhya Pradesh, Andhra Pradesh, Orissa, Bengal and Bihar. These labourers were brought till nineteenth-thirties as local labourers were not available. However, the recruitment of such workers virtually stopped before the start of the second world war. These people should have returned to their parent states after their contract period was over. But most of them did not go back. In fact, the tea-garden authorities helped them to stay behind and in many cases land was given just outside the gardens.

Another category of migrants was found in Assam. They are the traders mainly from Rajasthan and Punjab and also Nepalis to work as graziers. Their number was comparatively small.

In the 1931 census report of Assam, Shri C.S. Mullan, Superintendent of Census Operations, Assam, vividly described how the immigration to Assam took place at that time. Some of his comments are reproduced below:

Probably the most important event in the province during the last twenty-five years—an event, moreover, which seems likely to alter permanently the whole future of Assam and to destroy more surely than did the Burmese invaders of 1830, the whole structure of Assamese culture and civilization—has been the invasion of a vast horde of land-hungry Bengali immigrants, mostly Muslims, from the districts of Eastern Bengal and in particular from Mymensingh. This invasion began sometime before 1911, and the census report of that year is the first report which makes mention of the advancing host. But, as we now know, the Bengali immigrants censused for the first time on the Char lands of Goalpara in 1911 were merely the advance guard—or rather the scouts—of a huge army following closely at their heels. By 1921 the first army corps had passed into Assam and had practically conquered the district of Goalpara.

I have already remarked that by 1921 the first army corps of the invaders had conquered Goalpara. The second army which followed them in the years 1921—31 has consolidated their position in that district and has also completed the conquest of Nowgong. The Barpeta subdivision of Kamrup has also fallen to their attack and Darrang is being invaded. Sibsagar has so far escaped completely but the few thousand Mymensinghias in North Lakhimpur are an outpost which may, during the next decade, prove to be a valuable basis of major operations.

Wheresoever the carcase, there will the vultures be gathered together—where there is waste land thither flock the Mymensinghias. In fact the way in which they have seized upon the vacant areas in the Assam Valley seems almost uncanny. Without fuss, without tumult, without undue trouble to the district revenue staffs, a population which must amount to over half a million has transplanted itself from Bengal to the Assam Valley during the last twenty-five years. It looks like a marvel of administrative organisation on the part of Government but it is nothing of the sort:

the only thing I can compare it to is the mass movement of a large body of ants.

Mr. Mullan also mentioned in his report that the amount emigration from Assam was very small. The net figure of immigration was always in favour of Assam, which means in-migration to Assam was much more than the out-migration.

The population growth rates in Assam and India from 1901 to 1941 is given below to gauge the extent of migration into Assam:

Table 9.1

Year	*Population growth rate*	
	Assam	*India*
1901	—	—
1911	+16.99	+ 5.75
1921	+20.48	- 0.31
1931	+19.91	+11.00
1941	+20.40	+14.22

Note: Assam's population is adjusted to the present boundary.

The difference in growth rates between Assam and India during the pre-independence period was quite significant. Assam's population grew at the rate of 103.51 per cent while the country's growth rate was only 33.671 per cent during 1901–41. Thus the difference of growth between Assam and India was due exclusively to migration.

It may be mentioned that the pre-independence Assam included the present north-eastern region except Manipur and Tripura. However, a large part of Sylhet district of Assam was transferred to East-Pakistan at the time of partition. During 1901–41, the population growth rate of Manipur was just over 80 per cent. But in Tripura the growth rate was the highest, being 195.98 per cent. Most of the migrants to that state were of Hindu community.

After independence the affect of migration to Assam was the highest. The rate of migration may be divided broadly into two parts, pre-1971 and post-1971. Post-1971 period refers to the trend of migration after the creation of Bangladesh. Large-scale immigration did take place between 1951 and 1971 in the entire region. These migrants were both Hindus and Muslims.

During 1951–61, the population growth rate of Assam was the highest among the major States. The other States of the north-eastern region also recorded high growth rate except Nagaland, where growth rate was only 14.07 per cent. On the other hand, Tripura's growth rate was as high as 78.71 per cent. Hindu refugees from the erstwhile East-Pakistan came to Tripura in large numbers immediately after independence. In fact, the growth rate during 1951–61 in the north-eastern region except Arunachal Pradesh, where census was conducted for the first time in 1961, was as high as 38.04 per cent. It was revealed that during 1951–61 the growth rate of Muslims in Assam was 38.37 per cent, compared to 33.87 per cent for the Hindus. As per estimates made by the Census Actuary and Deputy Registrar General, India, Shri S.P. Jain, who later became the Director, International Institute of Population Studies, Mumbai, the natural growth rate of Assam was about 22.4 per cent for that decade. Even if was assume that the natural growth rate Muslims is slightly higher than those of other communities and that some of those who left the state immediately after partition returned after 1951 census, the growth rate of 38.37 per cent for that community clearly that a sizable number of Muslims entered Assam along with those who had fled immediately after independence. The growth rate of Hindu population also confirmed that the flow of refugees, coupled with the immigration of Nepalis and persons from other parts of India remained unabated during that period. If the population growth rates of Hindus and Muslims of East-Pakistan (now Bangladesh) during that period is used as a basis for comparison, being 26.88 per cent for Muslims and 1.53 per cent for Hindus, the extent migration into India can easily be gauged.

During 1961–71, the population growth rate of the entire region continued to remain high, being 35.04 per cent. The whole region felt the effect of migration, particularly from what is now known as Bangladesh. Large number of Hindus continued to cross-over to Assam. This is the only plausible explanation for the high growth rate of 37.18 per cent for Hindus in Assam during 1961–71. Although a large number of illegal migrants, mostly Muslims, were pushed back across the border between 1964 and 1969, after the formation of the Foreigners' Tribunal in 1964, there were instances when many of them re-entered Assam surreptitiously. The growth rate of 30.99 per cent for Muslims clearly indicates that the infiltration of people of that community continued during 1961–71 too, at a slightly reduced rate. The process of detection and deportation suffered some setbacks and had to be stopped later due to political interference and legal complications. People of other religious groups constituted only about three per cent of the total population. The variation of their numbers is dependent, to some extent, on conversions to and from other religions but their numbers bear very little significance in the State's religious composition.

After the emergence of Bangladesh the immigration pattern has undergone changes. Census could not be conducted in Assam in 1981 due to disturbed condition prevailing at that time. So, our study for post-1971 period is restricted to the entire twenty year period i.e. 1971–91. Census was, however, conducted in the other north-eastern States in 1981.

Table 9.2 gives the growth rate of population in the north-eastern states in the post-independence period.

Table 9.2 : Growth Rate of Population During 1951–2001 in the North-Eastern States

State	*Growth rate of population during*				
	1951–1961	*1961–1971*	*1971–1981*	*1981–1991*	*1991–2001*
1	2	3	4	5	6
Assam	34.98	34.95	**23.36	**24.24	18.85
*Arunachal Pradesh	—	38.91	35.15	36.83	26.21
Manipur	35.04	37.53	32.46	29.29	30.02
Meghalaya	27.03	31.50	32.04	32.86	29.94
Mizoram	35.61	24.93	48.55	39.70	29.18
Nagaland	14.07	39.88	50.05	56.08	64.41
Tripura	78.71	36.28	31.92	34.30	15.74
N.E. Total	38.04	35.04	26.40	27.46	22.02

* Census was conducted for the first time in 1961.

** Since census was not conducted in Assam in 1981, the rates for 1971–81 and 1981–91 are estimated on the basis of interpolation.

In all the hilly States, the growth rates of population were quite high, which apparently suggest large-scale migration to these States.

But, if we study the growth rates of scheduled tribe population it is revealed that their growth rates are higher than that of the general population. For example, in Meghalaya, Mizoram and Nagaland the growth rates during 1981–91 were 32.86, 39.70 and 56.8 per cent, whereas the growth rates of scheduled tribe population were 41.02, 41.54 and 62.99 per cent respectively. It is known to all of us that the scheduled tribe population has not migrated to these hill States in large number during 1981–91. These high growth rates are due perhaps to under enumeration in the earlier census, rather than in-migration. However, a small number of Muslims have entered to these states during this period. The following figures in Table 9.3 for 1981 and 1991 relating to N.E. States (except Assam) give an idea on such migration.

Table 9.3 : Muslims Population in 1981 and 1991, Their Growth Rates and Percentage to Total Population

State	*Muslim Population*		*Growth of Muslims 1981–91*	*Percentage of to Total Population*	
	1991	*1981*		*1991*	*1981*
1	2	3	4	5	6
Arunachal Pradesh	11,922	5,073	135.01	1.38	0.80
Manipur	133,535	99,327	34.44	7.27	6.99
Meghalaya	61,462	41,434	48.34	3.46	3.10
Mizoram	4,538	2,205	105.80	0.66	0.45
Nagaland	20,642	11,806	74.84	1.71	1.52
Tripura	196,495	138,529	41.84	7.13	6.75

In terms of percentage, the growth rates appear to be quite high. But in absolute number the effect of migration is minimal in all these States. It is, therefore, necessary to discuss about migration in detail only for Assam State of the north-eastern region. In Assam not only the extent of migration is quite high, the proportion of Muslims to the total population is also significant.

The pattern of migration to Assam has undergone changes during 1971–91. The twenty fifth of March 1971 is considered to be most crucial date for determining the legality of the entry of Bangladeshi nationals into India. The reference date of first April for the 1971 census is, therefore, quite ideal as a benchmark for the study of the growth of population and the extent of illegal migration to Assam in particular.

Normally migration data collected in census should give the extent of migration. Unfortunately these data are not at all reliable. As already discussed in the 1961 census report of Assam that the illegal migrants are unlikely to respond truthfully for fear of deportation. It is, therefore, not possible to correctly estimate the size of illegal migrants. The data on the natural growth rates for different religious groups in all the States are not available. Therefore, the extent of migration is to be estimated indirectly. Such estimates are always approximate.

The growth of population of three major religious communities during 1971–91 is given in Table 9.4.

Table 9.4 : Growth of Population of Three Major Religious Communities, Their Growth Rates and Percentage to Total Population, 197.1–91—ASSAM

Religious Community	*Population*		*Percentage to total Population*		*Growth rate during 1971-91*
	1971	*1991*	*1971*	*1991*	
Hindu	10,604,618	15,047,293	72.51	67.13	41.89
Muslim	3,592,124	6,373,204	24.56	28.43	77.42
Christian	381,010	744,367	2.61	3.32	95.37
Others	47,400	249,458	0.32	1.12	426.28
Total	14,625,152	22,414,322	100.00	100.00	53.26

The high growth rate among the Christians was largely due.to conversion from other religions, mostly from Hindus. If the figures of all the non-Muslim communities are combined together, the growth rate comes to 45.39 per cent for the twenty year period. The decadal growth rate is, therefore, calculated at about 20.38 per cent. The natural growth rate of Assam in 1991 for all the religious groups combined, is estimated as 19.4 per thousand. If the natural growth rate for the non-Muslims is slightly lower than 19.4, say 19 per thousand, then the excess of about four lakhs non-Muslims may be due to migration for the entire twenty years from 1971 to 1991. If the decadal natural growth rate for the Muslims during this period is considered to be 20.5 per cent, then the growth rate for this period is calculated at 45.2 per cent. In that case, the excess of about 11.5 lakhs may be considered as illegal imigrants of Muslims, mostly from Bangladesh. It may be mentioned that only a few entered Assam with passport during this period.

Some of us think that the growth rate of Muslims is much higher than the rate estimated above. Before discussing the merits of this presumption it is appropriate to study the population pattern and growth rate of two major religious groups of Bangladesh during 1981–91. Since earlier census of Bangladesh was conducted in 1974, our discussion will be restricted to the data of 1981–91 period only.

Table 9.5 shows the population growth rate and Hindu/Muslim growth rate for 1981–91 in Bangladesh.

Table 9.5 : Population Growth Rate and Hindu/Muslim Growth Rate, 1981–91 in Bangladesh

(In thousands)

Country/ District	*Population 1991*			*Growth Rates, 1981–91*		
	Total	*Muslims*	*Hindus*	*Total*	*Muslims*	*Hindus*
1	*2*	*3*	*4*	*5*	*6*	*7*
BANGLADESH	106,315	93,881	11,179	22.03	24.39	5.76
Bandarbon	231	110	8	35.09	54.93	60.00
Chittagong HT	744	320	80	28.28	70.21	21.21
Chittagong	6,715	5,752	808	22.29	24.02	13.17
Comilla	8,207	7,609	578	19.27	20.64	2.30
Noakhali	4,626	4,339	282	21.23	22.26	7.22
Sylhet	6,765	5,605	1,122	19.61	21.90	10.11
Dhaka	13,232	12,167	986	32.14	34.19	10.79
Faridpur	5,424	4,551	849	13.85	18.15	(-)5.03
Jamalpur	3,013	2,920	72	22.88	23.00	10.77
Mymensingh	7,994	7,401	515	21.71	22.78	6.40
Tangail	3,002	2,748	236	22.93	24.12	7.27
Barisal	5,413	4,704	692	15.98	19.27	(-)1.84
Patuakhali	2,050	1,871	174	11.23	12.37	1.16
Jessore	4,848	4,077	760	20.60	26.34	(-)3.43
Khulna	5,039	3,834	1,176	16.40	23.24	(-)0.17
Kushtia	2,801	2,698	94	22.21	23.82	(-) 8.74
Bogra	3,434	3,147	261	25.88	26.64	13.97
Dinajpur	3,983	3,073	835	24.47	26.57	19.12
Pabna	4,183	3,741	232	22.17	18.12	(-)7.57
Rajshali	6,594	5,924	549	25.12	26.93	9.15
Rangpur	8,015	7,092	871	23.12	23.81	15.36

From Table 9.5 it is clearly seen that the growth of Muslim population in Bangladesh is much lower than the border districts of Assam. Statement 6 will give an idea about growth rates of Muslims in some of the border districts of Assam.

Table 9.6 : Statement Showing the Growth Rates of Muslims in Some of the Border Districts of Assam during 1971–91

State/ District	*Growth rate of Muslims, 1971–91*	*Estimated decadal growth rate for 1971–81 & 1981–91 of Muslims*
1	*2*	*3*
Assam	77.42	33.20
Dhubri	71.13	30.83
Kolkrajhar	100.83	41.71
Bongaigaon	92.78	38.83
Goalpara	86.52	36.58
Barpeta	65.19	28.52
Nalbari	93.40	39.06
Darrang	108.10	44.25
Sonitpur	131.73	52.23
Marigaon	70.26	30.47
Nagaon	81.91	34.86

From Tables 9.5 and 9.6 it is clear that not only the Hindu migrants have entered India, Muslims have also migrated to our country in large numbers. The natural growth rate of Muslims should not have much difference between Bangladesh and Assam. But the difference in actual rate clearly confirms the migration of Muslims to Assam during 1971–91.

Mother-tongue data would have helped in assessing the extent of migration from Bangladesh had the Muslim migrants returned their mother-tongue properly. In the pre-independence era, the mother-tongue returns were recorded more or less properly. The proportion of Assamese speakers in Assam was 39.74, 37.13 and 35.69 per cent during 1911, 1921 and 1931 respectively. But from 1951 to 1991, the trend of Assamese speakers has changed from minority to majority.

Table 9.7 shows the mother-tongue figures of 1961, 1971 and 1991 in Assam.

Table 9.7 : Growth Rates and Proportion of People of Major Linguistic Groups in Assam in 1961, 1971 and 1991

Mother-tongue	*Growth rate*		*Percentage to total population*		
	1961–71	*1971–91*	*1961*	*1971*	*1991*
Assamese	31.78	45.52	62.36	60.89	57.81
Bengali	43.57	68.51	18.54	19.71	21.67
Hindi	54.19	30.66	4.74	5.42	4.62
Bodo	90.54	121.95	2.58	3.65	5.28
Nepali	93.01	23.89	1.67	2.39	1.93
Karbi	27.28	85.54	1.39	1.31	1.58
Oriya	3.41	(-) 6.27	1.34	1.03	0.63
Mising	30.02	115.30	1.26	1.21	1.70
Santali	28.65	57.94	0.62	0.59	0.61
Garo	53.21	51.02	0.46	0.52	0.51
Rabha	15.94	246.99	0.26	0.22	0.50

The proportion of Assamese speakers has come down gradually from 1961 to 1991. The abrupt growth of Assamese speakers from 35.69 per cent in 1931 to 61.60 per cent in 1951 is quite surprising. After independence the growth of Assamese speakers was due mainly to the return of Assamese as mother-tongue by most of the migrants of Muslims community in the Brahmaputra valley. The definition of mother-tongue used in census is such that there is very little scope of changing one's tongue. But there is a provision under which the field-staff is to write whatever is returned as mother-tongue by the respondent.

It is significant that from 1961 to 1991, the proportion of Assamese speakers has come down slowly. If we observe the Table 9.7 carefully, we find that the local tribals like Bodo, Karbi, Mising, and Rabha have returned their own language or dialect in 1991 instead of Assamese, which they recorded in earlier censuses. Most of the 1971–91 migrants in the Brahmaputra valley returned their mother-tongue as Bengali, which accounted for the increase of proportion from 19.71 per cent in 1971 to 21.67 per cent in 1991. These are the major reasons why the proportion of Assamese speakers has gone down in 1991. The percentage would have gone down further had some of the tea-tribes, who are in their second and third generations in Assam, not returned their mother-tongue as Assamese instead of their original mother-tongues. However, the affect of such change-over is very marginal. Thus the mother-tongue figures will not help in assessing the extent of illegal migration to Assam.

Majority of the Muslim migrants from Bangladesh are illiterate. Initially they worked in the *char* areas of the lower Assam districts as cultivators. Gradually they are infiltrating to the urban and semi-urban areas in search of job, mostly as daily wage labourers. Practically all the *char* areas have been occupied by the earlier migrants. This group of people is considered as vote-bank in the electoral politics of Assam and every political party, both national and regional, tries to woe the voters in its favour. This is the main reason why these people could stay without any fear in the State.

The IM(DT) Act of 1983, which is applicable only in Assam, is considered deterrent in detection and deportation of illegal migrants. The All Assam Students' Union (AASU) tried to repeal the Act without success. The main reason why the Act could not be repealed was due to the opposition by the Congress Party and that party is in majority in the Rajya Sabha.

It should have been possible to restrict the entry of illegal migrants had the border been sealed and protected in a full-proof manner. At present the border is quite porous and one can easily move in and out without much difficulty. The huge influx of illegal migrants will naturally alter the demographic pattern of Assam, in not so distant future, if proper steps are not taken to detect and deport such infiltrators and arrest the flow of further immigration to Assam in the coming years.

10

Illegal Infiltration in The North-East India's Internal Security Perspectives

K.P.S. Gill

A few years back when I was still in service, I think it was in 1994, Prof. Bharat Karnard of the Center for Policy Research, New Delhi, had published a book entitled *Future Imperiled,* focusing on security perspectives for this region of the world. I had contributed an article on India's internal seurity perspectives in the years to come. I had mentioned there that, more than terrorism, more than any other activity, the major threat to India's security is from illegal migration, illegal infiltration, into the North-East.

The history of infiltration from what is now Bangladesh, but which were certain selected districts of the erstwhile Imperial administrative region of Assam, and subsequently of the undivided Assam province in the years after Independence, is now a fairly well-known story. It started long time back in the nineteen twenties I think, and then quite a number of British analysts writing on the Assam situation mentioned about how, when the ministries were formed after the first General Election of 1937, a deliberate policy of sending a large number of infiltrators into various areas of Assam was adopted. One of the writers of the time said, in the name of "Grow More Food," what the government was trying to do was, to use what is not a fashionable political term, to "grow more Muslims." And this was noted long time before anyone else noted it.

Thereafter, it was a policy of linguistic reorganisation of States in which the Bengali Hindu gave his language as Bengali and he had been trying to make out for years that Assamese was only a derivative of the Bengali language. This had created a lot of animosity towards the Bengalis within the Assam valley. On the other hand, the migrant Bengali Muslim gave his language as Assamese. In the nineteen sixties there was an agitation which was an anti-Bengali agitation, in the main. I remember the murder and mayhem which took place then, and ultimately Assamese was made the official language of the State of Assam except in certain areas.

The 1962 Chinese aggression was an eye opener. It was very interesting to see the pattern of exodus from Tezpur. I am going to use politically unfashionable terms which will not satisfy the secular mind, but otherwise you cannot speak the truth. The pattern of migration from Tezpur was very interesting. It was the Hindus who had fled. There was no exodus of Muslims. I am talking of the migrant Muslims because, between the Assamese Hindus and the Assamese Muslims, you cannot distingush who is who. They are like one people. Their language and their culture is almost—99 per cant—similar to each other's and there has never been a conflict between the two. At least, I have not seen a conflict between the Assamese Hindu and the Assamese Muslim. I would say that, if there ever was an example of secular co-existence with a lot of respect for each other, it was among the Hindus and Muslims belonging to the Assamese culture. But there was no exodus of migrant Muslims who were present in many areas of Tezpur. So that was an interesting observation, which I had noted. I was residing, posted very near to Tezpur and I was asked by the then IGP (Inspector General of Police) to go across and find out what was happening in Tezpur, because the police wireless operators had fled, the telephone lines had been cut by ourselves (the police) and there was no contact. So I went across and talked to the people there. The only thing functioning there was the police station in the centre of the small little town. Thereafter, after serving in Nowgong, I went to Tezpur as an SP. But a similar phenomenon, not to the extent of the exodus of people but to the extent of alarm in the minds of the people was noticed in Nowgong also.

By that time, a certain section of the leadership in the Congress party itself had realised that migration, or infiltration as it was called, was a very serious matter for Assamese identity and it needed to be addressed. This, probably, to some extent, strengthened their feeling and that is how it came about that we received intructions to identify and deport the illegal infiltrators who sneaked into Assam, who at that time were East-Pakistanis. It was a very difficult process (detecting and deporting) and that is why it is difficult to make a correct assessment—of what really happened, what was the number of infiltrators, which were the areas they had entered. So I decided to do it with the help of those migrants who were not illegal, who had settled there before a certain date, and by virtue of being in India at a moment in history they had become Indian citizens. So I took their help.

There was a very interesting phenomenon that they came at a time when the older immigrants were feeling threatened by the new migration itself. So I took advantage of that process and I said, "We are not going to raid your villages, we are not going to go house to house, please bring the people who do not qualify to be citizens and and who have migrated illegally into the country and we will deport them." So the deportation started and the task was given to the Superintendent of Police who could sign the deportation orders. When the deportation started, all the migrants who were deported were settled near the border in camps. East-Pakistan did not accept them. So large camps grew up along the border of East-Pakistan and these people started going out from their camps and attacking Hindu villages and there was a large scale migration of Hindus from that side who had settled down and who again were put in camps. I remember in 1964, there was a tremendous riot all over the North-East and Bengal, parts of Bihar and Assam. Mine was the only district in which there was no communal riot. But otherwise the whole area was a sea of violence.

Thereafter there was a conference between the Home Ministers of India and Pakistan. Mr. Gulzarilal Nanda, I think, was the Home Minister of India at that time. Prior to that (the conference) I had visitors in the then DIB (Director of Intelligence Bureau, Mr. Mailk) and the then Home Secretary. I think it was sometime in 1963–64. It was more or less at the same time when this large-scale rioting had started. They had come to see this phenomenon which took place in many rural areas of Assam. The migrants, (mostly Muslims) feeling threatened, would collect at a place and village after village would shout "Nara-e-Taqbir, Allah Hoo Akbar" and this would lead to tremendous panic among the Hindus. So, we were on our toes, moving at night from village to village to calm the situation. At times there was an internal migration of people. People would leave their village and go to a nearby village, or go to the local school and camp there under police protection. This created a sense of insecurity in the rural areas of Assam. So, pursuant to that, Mr. Malik (the DIB) and the then Home Secretary came down. I had prepared a note and I gave it to them saying 'this is what has been happening.' They were travelling in a car and I vividly recollect the dilemma that was confronting them. Their dilemma was happening on the ground. They said,"Look, we never knew that a situation of this nature exists in any part of the country." So I said, "You are free to go and verify these facts for yourself." My advantage was that I enjoyed the confidence of all the communities, whether it was the Hindus or the Muslims, or the migrant Muslims.

So as I told you, we had these camps on both sides of the border. This conference (between the Home Ministers, as had been mentioned earlier) was held.The then Prime Minister's instructions in 1964 were to stop the process of deportation. I am not talking of the nineteen seventies and the nineteen eighties. I am talking of 1964. I happened to be a member of the Indian delegation (at the conference) as a very junior officer of the IPS. We were all staying in Assam House and, when I went back, I found there was gloom all-round, because the Prime Minister wanted this as a matter of policy. Mr. Kidwai was the Chief Secretary (of Assam), Mr. Rana K.D.N. Singh was the additional Chief Secretary, the then IGP, Bhavani Barua, and Ghanakant Medhi... all of us were there. When I reached there I found all of them sitting with their heads hanging and apprehending all sorts of things. Then Rana K.D.N. drafted a latter to the Prime Minister from Mr. Chelliha. Mr. Chelliha put down a half-page letter and sent it across to the Prime Minister. The talks broke down because he did not agree to the cessation of deportation. He said, it must continue. If some J.N.U. scholar can trace out this letter, it will be a great contribution to contemporary history because, in that letter, in a few sentences, he has pointed out the dangers posed by this migration to the Assamiya identity.

Thereafter, gradually, the powers of the Superintendent of Police were whittled down, the extent of their (police's) ability to deport went down and down, and, ultimately, the Government of

India sanctioned infiltration check post, to be located all over the State of Assam in the districts affected by this infiltration. It was a fairly large post, but I always found that, when you put up a special force for doing something, it does not tackle the problem; it somehow manages to create a tremendous amount of confusion. What started happening, and that is what made me withdraw myself from what we were doing, was that this special post that we set up became a centre of great corruption, great by Assam levels, not by Delhi levels. They started collecting money and all that.

Then, I also remember at that time Gulzarilal Nanda going round and championing issuing identity cards. At that time, the population of Assam was a little more than a crore. So I said, if you are going to have identity cards, you are going to have a great amount of corruption—if you calculate an average of a certain amount (to be shelled out to the corrupt officials) per identity card, specially in the migrant areas where it will exert a great psychological pressure on the people—that they must get a card, otherwise they are nobody— So I said that was going to lead to a tremendous amount of corruption and a feeling of alienation among those who have been here for so many years. The idea all along has been—how do you sift those who have been here and who qualify to be Indians and those who do not qualify. And that was the problem that was confronting us. It was very difficult to address that problem. But if you had good policing and the confidence of the community you were dealing with, it was not much of a problem because most of the infiltrators who I had sent out were voluntarily surrenderd to me by the village leadership that those were the people who had come in. We did not have to use any coercive methods. But the point remains that, having seen the actual collective activity of the migrants at certain important moments of history in the North-East, I have always felt that, as individuals who have come into Assam, they do not have stake in the State of Assam; they do not have a stake in the collective identity of what is Assam today—which is so many different communities, castes, languages etc. etc. That is why I have always felt that their presence was unwarranted...because ultimately the security of an atea depends upon the goodwill of the people living in that area and it depends on whether they have a stake. We are not talking of India, we are talking of Assam, do they have a stake in Assam as Assam, as we see it today? I don't think so. I have interacted with them at a very close level. I don't think they have a stake. And if that is the case, and if you would have observed the news during the past few months, the only area, apart from Kashmir, from where fundamentalist Islamist cadres went for training to Afghanistan was the State of Assam, and not from any other part of the country. That is a very significant point to note. Why should it be only from these areas? It is because, among them, the internal propaganda which takes place through various Tibliqi Jamaits, etc., is aimed at the internal subversion of this community. And I can tell you that, and interestingly so, there is a difference between those who have been here for two or three generations and those who came much later through an illegal process. So they (the second category) are more prone to be subverted by those who have been here for a while and who then develop a stake in Assamese society and in Assam as such. And if they have a stake in Assam, they have a stake in India. Fortunately, this development did not result in a chain reaction, because the boys who returned after training were persuaded by the village community itself to give themselves upto the police. But, if the first attempt has failed, it does not mean that successive attempts would not be made. Let me elaborate: It does not mean that more volunteers will not be recruited and it does not mean that such volunteers will always return and surrender. I feel, if there is a very grave threat to the North-East, it is from the subversion of illegal infiltrators.

How do we address this problem? At one time I had thought of it and suggested to Mr. Challiha, in the nineteen sixties, of a Sri Lanka—type solution—disenfranchise them (the infiltrators). I was also a witness to a great dual—the great verbal exchange in the most impolite Assamese between Bishnuram Medhi and Mr. Bimla Prasad Challiha, where they accused each other of inaction against illegal infiltrators. Later on, I did suggest that you cannot address this problem unless you disenfranchise the people. It was not that we did not have the documentation. We have the documentation. The 1951 census was treated as the national register of citizens and it was placed in police stations. It was kept as a permanent record. It was bound and it was a reference point. At least upto a degree of about 90 per cent, it (the census document) was factual. There was a possibility of a margin of error of 10 per cent. But if you conducted a conscientious investigation you would be able to more or less pinpoint that this gentleman did not satisfy the law according to the citizenship laws of the country, and this gentleman did. So it was not a difficult problem. But subsequent developments have now made it impossible to detect and deport foreigners.

The problem started when the mass movement for deportation of foreigners was launched. That was when the problem of impeding deportation came up. Those very people who won the elections on the basis of the deportation-plan did not manage to deport even one single person from Assam after coming to power. Now, probably, the only thing we can do is to cry for a halt to ensure that it does not go any further, and bring those people who feel threatened by the political currents and cross-currents in our country, from time to time, into the mainstream, and make them develop a stake in this side of the border, in the society as it exists here. That again would be very difficult for any political establishment to accept, beacuse no one can deny that there has been infiltration. No one can deny that we have failed, but the next step which, to me, seems to be a logical is, accept that we have failed, but let us stop the failure here and ensure that whoever is here becomes a citizen with a stake in the prosperity and the development of the Assamese community and the country as such. But I don't think any political party in the country can take that last step, which probably is the need of the hour. Having studied this problem for more than forty years, I see no other way. But till we do that, I think we have very grave security concerns staring at us in the face in the North-East.

11

Illegal Migration from Bangladesh and Security Scenario in the North-East

J.N. Roy

Unlike in the past, the illegal migrants from Bangladesh could now be used to cause security problems in the North-East. Existing linkages between Pak ISI and Bangladesh (BD) fundamentalist and terrorist groups are being strengthened. Approach of BD Government is becoming increasingly anti-India and pro-Pak. It does not bode well for us.

Growth of Islamic Fundamentalist and Terrorist Organisations

The illegal migration from Bangladesh has seriously affected the security scenario in the North-East. The Assam agitation had been started by AASU (All Assam Students Union) over the issue of illegal migration from Bangladesh in 1979–84. Although there is no definite information on the number of illegal Bangladeshis present in Assam, some regional bodies like AASU, AJYCP etc., claim the presence of an estimated five million illegal Bangladeshis in Assam.

The resentment of Assamese people against the illegal Muslim settlers triggered a reaction from the Muslims leading to the formation of a number of Muslim extremist outfits including Muslim United Liberation Army of Assam (MULAA) and United Liberation Tigers of Assam (MULTA). More than 186 cadres belonging to MULTA and 30 MULFA cadres have been arrested during the last five years.

Besides the Muslim terrorist groups, there has also been an increase in the Muslim fundamentalist groups. Several new fundamentalist organisations including Isamic United Reformation Protest of India (IURPI), Islamic Sevak Sangh (ISS) have come into existence. The activities of Harkat-ul-Mujahideen (HUM) and Harkat-ul-Jehad Islami (HUJI) have increased significantly. These groups are working in close liaison with the Pak ISI, Jamat-e-Islami Bangladesh (JEI-BD) and Islamic Chhatra Shibir (ICS) of Bangladesh. In August 1999, 4 ISI agents (Faizullah, a Pak national, Kari Salim Ahmed and Mausafah of Uttar Pradesh and Mohammed Akjram Khan of Kupwara (J&K) had been arrested in Guwahati city. During interrogation they revealed the activities of ISI and HUM in the North-East and the existence of HUM organisational network. The arrested persons confessed that they had been asked to cause sabotage on Manali-Leh road. They also disclosed that the ISI had established its network in Lower Assam districts including Dhubri and Gopalpara. Based on their interrogation several activists of HUM and HUJI were arrested.

Subsequently, the interrogation of 7 HUM/HUJI supporters revealed that the Muslim youths from Assam, North-East and North Bengal are taken to Bangladesh and later to Pakistan for arms training. These outfits target the illiterate and semi-literate youths from poor Muslim families for enrolment.

The Islamic organisations in Bangladesh have also been trying to distribute anti-India propaganda material in the name of propagating religion among Muslims in the NE region. During October-November, 2001 calenders showing photographs of Osama-bin-Laden were found in circulation in Karimganj District. Police also seized Laden CDs and cassettes at Tezpur in November, 2001. Recently in November, 2002 Karimganj Police recovered a large number of audio cassettes containing anti-India inflammatory and provocative speeches. The seized cassettes contained anti-India speeches of Maulana Dilavar Hussain Sayeedi, an MP and leader of JEI-BD. The cassettes were recorded in Bangladesh and were sent for free distribution among the Muslims in North-East.

Recent reports indicate increasing collusion of ISI with Bangladesh agencies. ISI is organising training to Muslim fundamentalist groups and equipping them with arms and explosives with a view to utilise these groups subsequently.

Support to Indian Terrorist Groups by Bangladesh and ISI

The Indian terrorist groups have been using Bangladesh camps for stay of their top leaders, channel for trans-shipment of weapons and various logistic support including preparation of fake passports, visa, air tickets etc., the Indian terrorist groups are staying in Bangladesh under the full knowledge of Bangladesh Government and its agencies including BDR (Bangladesh Rifles) and DGFI (Directorate General of Forces Intelligence). The interrogation of a number of surrendered/arrested terrorists have provided details of the activities of Indian terrorist groups in Bangladesh, the location of their camps and the support provided to these groups by the Bangladesh Govt. agencies.

Most of the important NE terrorist groups including ULFA, NDFB, NSCN-IM, NLFT, ATTF and ANVC have established camps in Bangladesh which are used as shelters, training camps, stores and Hqrs. of these outfits. The Tripura terrorist groups often take the abducted persons to their camps in Bangladesh and keep them there till ransom is received.

Bangladesh serves as an important route for trans-shipment of arms, ammunition and explosives. The arms and explosives are normally brought to Cox's Bazar in Bangladesh and transported from there to various terrorist camps in India and Bhutan.

ISI operatives in connivance with Bangladesh agencies provide fake passports, arrange for visa and purchase air tickets and also provide financial assistance for the arms training of NE terrorists in Pakistan. Important ULFA leaders including Paresh Barua, Arbinda Rajkhowa etc., have been using Bangladesh passports with Muslim names.

Bangladesh agencies, including BDR, often provide advance information to the Indian terrorist groups, present in Bangladesh, about their plans to conduct raids on their camps, which they have to do for the consumption of international community. The insurgent groups, last year (in 2002), were asked to move away from their camps, remove the wireless antennae etc., and keep them inside the house. They were also tipped off about the block period during which the raids would be conducted.

The ISI has been instrumental in imparting training to a number of NE terrorist groups in Pakistan and earlier also in Afghanistan. Several batches of ULFA cadres were taken to Pakistan in early 90s for training. Later, the ISI arranged some training programme for the cadres in Bangladesh itself. Besides ULFA, some NDFB leaders and ATTF cadres have also in the past been taken to Pakistan/ Afghanistan for training.

The ISI which has been maintaining close links with ULFA, NDFB and other outfits also uses them for spying activities. During January-February, 2002, when the Indian Security Forces were being moved to Western border, some BD-based Indian terrorist group leaders acting at the behest of ISI, were enquiring about the locations and details of various units of Indian Army and Air Force.

In this scenario a continuing flow of illegal immigrants, do pose a threat to the whole of NE region. Recent developments in Bangladesh, where the fundamentalist forces have been gaining ground and the Pak ISI is becoming more active than in the past, and its reported plans to create terrorist cells in Assam and other bordering states, the whole issue of illegal migrants assumes a security dimension. Migrants are always a vulnerable community and subject to exploitation. This aspect had earlier not received adequate attention.

(12)

ISI and New Wave of Islamic Militancy in the North-East

ONKARESHWAR PANDEY

The infiltration from Bangladesh and the consequent New wave of Islamic militancy in the North-East India is a matter of grave concern. The Influx of millions of Bangladeshi Muslims into N.E. and rest of India is posing the gravest threat to the unity and integrity of our county today. Our developing nation has not only been burdened with the responsibility of feeding millions of aliens, but is also facing serious threat to the security of the region by ISI sponsored Islamic insurgents.

The undivided Assam has been a Hindu Majority state. The history of the brave people of Assam living in the valley of Brahamputra dates back to the Vedic period. In ancient days Assam was known as "Kamrupa." Guwahati, known in ancient times as Pragjyotishpura was the capital of Kamrupa (Assam). Pragjoytishpura is frequently mentioned in the Mahabharata. The Ahoms came to Assam through Burma in 1228 A.D. and established their rule in upper Assam. Later on, they extended their reign to lower Assam. The Ahoms ruled over Assam for 600 years. In course of time, they embraced Hindu religion and adopted Assamese as their language. Dr. S.K. Chatterji, the renowned Bengali writer, has recalled "Rudra Singha (1695–1714), one of the greatest kings of Assam was the Shivaji of Eastern India.

After the first Burmese war, the Burmese signed the treaty of Yandavoo with the British in 1826 A.D. and handed over the control of Assam to the British, though the last Ahom king Purandar Sinha was allowed to continue his rule over upper Assam till 1839. In 1839

A.D., the British annexed upper Assam also. Annexation of the Assam including hilly areas was complete by 1892. Before advent of the British rule, there were six major Hindu states in North-East India: the Koch, theTripuri, the Jaintia, the Kachari, the Ahom and the Meitei in Imphal valley. Islam had almost no place in the region except through a few immigrants. "In fact the Muslims had been a microscopic minority till the partition. This fact is also supported by the decadal census figures. For example, the total immigrant population in Assam in 1911–21 and 1945–51 were registered at a mere 0.4 and 0.5 million respectively." (Dwaipayan—Assam Tribune, 22 March 2000).

Starting with the Turk attack on Kamrup in 1206, the Mohammadan's made 17 unsuccessful attempts to conquer Assam. But the Powerful Hindu Ahom Kings of Assam squarely defeated them in all the battles. In fact Assam was the only State of North India which withstood valiantly the onslaught of the Turk and Mughal invaders, and successfully preserved its cultural and political identity unimpaired. According to Dr. S.K. Chatterjee "Assamese Kings stopped the Muslim flood from penetrating into Burma and beyond, in a wave of aggressive warfare and conquest.... Otherwise the history of Burma and China might have been different."

In 1257 A.D., Tugril Khan attacked Kamrupa but failed to make any headway. However, he built the firstever mosque in North Kamrupa. Subsequently in 1498 A.D. Nawab Hussain Shah of Gour made successful inroads in Kamtapur and appointed his son to administer Hajo. Today Hajo has a prominent Muslim shrine known as 'Poamacca' established by one Giyasuddin Aulia who had then accompanied Hussain Shah. The number of Muslims increased with every successive attack on Assam during the Mughal period. This happened, particularly, with the attack of Mir Jumla in 1661. One of their descendants known as Gandhela Garial later took a prominent part in 1695 in repelling attack on the Ahoms. Some of them had also gained the confidence of the Ahom kings and were given titles of officials such as Phukan, Barma, Saikia, Bora, Hajarika, Khonikar etc. One such military commander known as Ismail Siddique Hajarika alias 'Bag Hajarika' fought distinguished battle against the Mughals under the leadership of the legendry Ahom figure Lachit Barphukan. The Ahom king Rudra Singha had also imported skilled

Muslim personnel in certain trades, including blacksmithy, architecture, Persian translation, tailoring, painting, drum beating, etc. A Muslim painter made beautiful pieces of painting in the famous "Puthi" (book) known as "Hastividyarnava, written under the patronage of the Ahom king Sib Singha. There were also a good number of locally converted Muslims in Assam.

A Muslim religious cleric popularly known as Azan Fakir came to Assam in approximately 1635 A.D. from Baghdad and acquired a legendary status in Assamese society not as much through his preaching of Islam but more from his identification with the culture of the land.

Though Assam has traditionally been free from the Hindu-Muslim animosity and religious fanaticism, the proliferation of the Muslim population in the past century has created a feeling that politics of number could eventually have its way. Today Bangladeshi immigrants can determine the poll outcomes in as many as 52 assembly constituencies in West Bengal, and in other 100 constituencies they can significantly influence the poll results. As far as the situation in Assam is concerned Bangladeshi immigrants are in majority in four districts.

At the time of partition, Mohammad Ali Zinnah, the architect of Pakistan had once expressed to his co-religionist colleague Moinul Haq Choudhary:

> **"Within a decade, I shall be able to annex Assam to East Pakistan by the dint of more infiltration of Muslims there..."**

Zulfikar Ali Bhutto the then president of Pakistan wrote in his book, *The Myth of Independence*:

> **"Our controversy with India is not on the problem of Kashmir only, there is the problem of Assam. In Assam, there are some Muslim majority districts which should have been given to Pakistan at the time of the partition, these districts were wrongly included in India."**

It all shows that the fanatic leaders of the Muslim League had malicious intentions regarding Assam. In fact, according to well planned scheme, Bengali Muslims were goaded to infiltrate into Assam to create Muslim majority enclave, so that another Pakistan might be carved out there in future. Now according to an official estimate, nearly 150–180 lakh Bangladeshi nationals have migrated from Bangladesh into India since 1971. This has resulted into abnormal population increase in districts bordering Bangladesh.

Sheikh Muzib-ur-Rahman, the then president of Bangladesh once expressed:

> **"The population of East Bengal (Bangladesh) is increasing at alarming speed. Their inhabitants face acute shortage of land. The Bengalis need land, which can be given by Assam. Assam abounds in good forests and beautiful scenes of nature. If some inhabitants of Bangladesh migrate to Assam and settle there permanently, they will be very happy. Actually Assam should have been included in East-Pakistan."**

This is also a fact that at the time of partition of the country Hindus constituted 30 per cent to the total population of East-Pakistan (East-Bengal; now Bangladesh). The fanatic Muslim leaders backed by the Muslim League Government of East-Pakistan barbarously persecuted the Hindus; they were compelled to leave their ancestral land and take shelter in Assam and elsewhere in India. Consequently, the population of Hindus in East-Pakistan/Bangladesh was reduced from 30 per cent to 10 per cent.

Massive movement of Muslims from East-Bengal started in the early part of the last century. It was speeded up during Muslim League's ministry in the State. Viceroy Lord Wavell in his diary noted in 1946 that Sir Sadullah's "grow more food" campaign with its open invitation to Muslim peasants from East-Bengal was turned into "grow more Muslims" campaign. After the partition, the Muslim population increased further. And the aftermath of the Bangladesh liberation war of 1971, opened floodgates of Muslim infiltration. The process continues even today, thanks to the support from hard-line communal Muslim politicians of Assam.

The fear of the indigenous Assamese people of being swamped away by the aliens compelled them to launch the 'Assam Agitation' extending for six years which culminated in the signing of the Assam Accord (1985). It contained many highly damaging provisions. The Assam Accord led to the passage of a new legislation called the IMDT (Illegal Migrants Determination by Tribunals) Act, 1983, which gave the death blow to the main objective of the agitation, as that Act, instead of helping in the detection and deportation of the foreigners, gave them protection only. Later on Sri H. D. Deve Gowda the then Prime Minister of the UF Govt. and Shri A. B. Vajpayee, the former Prime Minister, made commitments to repeal the IMDT Act, but nothing has been done in this direction so far, as the case is now pending in the Supreme Court.

The infamous IMDT Act shifts the burden of proof of citizenship of the alien on the complainant or the police. Thus, it gives freedom to an alien to enter this country, secure in the knowledge, that the country he is entering illegally will have to prove that he is an illegal migrant to deny him citizenship. Under the Foreigners Act of 1946, which applies to the rest of the country and which is in consonance with the practice followed the world over, the burden of proof of citizenship lies on the foreigner. Under this discriminatory Act, the police do not have the powers of search, seizure or arrest as available under the Foreigners Act. At present the Act requires two individuals living within the area of the same police station of a suspected illegal migrant to file a complaint accompanied with a deposit sum of Rs. 10 (earlier, it was Rs. 25). The police can also initiate suo moto action. But often by the time a complaint is received or the police initiates inquiry against a suspect, that person shifts to another area and is not traceable. Even if the person is available, he insists that he is an Indian National and while the police spares time from their routine duty and tries to collect evidence, he often disappears. During trial by Tribunals, prosecution witnesses do not appear because there is neither any protection to them nor any provision for paying them their travelling expenses. More so, the Tribunals setup under this Act has been starved of funds and resources. The Act caters for an Appellant Tribunal of two retired High Court Judges, and sixteen district Tribunals of two retired District/Additional District Judges with supporting staff. But out of 16 District Tribunals only 5 are functioning. The remaining 11 Tribunals have only one person each on the desk and as such are non-functional. During the last 15 years, Border Organisation (raised under PIP/PIF scheme) of 4000 policemen identified only 9,599 illegal migrants, and even out of these only 1,454 could be deported. These statistics amply establish the futility of continuing with IMDT Act. It may be recalled here that Article 6 of the Constitution gave citizenship to those who entered India before 1948, but through the IMDT Act, the Govt. of India extended the period by another 23 years (upto 1971) in case of Assam. Now taking advantage of the fact that identification of the foreigners through the IMDT Act is very difficult, infiltration from Bangladesh into Assam continues unabated.

Assam Governor, Lt. Gen. (Retd.) S.K. Sinha, who has made an indepth study of the problem of demographic threat to the region in his report submitted to the President of India on Nov. 8,1998, has lucidly focussed on the dangers that might arise out of such continuous influx. Unexpectedly and unfortunately, it is yet to receive due attention of the Centre. Gen. Sinha has observed in his report:

> **"The unabated influx of illegal migrants from Bangladesh into Assam and the consequent perceptible change in the demographic pattern of the state, has been a matter of grave concern. It threatens to reduce the Assamese people to a minority in their own state, as happened in Tripura and Sikkim. Its more dangerous dimension of greatly undermining our national security is ignored. The long cherished design of Greater East-Pakistan/Bangladesh, making inroads into the strategic land link of Assam with the rest of the country, can lead to severing the entire land mass of the North-East, with all its rich resources from the rest of the country. This will have disastrous strategic and economic consequences."**

Muslim population of Assam has shown a rise of 77.42 per cent in 1991 from what it was in 1971. Hindu population has risen by nearly 41.80 per cent during the same period. Muslim population had risen from 24.68 per cent in 1951 to 28.42 per cent in 1991. As per 1991 census, four districts of Assam

(Dhubri, Goalpara, Barpeta and Hailakandi) have become Muslim Majority districts. Two more districts (Nagaon and Karimganj) should have become so by 1998 and one district Morigaon is fast approaching the same position. As a result of population movement from Bangladesh, the spectre looms large of the indigenous people of Assam being reduced to a minority in their home state. According to a publication—"Assam towards Islamisation" by one Mrinal Kumar Saikia (of Assam) published in 1996, Assamese people are afraid. A new slogan among the Muslims: "Sylhet nelam gana bhote, Cachar nebo lathir jore" (We have annexed Sylhet by ballot, now we will take Cachar with the help of *lathis*) reflects the attitude of the aliens. Infiltration, if not checked, may ruin the entire Hindu population of the state in the coming days.

Till the Chinese aggression of 1962 the Congress Government, both at the Centre and the State did not bother about the continuous illegal infiltration of the Muslims to Assam from East-Pakistan. But when Indian Army deserted the frontier without firing a single round and hurriedly retreated, and the people of Assam received a 'farewell message' from their beloved and trusted Prime Minister, late Shri Jawahar Lal Nehru through All India Radio, in which he stated: "Our heart goes to the people of Assam," in some places of Assam in Darrang and Nagaon districts under exclusive occupation of immigrant Muslims, Pakistani and white flags were seen flown to avert possible Chinese air attacks. This had opened the eyes of some Indian Statesmen and made them think seriously about the danger from the unrestricted flow of Pak Nationals to Assam. It resulted in the drawing up of the PIP (Pakistani Infiltration Prevention) Scheme. After the creation of Bangladesh in 1971, the scheme was renamed PIF (Prevention of Infiltration of Foreigners) Scheme. The main thrust of the scheme lay upon detection and deportation of infiltrators from Assam. This scheme came into operation in 1964, and soon after, it was extended to the States of Meghalya, Tripura and West Bengal. The Border Organisation set up under this scheme was deployed in the interior to identify and deport illegal migrants after the 1965 war, when the Border Security Force came into being. But neither the BSF on the border nor the Border Organisation in the interior, could prevent large-scale illegal infiltration from Bangladesh.

The Pakistan's ISI found this fertile ground fit for its own plans. ISI has been active in Bangladesh supporting militant movements in Assam. Muslim Militant organisations have mushroomed in Assam and other North -Eastern States and there are reports that more than 25 Muslim Militia/fundamentalist organisations are active in the region.

The ISI's patron-client relationship with different militant outfits operating in the NE region has attracted attention only in recent years. But such relationship had their beginning in the mid-fifties, when A.Z. Phizo-led Naga National Council (NNC) sent an emissary to the then East-Pakistan on the way to Karachi, to seek support of the then Pakistani regime. This emissary, General Mamu Mosievilie, even met the then Chief Minister of East-Pakistan, Ataur Rahman of the Awami Legue. He was arrested by a Sub-Inspector of Assam Intelligence department at a place near Dhamcherra on the Cachar-North Cachar Hills boundary, while he was returning from East-Pakistan in the garb of a Buddhist monk. Many documents, besides a letter from NNC President A.Z. Phizo introducing him as an ambassador plenipotentiary of Nagaland to Pakistan, the copy of which was addressed to the *New York Times* were found in his possession. He was produced before a Magistrate's Court at Silchar for police remand. That was the beginning of a relationship between ultras of NE region with Pakistan. The Mizo National Front (MNF) of Laldenga was the second important rebel group that enjoyed Pakistan's support. But during the last one and a half decade the number of militant outfits of North-East having direct contact with the ISI has increased manifold.

Formation of Muslim militant outfits came to the notice in the beginning of the 1990's. The continuous agitation over foreigners' issue, communal/ethnic clashes (Nellie, 1983, Manipur, 1993, Bongaingaon, etc.) in which migrant Muslims were the prime victims might be construed as the main reason behind the formation of such groups. During 1992, the Muslim Fundamentalist groups became very much active throughout the country, including Assam mainly on *Mandir* and mosque issue. Revision of electoral roll in Assam was another cause for fear among illegal immigrants. A Muslim organisation, named "United Social Reform Army of Assam (USRAA)" was formed during that period. This organisation spread fear and suspicion in the minds of migrant Muslims for their vested interest, propagating that the minorities in India are being harassed and atrocities are also being committed on them. Because of this propaganda and mass mobilisation programme, they, to some extent, succeeded in achieving their goal of uniting the immigrant Muslims. A report indicated that this organisation was formed at Mankachar in Dhubri district of Assam and professed the object of safeguarding the interests of the Muslims living in Assam and to ensure their social upliftment. Further, it is learnt that they also formed some code of conduct for Muslim women. During this period this organisation held series of meetings throughout the state mostly in Muslim dominated areas.

An organisation named Saddam Bahini, comprising of the Muslim youths, reportedly came into existence during 1994 somewhere in the Barak Valley of Assam. Pak ISI has raised this Bahini at different places with a view to propagating anti-India feeling, which, in turn, may result in widespread violence. Barak Valley, Silchar, Kitigora, Karimganj (Neelam Bazar), Dhubri district and Cooch Behar are being used as corridors by the Muslim youths.

There were reports of large number of Muslim Youths (from Hojai, Nagaon, Dhubri, Gowalpara and Karimganj areas) being lured away in the name of religion to join militant Islamic Organisations to "protect" the religious minorities in the state. It has complicated the situation in North-East, especially in Assam, which has witnessed a number of communal clashes during the last few years. The involvement of the notorious Inter Services Intelligence (ISI) of Pakistan in organising Islamic militancy in Assam has come openly with the confession of one Kaju Ahmad arrested at Dibrugarh during Sept' 96.

"The ISI agents are trying to create all sorts of violent activities throughout the country (India) by carrying out various types of subversive activities. The ISI has, reportedly, been operating training camps at places near the Bangladesh border where members of separatist groups of the North-Eastern States, known as the United Libération Front of Seven Sisters (ULFOSS) comprising of National Socialist Council of Nagaland (NSCN-IM), the Peoples Liberation Army of Manipur (PLA), the United Liberation Front of Assam (ULFA), the National Democratic Front of Bodoland (NDFB), the

United National Front of Manipur (UNLF), and the National Liberation Front of Tripura (NLFT) receive training. The ISI strategy called the 'Internal Encirclement of India' is to Islamise the border with India to facilitate the influx of terrorists into the interior of the country. There have also been spurts in the number of *Madarsas* and mosques, which have come up in areas bordering Bangladesh, especially in West Bengal and Assam. There have been reports that these madarsas and mosques are being used for instilling fundamentalist ideas among the Muslim youth. The proclaimed aims of the Muslim fundamentalists are to ensure security, safeguard the over all interest of the Muslims and to form a separate state for themselves, with a view to establish a separate Islamic country.

After the Kargil failure, Pakistan is now attempting with the help of Muslim Fundamentalists of Assam to separate the entire northeast from the rest of India by cutting off the **"Chicken neck"** area between North Bengal and Assam (a narrow alley between Sri Rampur in Assam and Jalpaiguri in North Bengal.

In fact the general plan of Pak ISI is to stoke terrorist activity in the North–Eastern region with the help of well-trained and well armed fundamentalist groups and to cut off the chicken's neck that links the North-East to the rest of the country. It may be recalled that, "during 1965 Indo-Pak war, this was precisely what China had threatened to do. What prevented China from carrying out its threat was the stern warning of the Soviet Union of the consequences of any such action. It will also be recalled that Pakistan's deposed Prime Minister Nawaz Sharif had also warned that he could open several fronts similar to Kargil. As we know the Siliguri Carridor or the Chicken's neck area projects towards the east into the Brahamputra Valley, which connect the North-East with the rest of the country. Pakistan plans to control the area, which would make it easier for them to cut off the entire North-East from the mainland. The ISI has spread its tentacles from New Jalpaiguri to Assam and to 24. Parganas, Nadia, Murshidabad, Malda and Dinajpur districts. Security in the entire area is threatened by massive Bangladeshi infiltration under ISI influence. Hence the ISI has made a constant effort to support and gain sympathy of the Bodo Security Force (BDSF), as the Bodo dominated area is adjacent to the Siliguri Corridor."

There has been a mushrooming growth of underground organisations of this community, which is causing headache among the Government circles. There had been the North East Minority Front (NEMF), the People's United Liberation Front (PULF) and the Islamic Revolutionary Forum (IRF). The latest report is that yet another outfit of the Muslims in the name and style of the Government of Muhammadan Islamic National Front has come up. The leaders of the new outfit say that the main objective of the outfit will be checking crime at Kwakta, under Bishenpur district of Manipur and in some other Muslim populated areas. With this new outfit, Manipur can boast of about 21 Underground (UGs) organisations. Since it is the best way of earning easy money, more and more people in the NE region are forming the underground organisations. The main source of income of such organisations is the collection of huge amounts, particularly from rich Muslim businessmen of the respective areas. Besides, the linkage of the Fundamentalist groups backed by Pak ISI with underworld elements cannot be ruled out. The funds for procuring arms, providing training, shelter etc., to various Islamic Fundamentalists of India might have been canalised from underworld elements like Dubai based Dawood Ibrahim, Afganistan based Saudi Millionaire Osama Bin Laden, etc.

The various Muslim Fundamentalist organisations are holding all types of modern weapons like M-16, AK rifles, Rocket launcher, Carbines LMGs, SMGs, Pistol, .303 Rfiles, IEDs etc.

The sudden surfacing of more than a dozen Islamic Militant groups in Assam and the increased ISI activities cannot be explained as mere coincidence. The outfits like Assam Minority Liberation Army (AMA), Muslim Liberation Front of Assam (MULFA), Muslim United Liberation Tigers of Assam (MULTA), Saddam Bahini etc., are said to have enjoyed the covert support of the ISI. The recent arrest (July' 99) of the ISI agent Gauri Salim Ahmed alias Abdul Habib alongwith three others in Assam, revealed many untold stories of the ISI design. Hailing from Muzaffarnagar and blind from the birth, Salim Ahmad is considered most dreaded and committed ISI follower. Maulana Hafiz, another dreaded ISI agent from Kupwara region of J & K was also arrested. Their mission was to handover a large quantity of RDX to the Assamese insurgents as well as to other UG outfits of North-East to facilitate disruption on the eve of Independence Day Celebrations of 1999, during Lok Sabha Election, etc.

During interrogation, Gauri Salim Ahmad divulged that fake passports were used for going to Pakistan from Dhaka. If appropriate passports are not available, then chit system is used. In that system the person to be dispatched, is introduced to the crew of the Air Lines who are on pay roll of ISI. The crew gets him across immigrations. Quasim based at Dhaka is responsible for this job. After the big catch of four key ISI agents, 33 others have also been arrested from various parts of Assam. In fact, in the country as a whole, around hundred ISI agents are in various jails. But still, the number of arrested agents would not be more than 25 per cent of the total. In terms of modules (the word used for one group of ISI activists for particular mission), 13 have been smashed so far all over the country. Two of these modules were operational in Assam with active co-operation of the Muslim Fundamentalists. Reportedly, to execute the operations, ISI has organised about 24 active Islamic Fundamentalist groups in Bangladesh, Nepal and India who have been trained on the pattern of Laskar-e-Toiba and Taliban Malitia. These include groups like Muslim United Tigers of Assam (MULTA), Muslim United Liberation Front of Assam, Peoples Liberation Front (PLF), Islamic Liberation Tigers Force (ILTF), Muslim Liberation Militia of Assam (MLMA), Minority Volunteer Force (MVF), Mujahid Vahini and Jubo Command. The intents and purposes of these newly formed organisations are very much clear. The arrest of one militant named Kiranuddin at Pathar Kandi in Assam in 1999 has led to the sensational disclosure that there is a plan hatched by Pakistan and Bangladesh to Constitute a Muslim State comprising the districts of Nagaon, Hojai, Haila Kandi & Karimganj etc. Such bizarre plans should not be taken lightly. Nearly 5000 Bangladeshi youth have been trained by the ISI for executing Kargil type operations and their training was imparted by Mujaheed Vahini in Bangladesh by ISI of Pak. According to the reports, camps were also organised in Galamari area of Khulna district and Baghchara and Salim Bila area of Jessore district with strong support of Bangladesh's secret agency DGFI and Jamait-e-Islam-i-Hind. To oversee the entire operation, Pakistan had appointed one retired Major, Rustam Ali in

Bangladesh. Muslim Liberation Tiger of Assam (MULTA) has geared up its activities in the Muslim dominated areas of Dhubri district. MULTA cadres are collecting funds from the businessmen of Dhubri. They generally take shelter at Madrassas in Dharamsala and Chatrasal (Assam).

Some Muslim Fundamentalists are also entering Assam via Nepal and Bangladesh with the ISI's help. Most of such fundamentalists belong to suicide squad. The approximate number of the groups is about 350. They are responsible for organising powerful network in Jodhpur, Ahmedabad, Surat, Baroda, Bhuj, Jullandhar, Ludhiana, Pathankot, Jammu, Udhampur, Lucknow and Patna. Political leaders are their main targets. It may be recalled that the chief hijacker of the Indian Airlines Plane IC-814 (on 24-12-99) Syed Shahid Akhtar had used the Siliguri Route to reach Nepal. According to the Home Ministry report on November 1, 1999, Akhtar accompanied by Abdul Latif left Mumbai for Calcutta by Air. But from Calcutta they took a train to New Jalpaiguri and then went to Kathmandu by Bus. Abdul Latif returned after dropping Akhtar at Kathmandu one month later on December 1, 1999. Abdul Latif made another trip to Kathmandu, along with Shakir. But this time he travelled by train to Gorakhpur and from there onwards to Kathmandu by Bus. After the military coup in Pakistan, several MULTA cadres had been undergoing training at Qawa Islamic Institute in Pakistan. 15 MULTA cadres undergoing Guerilla warfare course in a Talibani Training Centre in Peshawar, returned to Assam via Bangladesh without completing their training due to US Operations in Afghanistan.

ISI has recruited Assamese Muslim youth from Hojai area (Nagaon district) for conducting their operations. ISI has planned employment and shelter scheme for them and is making payment for their work from the funds received from Saudi Arabia. To motivate these youths, ISI has promised them for their permanent settlement in Saudi Arabia in future. As a result, slogans such as "ISI Welcome," "Indian Army Hatao", "ULFA Jindabad" are gaining momentum in Hojai, Nagaon and Maibang areas.

A new Muslim Fundamentalist group "Islamic Force No. 786 Aslam" was formed in Aug'99 at Yairipok of Thoubal district of Manipur. This outfit, supported by ISI is to become active in

Manipur to spread the unity in Muslim community against threats to Islam.

With the aim of fighting for an Independent Muslim state in Assam, 120 cadres of MULFA and AMLA have sneaked into Char Chapori area of Mangaldoi district and Bura Chapori of Sonitpur district of Assam with weapons. This group was trained at Mahisasan, Samser Training Center in Bangladesh under the supervision of ISI. They entered into Assam in three groups via Karimganj after completion of 6 months training in first week of January 2000.

ISI-ULFA Nexus

The ULFA had consultation with ISI in Pakistan near Peshawar on 27 December '99. The meeting was attended by Ashanta Bagh Phukan, prominent leader of ULFA along with 5 cadres and one Mohd. Abdul Karim, retired Pak Army Officer representing ISI. Moulana Fazul Rahman of Hizbul Mujaheedin was also present in the meeting. The following decisions were taken:

(a) ISI will supply various kinds of arms and ammunitions to ULFA.
(b) It will train at least 800 cadres of ULFA by September 2000.
(c) All Muslim groups located in Assam will extend help to ULFA.
(d) ISI sought ULFA's support in carrying out sabotage activities in Assam.
(e) ISI has asked all the Muslim groups of North East to disturb Republic Day functions and all Madarsas have been asked to extend logistic support to cadres inducted into the region for taking sabotage activities.
(f) ISI has set up a printing press at Peshawar to help ULFA and other insurgent organisations to bring out various publications against Government of India.

Most of the insurgent group in the North-East supported by ISI stepped up sabotage activities in the region immediately after the

Kargil Conflict, as a result of which a spurt in violent activities such as kidnapping, killing, etc., have taken place in Assam, Nagaland, Tripura and Manipur.

Assam Police is in possession of plenty of evidence to show that the top ULFA leadership is in close touch with certain officials of the Pakistani High Commission in Dacca. The ULFA leaders have also been travelling to Pakistan regularly. Pakistani agencies have already imparted arms training to hundreds of ULFA cadres. According to the confessional statements of scores of arrested ULFA leaders including their self-styled Vice Chairman, Pradip Gogoi, the Pakistani officials in the High Commission in Dacca arrange for their passports in various Muslims names and send them to Karachi. From Karachi airport they are whisked away in unmarked vehicles to the training centres. Specific evidences of such trips by dozens of ULFA leaders are already available.

ISI procured different passports for Paresh Barua, the self-styled C-in-C of ULFA in different names. Assam Police was able to procure a copy of one passport issued to Paresh Barua in the name of Kamaruddin Zaman Khan. Documentary evidence suggests that this Bangladesh passport has been obtained by fraudulent means with the help of an official of the Pakistani High Commission.

During the recent Kargil conflict, the ULFA issued a statement condemning Indian Government's role in Kashmir. The language of the above statement was exactly the same as that issued by the Harkat-ul-Mujahideen, a Pakistan based terrorist outfit controlled by the ISI. This shows that even the drafting of the above statement was probably made by the Pakistani agency.

During second week of December '99, a joint meeting of heads of important UG organisations operating in the north-east region was held at Lahore, Pakistan under ISI. Arabinda Rajkhowa of ULFA and Ranjan Daimari of NDFB attended the meeting. ISI assured supply of arms for creating disturbances in NE region and also for use against ISF. ISI also assured to provide passports for their journey to other foreign countries, if required.

Even the United States is fully aware of the fact that Pak ISI is fomenting extremist violence in India's North-East. Much before the 11th September terrorist attack on the World Trade Centre, a high ranking US State Department official said that "We believe, the ISI is helping the militants of Assam, possibly working through dissident groups based in Bangladesh."

"Since they attack unarmed civilians for political purposes (the militants meet the classical definition of terrorists" said the US Official who spoke to "The Washington Times" on the condition of anonymity. The accusations come on March10, 2000 when the US president Bill Clinton was preparing to visit India, Bangladesh and Pakistan from March 19 to 26 despite recommendations by his secret services that he faced a risk from terrorists in Pakistan.

Very recently, Assam Police has seized a dozen VCDs that had been in circulation in the State and contain a documentary 'Path to Paradise' that talks about the Sept., 11 attacks on US. Intelligence reports in Guwahati said, Bin Laden is being regarded as hero in several pockets of Assam dominated by illegal immigrant Muslims from Bangladesh. Last month (October, 2001), several posters and calendars eulogising Bin Laden had appeared in Karimganj and Dhubri. According to a recent sensational report, over 20 Muslim fundamentalist organisations and militant outfits in the NE region are being funded and, reportedly, have links with Osama-bin-Laden's Al Qaida network. According to the MI report, the Al Qaida is funding these groups through the ISI of Pakistan to keep the secessionist movements in NE alive.

The explosive situation in Assam arising out of the continued influx of Bangladeshis over the decades, their unhindered settlements in the state, the growing menace of Islamic Fundamentalism and the activities of the ISI indicate that in Assam a Kashmir like situation is very much on the cards.

REFERENCES

(1) Muslim Politics in India—S.K. Ghosh.
(2) Secessionism in India—K.M.Talreja.
(3) Demographic Aggression against India—Baljit Rai.
(4) Assam Muslims—Politics & Cohesion—B.J. Dev/D.K. Lahiri.
(5) Report on Illegal Migration into Assam—The Governor of Assam, Lt.Gen. (Rtd.) S.K. Sinha.
(6) Assam Minorities holding balance—Anirban Roy (Eastern Panorama, February 1996).

13

Illegal Migration from Bangladesh and the Electoral Politics

ARUN K. SARMA, M.P.

Much has been discussed on this particular aspect of illegal immigration. If one goes through history, the phenomenon on the border of East-Pakistan with the neighbouring States was different. The policy of Government of India had two directions. It was very serious so far as the Western border with West-Pakistan was concerned where there were shoot at sight orders, while on the Eastern border with East-Pakistan, it was a localised area and at any point of time this area could be manipulated. That was how the political thinkers thought at that time. So East-Pakistan was taken very easily, the main control from West-Pakistan was minimal on East-Pakistan, so it was taken in a different direction, there was very liberal approach on the control of the border and exchange of population. It helped migration of both Hindus and Muslims in the beginning. The people displaced from Bangladesh were mostly Hindus and partly Buddhists, who are called Chakmas. There was even a resolution in the Assam Assembly accepting a quantum of refugee population in the State of Assam. There was hue and cry at that time in the sixties how Assam could bear this burden because there were crores of Hindus in East-Pakistan and they would continue to come because of the social problem. That problem did not get resolved though during the Congress period some action was taken in the name of PIP (Prevention of Infiltration of Pakistanis) Scheme. It was an administrative mechanism where the Pakistanis were identified and thrown out to East-Pakistan from various border point. But they came back and the process of their enrolment in the voters' list started in the late sixties. The phenomenon started with the Congress Party which was the ruling party in the country. They had a division and to retain power at the Centre and the States, they had to have certain pocket votes. One such pocket vote was that of the tea garden labourers. They had a lot of appeasement policies as a result of which they could get these votes. The second category was that of immigrants. They were threatened that if they did not vote for the Congress, they would be expelled to Pakistan. So under this threat, they fell an easy prey to the ruling party, the Congress, who made them into readymade vote banks. When some other parties, including the socialist parties, emerged in Assam, the situation got aggravated, Congress was pushed to the corner and they became much more possessive that they must have their vote banks in order to retain power. That was the limit of selfishness. Without thinking about the sovereignty and integrity of the country, these people were allowed to be enrolled in the voters' list in large numbers.

In 1979, for the first time, the All Assam Students Union started an agitation on this particular issue. The situation had got more aggravated in 1971 when Bangladesh was created. A lot of population from East-Pakistan had migrated to our side at that time due to the liberation movement launched by the Awami League. The repatriation of those people has not really been effected. So a lot of people stayed back. They imgrated from camps to various other places and started settling down. After getting the voting rights they started having mileage in the Assam Assembly. One after another they started being nominated or getting elected to the Assam Assembly. Out of 126 constituencies of Assam, now there are more than 40 constituencies in which the population statistics are such that if they are united under one party banner, they can enter the Assam Assembly easily that is they can capture one-third of the seats in the Assembly as of today.

That being the situation, the Assam agitation started which lasted for more than 6 years and it ended with Assam Accord. As has been rightly pointed out by Mr. Bezbaruah, by unofficial enrolment of non-citizens, a vote bank was created and they were given some right on land in addition to the right to stay and vote. So this right to franchise gave them automatic citizenship. That was the impression through the Assam Accord. I am a party to it. I was in the AASU, I was there at the time of signing of Assam Accord. Subsequently I have been in the political level in between. I have an academic background, I am an academic man, I still have a lien. Anyway the situation was when there was gradual increase in the number of voters in every constituency, in 40 constituencies (i.e., one-third of the assembly seats) they could nominate their candidates to the Assam Assembly and in another 20, they could influence the outcome of the election. If other votes get divided, the illegal immigrants could determine whom to elect. That is the reason why some of the politicians have become dormant on this issue. Nobody wants to take the risk of telling the unpalatable truth. No political party wants to tell facts correctly because of this numbers game. They blame the AGP and other parties, including the BJP, which advocated driving out the foreigners. Still the number factor is so high even today that to get a political mileage or political power in Assam, the votes count a lot and minus these vote banks, nobody can form the Government in Assam. This is the situation today.

And the prolificacy of this population is so high. They marry three or four women, there is no limitation. They need only bread and butter and nothing else. So because of the social habits and their prolificacy being so high, they are coming in large numbers from Bangladesh. And secondly they are having more propagation within Assam and other parts of the North-East. Maybe in 10 or 15 years, in many of the constituencies of Assam they will outnumber the locals if we continue allowing them to get enrolled in the voters' list. We have to get rid of this particular thing.

There are lot of reports in newspapers and even in certain secret documents of the Government of India that in Bangladesh they have a strong determination to annex Assam and a part of the North-East because there is a historical background. Assam was grouped in a category which was to be attached to Sylhet at that time. But ultimately at the initiative of certain political leaders of Assam, the State was not tagged to East-Pakistan at that time but was retained in the mainland India. That particular psyche is very strong in Bangladesh which we cannot visualise.

This political enrolment has led to a situation that when Government of India is giving more priority to the Kashmir issue, with West Pakistan, that Kashmir is the only problem of India, ISI is the main problem of India. The ISI knowing fully well that India's military and other forces are concentrated on the Kashmir border, have shifted their site of operation to Bangladesh. They have a sizable number within India and also some of the extremist outfits are given shelter in Bangladesh, where they get the money from them for giving shelter. They can also sell the arms, get more money by selling arms. Thirdly, they can also send the drugs and other things which can destroy the society. They also have a strong network within Indian territory with various extremist outfits recently formed in the name of minority organisations. I have a list of such minority organisations which was submitted by the Government of Assam to the Indian Parliament. More than 12 minority militant groups have been formed so far. They are also being trained and they have a tendency that at any point of time there will be chaos in the situation in the North-East today.

So far as Assam Accord is concerned, upto 1971 everybody, who immigrated, was regularised. The Government of India was very fast to regularise those who had migrated from Bangladesh to Assam till 1971. They took only one week to implement that. But on the contrary, to drive out those people who migrated to Assam after 1971 as per the Assam Accord, they are still not detected. They have not driven out a single foreigner in a very practical manner. Only for name sake, some IMD Tribunals have been created. Hardly any business is going on there and yesterday my President told the pressmen that the IMDT Act is so ridiculous that if Laden comes and enters Assam and if somebody says that he is a foreigner, then he has to prove that Laden is not an Indian, he has to be driven out.

Then the appeasement policy about the minorities is such that there is no clear-cut definition who is the Indian minority and who is the minority migrated from Bangladesh. There are so many advocates at the political level that whenever there is identification and the names of illegal migrants are being deleted from the voters' list, there is a hue and cry that Indian minorities are being harassed. These advocates are more prevalent in Delhi and in some part in Calcutta. Then there is a tendency to blame the political leaders for all things, social degradation and everything. I agree to that to some extent; the political situation is more prominent. But is there not any responsibility on the citizens? Every citizen of the country has a duty to see that nationalism grows. Because we do not have nationalism inherent in our mind, everybody feels that government is the machinery where every citizen has to acquiesce for their own selfish benefits and nobody bothers what happens to the country. There is no accountability at any level. Take the BSF which is entrusted to man the border. In exchange for a small bribe, they allow the Bangladeshis to enter our side. Even in the media, when the Assam agitation started, there was a hue and cry in the Calcutta media that "this is anti-national, anti-Bengali and anti-Indian agitation, this is parochial, mere Assamese chauvinistic. So many terms were given by the media. So why blame the politicians alone. At every level, people are responsible; at administrative level people are responsible; at media level people are responsible; so let us not generalise it as Mr. Bezboruah did. Maybe there are bad people at all levels—political level, media level—but we have to come to a solution.

What is the solution now? First of all, the greatest problems is related to the question that Dr. Misra has raised—the question of identification of the foreigners. What is the problem? When there was agitation in Assam, all the Bangladeshis started thinking how to protect themselves in this land. They started getting equipped with a number of documents, including PRCs, forged citizenship certificates, false voters' list being printed by them etc. For entry in the voters' list there is a system that any young man who attains majority at the age of eighteen, has to provide proof of the identity and place of residence his father to ascertain that he is a bonafide Indian and his name is to be entered. When he is 18 years of age, at that time his father's name, the parents' names are referred. Where from these will be referred? They will be referred in any of the earlier voters' list. When they refer it, a person claiming entry in the voters' list of a particular district says that his father/fore-father stayed in another district and this is the voters' list of the other district. Suppose I claim my enrolment in the voters' list of district A. I will give a voters' list of 1966 of district Z. I produce it before the Electoral Registration Officer. Now this officer has to scrutinise the citizenship status of more than ten thousand population whether they are citizens or not, whether their names can be entered in the voters' list or not. There are a number of revisions of voters' lists in Assam.

So at no point of time the voters' list could be cleaned up because of this factor whether they are equipped with citizenship. When there is identification process going on and when his name is temporarily deleted, he comes forward with a document that in Cooch-Behar in 1974 his father lived and here is the citizenship of his father, you cannot deny his voting right. Now who will go within seven days to probe whether that citizenship certificate is bogus or genuine. So this poor Electoral Registration Officer has no other option but to enter the names of all people who are enumerated. So everybody becomes a voter and everybody becomes a citizen.

I put a question in Parliament about the number of rackets of forged citizenship certificates and forged voters' lists in Assam. The Home Minister said that more than five rackets involved in manufacturing forged documents have been busted. They have the seals, they have signatures, all kinds of printed documents to show that a particular person is a citizen and he resided in some other part of Assam or India and he is a bona-fide Indian citizen. Today everybody is well equipped with all this. How to go about solving this problem? Every developed country probably maintains a list of citizens who are citizens by birth or by domicile or other process of application or whatever. But in India we do not have it. We had a list in 1951; this was never updated. The Home Minister of the present government at the centre has declared on several occasions that they will go in for a register of citizens but it has not come up till today. Every time I asked a question in every session, he gave me the same answer that it is under consideration of the government. Now the government cannot take a decision to prepare a list of citizens of the country. If the names of citizens are registered in a particular register, anybody who comes after that at least can be traced out. That is one solution which we can still do today provided there is a political will to do it. But these advocates will come to their rescue and they will rusticate the tribals, "You are tribal, you are aboriginal, you have to identify yourself as a citizen now." This is a retrograde step. There are so many advocates to nullify this issue.

Anyway we have to find out a solution. So far as identification is concerned, we must have a computerised system of keeping records for tracing out the documents. Suppose somebody has given a false document, the signatures of the particular magistrate issuing that document of that particular year should be there and it should be scanned. Also it should be cross-verified.

Secondly, the voters list of every constituency should be circulated in the whole of Assam. Likewise it should be done in other States in the region. Then cross-checking will be possible and that is possible only when it is computerised. Then mostly in Muslim communities we have noticed that in the case of certian people, the father's name is "Hussain" and the son's name bears some other title, because he comes from a different mother, so he has a different title. So if he claims that 'Hussain' is my father but I am not 'Hussain' I am Saikia or Sircar or have any other title, the Electoral Officer cannot say that you are not son of a particular father you have referred to. So there is a huge problem and it is a technical problem. This can be solved by technical means by having a very foolproof system of maintaining a list of citizens. From Pakistan so many people have migrated, we do not have any records, so many people were arrested, we do not have any record.

Secondly, there should be an identification machinery with the police and all other administrative mechanisms. What has happened that in 1966 some Tribunals were created as per the Foreigners Act. Why were these tribunals created? The Assam Police was blamed that they were sending people indiscriminately. They were only looking if somebody was a Muslim, he was to be sent back to Pakistan. But so many bonafide Indian citizens were also pushed back to Pakistan. On that plea, the Government of India decided to have tribunals so that their citizenship status could be scrutinised. These tribunals take a lot of time and by that time these people migrate to other districts and it is very difficult to trace them. I fully agree that this IMDT Act must be scrapped. In fact I have also mentioned this to some other political leaders who are at the helm of affairs and that for POTA. When the BJP does not have majority in the Lok Sabha and they are going to make it a joint session so that the total number is there to pass the bill, likewise IMDT Act is an old issue, this can be tagged to POTA and both the Acts can be got passed. They can very well do it if they have the political will. Once IMDT Act is repealed these tribunals will go away. As Mr. Bezboruah has pointed out, these Tribunals have only helped regularise some of the illegal migrants as legal migrants. So this process has to be totally stopped.

Thirdly, on the electoral side, I do agree with some of the previous speakers that it will be a very unpalatable, very hard decision but we have to take it. Number one, we have given shelter to those people who have come due to economic reasons or due to their social problems in Bangladesh. This is all right. Due to Economic reason we have allowed, that is all right. Even land, this is all right. But why should we allow them to decide our political destiny? Like one Mr. Moni Kumar Subba. He is a Nepali citizen. He migrated first to Sikkim, then to Arunachal Pradesh and Assam. He is an MLA, now he will become Member of Parliament. Tomorrow he may become Prime Minister, who knows. He is an illiterate man. Otherwise he would be facing the same fate as Sonia Gandhi is facing now. The question is, many of the Bangladeshis who migrated recently or in earlier times are entitled to be elected to the highest forum of our country. So how to prevent it? Mr. Pranab Mukherjee told in the Rajya Sabha when this kind of debate was going on, "These are our people, this is undivided India, they are our brothers, why should we harass them? Why should we not give them citizenship status, why should we deprive them of that?" But this has created the political identity crisis of many ethnic groups. The resentment in these ethnic groups is reflected in insurgency and the Government of India has to pay a lot of price for that. We must have a solution for this. These persons should be declared stateless persons. At least they should be deprived of the voting rights to decide our political destiny. We should have a strong political will.

And I have already pointed out what is the problem of the political parties. In Assam they are in such big numbers that nobody can deny their presence, otherwise nobody can form the government. If AGP comes out very strongly, they would become AASU, that means they would have to take to streets and launch agitation. But they will not be able to form the government. The statistics say this. But it is not that AGP has compromised. Whatever it may be, there was some compulsion to keep the Congress out of power. Because whenever Congress will come to power, they will bring in more people and get more immigrants with voting rights. So to stop Congress from coming to power, that was a temporary arrangement.

Anyway it is very easy to blame people, but to find a solution you have to take a nationalistic view of the entire problem. They have not only taken over our political destiny and economic values, they have spoiled the society because of their easy availability on cheap wages, their hard work any time, day and night, with less money and in any situations, and without any expectations, people have a tendency to employ them. By this, our younger generation is devoid of work culture. By this way, we are destroying our young generation, that they are incapable of cultivating, incapable of doing small trade. Even today fish produced in Andhra Pradesh is brought to Assam. These are being traded by some of the Bangladeshi migrants in the various streets. The cultivation done in the char areas is being traded. So trade, economic and even government jobs. The defence minister gave reply in Parliament last year that they have some records that many Bangladeshis have become Indian citizens and got enrolled in the Indian army. They have got enrolled in para-military forces, in many of the banks and financial institutions. So they have entered all levels. If they have entered our security level, how can we go about it and how much generosity can we show that they are a minority, they are our brothers and we fill feed them for all time to come at the cost of our future generations, at the cost of our political sovereignty, at the cost of our economic well-being and all that. So there should be a limit to everything. They should be deprived of the political rights. And also the concept of dual citizenship may be explored. If at all they are to be given voting rights, they should be allowed in a particular locality, so that they can elect only one member to Parliament to raise their voice. That is another kind of citizenship or voting rights. But not the mixing with the other indigenous groups that they can decide the political destiny of a particular State because States are organised on the basis of language. This is being jeopardised in many of the North-Eastern States and this has created social problems and it will continue to do so.

And we should have a specific definition of the "minority." Who is an Indian minority and who is a minority which has migrated from East-Pakistan? Nobody speaks of Christians as a minority, nobody speaks about the ethnic minorities. Everybody speaks that minority means Muslims migrated from Bangladesh or some Muslim population of our undivided India. But that is not the point. The point is, a minority is a minority. If he is a foreigner, he is a foreigner, he may be minority or majority. Or if he is a refugee, all right. If he is accepted as a refugee, he should be divided equally to all the States of India. Why only dumping them in Assam and other parts of the North-East? The entire country has to share this burden. Now in Assam, one-fourth of the population is from erstwhile East-Pakistan and now Bangladesh. Now they are enjoying our entire economic benefits. Whatever money goes from New Delhi, they are getting the share and they are given more political mileage because they are minority. To safeguard the minority, a lot of steps are being taken by all the governments. And who thinks for the majority and who thinks for the ethnic minorities? Ethnic minority is facing crisis, and that crisis has to be resolved if we want to keep India as an integrated whole. Otherwise the process of disintegration will set in. With the help of external forces, they may try to destabilise India not from the Kashmir side, they are trying to do it from the North-East side through Bangladesh.

That is the danger before the country. All people have to be cautious on this issue. And also reservation of seats in the Assembly and Parliament can be thought of, as suggested by many of the speakers. That is one possible solution, but there is the problem of identification. If we say that these particular constituencies are reserved for the Assamese or indigenous people, then who is an indigenous? A migrant who came before 1950, who migrated to Assam from East-Pakistan, whether he is indigenous or not? That question is also very important. It is very difficult to eliminate the non-indigenous. Who is non-indigenous? And anybody who has migrated from other States and who has been living there for more than fifty years, whether he is an indigenous or not? So there is a problem of identification. That is why a blanket cheque of making them stateless persons and identifying the Indian citizens and keeping a register in the computer and everything, we can set this for the time being.

I hope I have met most of the points I wanted to meet and at the political level still there is a possibility, there should be a national debate on this particular issue. This particular issue has affected most of the States in the country. It is no longer an issue of Assam or

North-East. As rightly pointed out, in many tribal areas, the lands are owned by the tribals, and not owned by the Government in the Sixth Schedule States in the North-East. So these Bangladeshis go in for marriage. They marry a Naga girl, or a Manipuri girl or a Mizo girl and through marriage they occupy the land. And in the particular locality, they know how to do it, they exploit the particular locality, its trade, its agriculture and economy and all other things. This will create a lot of problem in the near future. We have to be very cautious on this particular issue.

I thank Astha Bharati for inviting me to speak on this particular issue. No doubt I have heard somebody telling that everybody is responsible for what has happened today, but I think the generation which ought to have taken this issue long before did not take it up. We, AASU and AGP, have taken it. AGP could not succeed through the process of being in political administration till today. I do not say it is a failure, but the expectation was not met by them. But if the entire blame is laid on AGP and AASU and everybody else becomes a good man, I do not agree to that. At least let us go practical and find out a solution.

14

Illegal Migration and the Economy of the North-East

JAYANTA MADHAB

Although most of the North-East has suffered from immigration, my talk however is limited to the experience of Assam. Assam had two main streams of immigration in the twentieth century. Cultivators from the erstwhile East-Bengal were encouraged by the British Government to come to Assam during the first-half of the twentieth century to cultivate land and later to participate in the "grow more food" campaign. In the second-half of the twentieth century in the wake of partition (1947) and subsequently with the increased presence of land in the then East-Pakistan and Bangladesh and the density of population per square kilometre of land is being much lower in Assam and in the North-East than that of East-Bengal or Bangladesh, migration continued.

In addition to the Bangladeshi migration, immigrants from Nepal were going on at the time mainly looking for economic opportunities. Nepalis formed the next largest immigrants community. The other immigrants communities were Marwaris and Biharis. The British Tea Planters brought indentured labourers from Bihar and Orissa during the nineteenth and early twentieth century.

The Marwaris ultimately controlled the entire trade and now, after the British left, a major part of the tea and other industries. The Biharis were mainly manual labour such as porter, construction labour, brick-layer, cobbler, barber, rickshaw puller, etc. The Nepalese contributed at the beginning in the livestock and dairy industry. Later, they branched off to many other sectors.

Here, I shall be concentrating on the economics of Bangladeshi migration.

My hypothesis is that Bangladeshi immigrants contribute to the economy of the North-East. Basically most of the Bangladeshi immigrants came from the cultivator class in the erstwhile East-Pakistan and as you have heard and most of you know, they were brought, in early in the twenties and thirties, for the "Grow More Food" campaign and later on of course this continued for other reasons. So these Bangladeshis were essentially cultivators and they occupied what we called "the char areas" and degraded forest areas. You are all probably familiar with the char areas and also the degraded forests.

Of course, the early settlers who were brought in were put in different districts to grow more food during the "Grow More Food" campaign. These char areas were not inhabited by the locals. They were essentially the first inhabitants. The same is the case with the degraded forests. Only now we have utilised degraded forests, primarily for small holder tea plantation and other cultivations. Earlier degraded forests were unutilised. Most of the immigrants worked originally as agricultural labourers and then they became land-owners later. In the char areas, the zamindari or more precisely the Matabar system is prevalent. In fact in the char areas, practically it is the mafia who rules. Poor people remain poor. Although they came from East-Bengal or East-Pakistan or Bangladesh, they are no better off, they remained poor, only the Matabar or the zamindar became rich. Overtime, these migrants due to pressure on land and fresh entrants, extended to other areas. First, they started as agricultural labourers; eventually, because of their hard work, they got hold of these lands and then they became land-holders. This is an important point to remember.

The second point, I would like to emphasise is, wherever they were their productivity was higher than that of the locals. They cultivated normally three crops or even four crops whereas the locals cultivated one crop or at the most two crops. Therefore they had, to that extent, contributed to the State's economy by producing a higher amount of produce. And to that extent, of course, the State Domestic Product had increased.

That does not mean that the agricultural labourers or these people are better off because of the zamindari or Matabar system. Next, what happened was that pressure on land in these areas became really intense and as a result the second and third generation had moved out of agriculture. Some remain in the agriculture, but many of them had ventured outside. In fact what happened in Assam now is that particularly in the cities we see a lot of Bangladeshis in the form of construction workers, day labourers, rickshaw pullers, porters and household helpers. This visibility is noticeable. As a result, our perception is that Bangladeshis have really increased which may or may not be true. In have a suspicion that it is not true. What has happened is that these char area people or degraded forest people, because of lack of opportunities within that area, they have ventured outside to take over those trades and services previously manned by the Biharis. They did not replace the locals as much as they have replaced the Biharis. The Biharis were the construction workers, rickshaw pullers, porters and vegetable vendors. But now more and more these Biharis have been replaced by these people. Because of their productivity and also because of their cheap wages, more Bangladeshis are employed. That is the other thing has happened.

The point here is that the local employment opportunities have really not been taken over by these Bangladeshis. It is however true that they have restricted the employment opportunities. The problems in Assam is that we have acute unemployment problem. About 10 per cent of our population is unemployed and much of which is educated unemployed. But the irony is that we cannot find people where employment opportunities are there and we have people where employment opportunities are not there. This is the irony of the situation and the Bangladeshis have exploited this vacuum.

Thirdly, one has to admit that minorities everywhere, and not just the Bangladeshis, have to struggle for their existence. We have seen that all over the world and to that extent, Bangladeshis do struggle for their existence. As a result, they are hard working people, they are more productive. The second and third generation Bangladeshis, who are no longer Bangladeshis actually, though they are called Bangladeshis have in fact contributed not only to the economy but also to the other aspects of Assamese life, like literature, in government service and others. Quite a number of them have become professionals.

On the other hand, let us look at this: If we do not have one common figure on how many Bangladeshis are in Assam, let us assume that it is 40 lakhs in Assam which is mentioned by the Home

Ministry. Now 40 lakh is about 18 per cent of the total population and to provide infrastructure to this 18 per cent extra population, costs to the Assam Government in terms of roads, power supply, water supply, schools, hospitals etc., is very high. Of course, one must admit that this infrastructure hardly exists in char areas; char areas are in primitive conditions. Hardly water supply is given, roads hardly exist. Even if there is a road the next floods takes away the road. Therefore, not much is there, but, theoretically yes, the Government of Assam has a department called Char Area Department and a Minister-in-charge looks after the areas. There is a budget, though not much. Therefore to that extent, Assam Government spends some amount of money on this extra population which was originally not there. Now there is also a Minority Development Corporation. That also looks after the development of the char areas.

Lastly, I would like to say that the Assam Government do not earn any revenue out of these people. They are hardly taxed. On agriculture there is no tax. Of course, agricultural income tax is there but that is essentially on Tea. Therefore, they contribute no direct tax. And in the trade, they are in the lower trades which are hardly taxed. Therefore as far as tax revenue is concerned, there is hardly any benefit to the Assam Government.

To sum up, I would say that on agriculture they have their contribution which is noteworthy and they certainly have contributed to the National State Domestic Product of Assam. While the cost to maintain them by the Assam Government is quite a lot, but unfortunately it cannot be quantified and the Assam Government does not earn anything by way of revenue etc.

Having said this, I would like to say a couple of other points. One, we have been talking about immigration from Bangladesh since quite a long time. It was in 1979 that it was first discovered that we have so many Bangladeshis amongst us. Now it is about 22 years that we have been talking about it and AASU and others have made big movements and DN Bezbaruah has been writing all the time about it and many of us are involved in it. But nothing much has happened as we all know. I think what is really needed to be discussed in my opinion—I hope Dr. Arun Sharma will throw some light on this—is the politics of it, why is it that nothings gets happened on this issue politically and administratively.

15

Illegal Migration in The North-East: The Economic Aspects

ARUN K. SARMA M.P.

We have been much benefitted by the previous speeches about the impact of illegal migration on the Indian economy. There is a large scale impact of the additional population which has been migrating since long from East-Pakistan and Bangladesh to Assam and parts of North-East India and also West Bengal. Our country has to share a part of the national budget for them. That is a macroscopic observation.

So far as microscopic observations are concerned, there is a lot of pressure on our land because of this illegal migration of population and also on several social aspects. Now what is the impact on our Indian society as a whole and ultimately on our economy. They are very cheap labour, they can work day and night, they can work in any adverse situation, they have no fascination for education or good way of living. This has helped them to get employment everywhere in the country, not only in Assam or the North-East, but they get employment in New Delhi, Mumbai, in Punjab. Wherever organised sectors are there, they can work and work in any adverse situation. In Assam and parts of the North-East, they have occupied the traditional cultivated areas. As Dr. Jayanta Madhab has pointed out, there are char areas and degraded, abandoned forest areas. But how they are going into areas beyond the char areas and other areas is matter of serious concern and need to be discussed. What happened was that they had a kind of particular social habits—to commit dacoities, thefts, arson, intimidation of local cultivators. On account of intimidation, the local cultivators who had a farm house in a particular locality were being uprooted to the urban areas and they became jobless. Thus they have added to the increasing number of unemployed.

Secondly, because of the impact of rising population, it is mostly affecting the ethnic groups. There is a crisis of identity in the ethnic groups all over the North-Eastern States. Because of that insurgency started. When insurgency started, it has a manifold impact on the economy. The money which has gone for development work in those areas through the government machinery is being extorted. The government officials are kidnapped or businessmen are kidnapped and the money gets extorted. This money is utilised for the purchase of arms and guns and all that is required for continuing insurgency and for giving shelter to insurgents. For instance, in Bangladesh, four hundred crores were looted from the Lotimi Bank by some of the extremist groups. This was Indian money. So this has not only a direct impact on our exchequer, but as Prof. Saha has pointed out, the medical benefits which are being subsidised by our government have been enjoyed by them. The subsidised food items at our fair price shops are also largely being taken away. This also goes to Bangladesh. These are very cheap.

Thirdly, the greatest danger to our society is the threat to our work culture. What happens is that every average Indian family is keen to send their boys for school education and we are creating a very elite class society where they get white collar jobs or government jobs. Now everybody has given up the traditional cultivation work and this gap has been filled by the Bangladeshis, not only in Assam or the North-East but all over the country. As has been rightly pointed out, they have gone to European countries because of their hard working nature and the work culture that they have. Now the work culture which we had traditionally, for that we now rely on Bangladeshis for our day to day work in our family. Maybe the older generation had that kind of work culture in the family, but the youngsters who are growing cannot do any of their household works. They are totally dependent on this migrant population. Had there not been this population, they would have continued their work culture. This has a great impact on the Indian society. We have hundred crore population, still we are hiring people from Bangladesh as it is cheap labour. This has harmed the Indian economy to a great extent. So this is an important aspect which we have to note seriously. Secondly, mostly they are occupying forest areas. They are very much inclined to do processing and deforestation. Because this is not their country, they have only come to earn money and livelihood. They can go and destroy everything. Traditional Assam was fish surplus area. Now even at the seedling stage, all fish are being fished out and sold. Now Assam has become a fish deficit area and fish is being brought from Andhra Pradesh and other parts of the country. Like that it has a great impact on the entire system.

I hope we must have a particular agenda for the entire country to rebuild our work culture. We are not against anything politically, but we have to rebuild and regain our traditional work culture so that we are not dependent. Our dependence on Bangladesh will definitely make them come here and occupy our employment opportunities and affect our economy.

16

A Note on the Economic Consequences of Immigration of Bangladeshis into Assam

H.N. Das IAS (Retd.)

The British Government and the Muslim League Government of Sir Md. Saadullah brought cultivators from East Bengal, now Bangladesh, especially from its northern districts of Mymensingh, Rangpur, etc., and got them settled in sparsely populated areas of Assam for their 'Grow More Food Programme' during the period between First and the Second World Wars. The flow of the immigrant settlers continued due to easy availability of land in Assam and the encouragement given by the Saadullah regime of the State. Moreover, the indigenous cultivators lacked the dogged energy of the immigrants.

The immigrants form more than forty per cent of Assam's present day population of 2.3 crores. Their number is increasing rapidly because they procreate more and do not take any birth control measures. Another reason of the rapid increase in their number was their illegal immigration even after partition of the country. The immigrants who came to Assam after the 1971 cut off date number 49 lakhs as announced by the then Assam Chief Minister Hiteswar Saikia.

The immigrants from Bangladesh remain actively engaged in the food production, including production of vegetables, pulses, oil-seeds, and the cash-crop, jute. They are employed in the construction of roads, railways, buildings, etc. Unfortunately, local people are hardly seen engaged in such activities. They also provide cheap casual labour in Assam. Naturally, the food and cash crop production and casual labour market may suffer to some extent by their withdrawal. But their withdrawal will bring more economic benefits to the state and the people of Assam will be certainly benefited by the same. Their withdrawal will immediately result in the increase in the per-capita income of Assam. The land occupied by the illegal immigrants may be distributed among the local people, as a result of which their income and wealth will go up.

Assam suffers due to perennial flood. Millions of people get displaced during the floods and spend their days and nights under open sky on embankments and railway tracks for many days. They need safer place for their settlement. Moreover, the natural growth of population of the state has made it impossible to accommodate more people. Under such circumstances, the illegal migrants are an extra burden for the State's economy. Apart from the *sar* (river islands) land, the aliens also settle on the forest lands and destroy them and the natural vegetation. This has adverse effect on the economy of the State.

17

Illegal Migration from Bangladesh: A Case Study of West Bengal

BIMAL PRAMANIK

Introduction

A new dimension in the political and social arena has emerged in this eastern and north-eastern region of India after independence of Bangladesh in 1971. A novel phenomenon of demographic pressure started looming larger and larger on the border region centering around Bangladesh. During the last three decades illegal migration from Bangladesh to India are going on unabated. In Bangladesh era, Hindus are coming as usual like in the days of Pakistan due to religious persecution and political pressure but a new feature also started emerging as people from majority segment (Muslim) for different reasons and purposes started coming to West Bengal. Both the Centre and West Bengal governments were generally aware of this development yet no notable concern was visible before November 2002. Of late, Deputy Prime Minister and Prime Minister of NDA Government and Chief Minister of West Bengal and even the President of India have expressed their grave concern and agony on the issue of illegal Bangladeshi migration and its implications regarding internal security issues.

The secular state of India promised to protect all religions equally having no religion for itself—but Bangladesh Republic assures for arbitrating the process of peace and harmony under the shadow of state religion Islam. Under such codified and arbitrated policies, practised by any government of Bangladesh, the features of silent Muslim migration to neighbouring states of India shall largely depend upon how agreeably they are committed to respond to the incumbent situation. Our experience will show that states of West Bengal and Assam have been considerably shy and indifferent to the consequences of such socio-religious process. But little deeper, it may be observed that certain states surrounding Bangladesh, very calculatedly derive political benefits when their main thrust of the political existence are basically against the power of Central Government and out against the political party of the Centre.

Bangladeshi rulers, whosoever, with essential Islamic orientation possibly shall not rely or depend on Assam because of its more or less nationalist moorings of the government, but they would not be hesitant to keep their confidence and faith on the Marxist dominated Bengal to fight against Delhi. Ideologically, Pakistan was conceived on two-nation theory shaped out of the Marxist understanding of Stalinist thesis on right to self determination. It means that basically a religious approach got a blessings of ideological goodwill when the idea of Pakistan was considered to be a powerful instrument first to divide the country on the unreal sense of total freedom.

A fall out of a shift in the paradigm out of 11 September 2001 event, the new elements to influence a new world order have started working more as a deterrent to Islamic forces than to consolidating a further aggressive expansion. It is altogether a new experience in the world of Islam when they rally under a flag of fighting against USA with so many splits in their own international forum and without a Soviet Union beside them. The possible outcome of this emerging situation might be a multiple with many loose ends. For example, one such outcome might be shaping under highly stringent changing pressure from the donor countries upon Bangladesh to re-fix their political outlooks for management of their economy with regard to India particularly. There can be a second probable outcome by stalling and discouraging export of poverty-nourished cheap labour to adjoining Indian states by depressing the wage earned by the Indian counterpart. Sequentially, there might come up additional pressure of Bangladeshi redundant labour on Bangladeshi economy itself thereby generating new kind of resentment, disillusionment and anger of the rural and urban masses of Bangladesh.

Demographic, Socio-economic and Political Problems in West Bengal due to Illegal Migration and its Consequences

Reports have also been received about the purchase of lands in the border districts by infiltrators as well as Bangladeshi nationals. Till some years ago reports used to be received about the buying of land by Hindu migrants, primarily for providing a roof over their heads. But from eighties onwards, reports are being received about the large-scale purchase of agricultural lands in the border districts of West Bengal by rich Muslim Bangladeshi agriculturists with the connivance of local influential Muslims. In this context a memorandum on the subject was submitted to the former Chief Minister, Shri Jyoti Basu, and Land Revenue Minister, the Late Benoy Chowdhury, on behalf of the State Committee of the CPI. It was stated in the memorandum :

> "As the Chief Minister is possibly aware through his Home Secretary, the entry of hordes of infiltrators from across the border has been constantly creating problems of law and order in this State. By taking advantage of the loopholes in the laws governing the purchase of lands in this State, the rich people from across the border are buying up lands in the bordering areas of this State by paying two to three times the normal price, and by depriving the Indian agricultural labourers of their work, they are bringing over people from the other side of the border to cultivate those lands. This incident took place last year at Khanpur in the Balurghat Police Station of West Dinajpur District. A problem of law and order arose when local agricultural labourers wanted to harvest the paddy crop in the land which had been bought by the Bangladeshis."
>
> "Last year, a settlement was reached through the intervention of the District Administration. This year, again, there are apprehensions about discord and clashes over the cultivation of that land. Such incidents are on the increase. The buying of lands by foreigners in this State should be stopped by enacting a legislation and also by declaring all such purchases as illegal. There should be a law for the detention of all those

Bangladeshis who have been living in the border areas for quite some time. We hope you will take a serious view of the matter."[1]

In this paper an attempt has been made to explain the emerging picture consequent upon the internal demographic changes in the state as well as districts of West Bengal. During 1951—2001 period, the contrast between a decline in Hindu population and an extra-ordinary upswing in Muslim population is indeed remarkable in every district of the state. In a number of districts, the rate of growth of Muslim population is double or more than double than that of Hindu population during the last five decades. Growth rate of Hindus and Muslim's are 198.54 per cent and 310.93 per cent respectively during 1951—2001. Population share of Hindu and Muslim in 1951 was 78.45 per cent and 19.85 per cent respectively, but during the last fifty years, share of Hindu in West Bengal has come down to 72.47 per cent decreasing by 6 per cent whereas the share of Muslim has increased to 25.25 per cent an enhancement of 5.40 per cent. (See Chart No.1).

Chart No. 1: Trend of Population share of Hindus and Muslims in West Bengal during 1951–2001

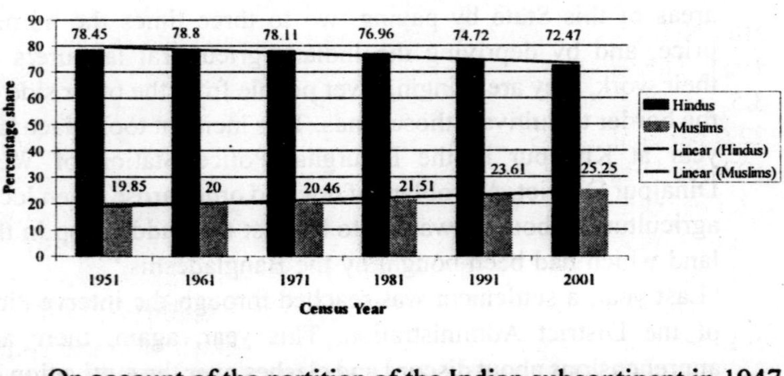

On account of the partition of the Indian subcontinent in 1947, Hindu refugees moved from East-Pakistan, without much interruption, to various parts of India, especially to West Bengal, till 1971, when political boundaries in South Asia were re-drawn. Even after the emergence of Bangladesh as an independent country in

1971, the march of refugees to West Bengal appeared to be ceaseless. In the days of Pakistan, most of the refugees coming to West Bengal were members of the minority communities in East Bengal (East Pakistan), viz. Hindus, Buddhists and Christians. But after Nehru—Liaquat Agreement on 8th April, 1950 in the context of displaced migrants from East Bengal, West Bengal, Assam and Tripura, where communal disturbances occurred, most of the Muslim migrants who crossed over to East Bengal came back again and settled in their ancestral places in the above mentioned Indian states during the entire period of undivided Pakistan i.e. 1950—1971. According to Agreement, "Indian Government ensured to the minorities throughout its territory, complete equality of citizenship, irrespective of religion, a full sense of security in respect of life, culture, property and personal honour, freedom of movement within each country and freedom of occupation, speech and worship, subject to law and morality." India also assured minorities 'equal opportunity with members of the majority community to participate in the public life of their country, to hold political or other offices and to serve in their country's civil and armed forces.'

On the other hand, Pakistan government neglected to implement the agreement or failed to enforce the fundamental rights of minorities in their country, mentioned in the agreement. As a result, no Hindu migrants returned back to East Pakistan/East Bengal after Nehru—Liaquat Agreement. As a consequence, during 1951—1961, Hindu share of population in East Pakistan came down to 3.5 per cent with growth rate of only 1.53 per cent. [i.e. from 22.0 per cent in 1951 to 18.5 per cent in 1961]. Even during 1961—1974 period Hindu population share further declined by 5 per cent to 13.5 per cent in 1974. A large number of Hindu families who crossed over to India during the liberation war of Bangladesh in 1971 did not return.

The Hindu community in Bangladesh participated in the War of Liberation with the expectation that in the newly liberated country they would enjoy equal status and rights along with the Muslim community. But in practice, the persecution of the minorities continues even after independence. The forms of oppression of the religious minorities in Bangladesh are manifold. Constitutionally they have been downgraded; economically they have been crippled through different discriminatory laws; politically they have been segregated and alienated from the main stream, culturally they have been made non-entity in different government and non-government services and socially they are insecured. They are totally deprived of the privileges of participation in top positions of government and nationally they are used as subjects tortured through communal riots organised by government for subsiding political unrest against the ruling party. ... As a consequence of the discriminatory policies combined with land grabbing, looting, arson, rape, murder and attack on religious institutions of the religious minorities under the protection of the government or government agencies, there has been continuous exodus of the minorities from Bangladesh.

After the emergence of sovereign Bangladesh in 1971 the Muslims in West Bengal did not feel any urge to migrate to Bangladesh because of diminished Islamic fervour in comparison with Pakistan. On the contrary, many Muslim families who had migrated to the then East Pakistan came back and started living in the several districts of West Bengal with the help of a section of influential local Muslims in all possible ways and ultimately settled in these areas since they could not fit in with Bengali Nationalism emerged from the liberation struggle of Bangladesh in place of Islamic fervour. Side by side hordes of Muslim infiltrators found a new haven in this region. Consequently, the Muslim population in the border districts as well as in other interior districts of West Bengal increased in geometric progression. In the eighties, Muslims in the border areas were further encouraged for community consolidation by the ruling parties of West Bengal. Demolition of the Babri Mosque in 1992, came as a great plea in committing organised crimes/dacoities by local Muslims and in some cases assaults on the Hindu families in connivance with Bangladeshi Muslims particularly in the bordering districts with Bangladesh.

It is observed from the ***Bangladesh Population Census 2001***, Hindu population share has come down to 9.2 per cent only. During the last 50 years since 1951, very lower growth rate indicates massive migration of Hindu population from Bangladesh to India, particularly in the state of West Bengal. On the other hand, a steady growth of Muslim population since 1951 has enhanced their population share to 89.7 per cent in 2001 from 76.9 per cent in 1951. During the last five decades (1951—2001) growth of Muslim population in Bangladesh is 244.68 per cent as against 23.16

per cent growth of Hindu population. Side by side, growth of Muslim population in West Bengal during the same period is 310.93 per cent, i.e. much higher growth rate than Bangladesh. When growth rate of Hindus in West Bengal in the same period is 198.54 per cent in spite of massive migration from East Pakistan/ Bangladesh. How it can be possible? It clearly indicates massive Muslim infiltration from Bangladesh to West Bengal.

Table 17.1 : Hindu-Muslim Proportion in the Border Village Significantly Changed due to Migration[2]

Period	*Gunarajpur*	*Keutsa*	*Mathurapur*	*Hogolbaria*	*Routbati*
(1)	*(2)*	*(3)*	*(4)*	*(5)*	*(6)*
1950s and 1960s	2:3	2:3	4:6	7:3	4:6
1970s and 1980s	2:3	2:3	5:5	6:4	5:5
1980s and 2000	1:4	1:2	3:7	5:5	3:7

Source: The above 5 border villages have been taken from P.S. Swarupnagar, Baduria (district 24-Parganas), Karimpur, Hogolbaria and Muturia (District Nadia).

Table 17.2 : Nature of Administrative Management[3]

*Total No. of case study family**	*No. of Incidents*				*Complaint lodged*	*Police action*	*Action of Panchayat etc.*	*Remarks*
	Dacoity	*Rape*	*Murder/ wounded*	*Other atrocities*				
(1)	*(2)*	*(3)*	*(4)*	*(5)*	*(6)*	*(7)*	*(8)*	*(9)*
30	28	3	15/3	10	Each and every case	Partially in three cases only	Nil	No punishment in any case

* All the 30 families who have migrated during the last two decades are from following police stations: Karimpur, Hogolbaria, Murutia, Thanerpara and Swarupnagar under Nadia and 24-Pargans districts.

Out of all the 59 incidents as referred to in Table 17.2, 49 cases are related to the worst form of crimes like murder, rape, dacoity, etc., but necessary administrative measures by the concerned authorities are very bleak by any standard.

Incidents of organised crimes in connivance with Bangladeshi Muslim and other criminals, coupled with non-cooperation of the local administration (the police, the panchayats, etc.) and the party in power to keep intact the Muslim vote-bank have forced many Hindu families to move to other interior Hindu dominated areas rendering these areas densely Muslim populated mainly by Bangladeshi

Table 17.3 : Population of West Bengal and Districts, 1981 and 1991 Illegal Migration and its Impact on Demography of District of West Bengal

(Religion-wise break-up)

		1981	*1991*	*Net Increase (%)*
West Bengal	Total Population	54580647	68077965	
	Hindu	42007159 (76.96)	50850000 (74.69)	8842841 (21.05)
	Muslim	11743209 (21.51)	16050000 (23.57)	4306791 (36.67)
District		*Rise in the number of Hindus 1981–91 (%)*		*Rise in the number of Muslims 1981–91 (%)*
(1)		(2)		(3)
Cooch Behar		18.51		37.43
Jalpaiguri		22.54		44.58
Darjeeling		24.50		58.18
Midnapore		19.74		53.08
Bankura		14.33		38.71
24-Parganas (North and South)		16.49		35.15
West Dinajpur		28.49		33.48
Maldah		24.36		36.09
Murshidabad		19.55		34.15
Nadia		28.43		34.49
Howrah		22.30		38.35
Hooghly		20.90		29.11
Purulia		18.93		31.62
Burdwan		22.38		38.67
Birbhum		18.36		30.00

Source: Census Report, Government of India, 1981 and 1991 and Satchidananda Dutta Roy, *Paschimbangabashi,* K.P. Bagchi & Company, Calcutta, 1994.

infiltrators. For the same reasons many of the one-time Hindu majority border villages have now turned into Muslim majority villages. It needs mentioning that the incidents of dacoity, cattle lifting, rape and murder are more or less non-existent in the Muslim inhabited border villages of West Bengal. On the contrary where the population is mixed, Hindu families are specially subjected to coercion and dacoities by the Muslim criminals and in some cases in connivance with a section of the Bangladeshi Muslims. In most of the Hindu majority villages the entire cattle population are left to the care of the Border Security Forces (BSF) or under the protection of local police before it is dusk and taken away by the owners at dawn.

Regrettably it may be mentioned that entire management of rural society run on the ground rule of law, more or less replaced by spasmodic arbitrary and also authoritarian local decisions of the party-administration nexus—the local self government remaining on the surface as such. Now almost both sides of the Indo-Bangladesh border region are inhabited by a population, which is ethnically, culturally, linguistically and religiously identical[4]. Already it has taken the shape of a demographic expansion. This changed demographic scenario is quite capable of disrupting social harmony of this region.

Secondly, the process of Islamic fundamentalist orientation through madrassah education, Islamic *Jalsa* (fundamentalist preaching for Islamic consolidation), anti-Indian propaganda by speeches and literatures mostly from Bangladesh, etc. not only alienated other religious sects and ethnic groups but is also strengthening the Islamic militancy and Inter Services Intelligence (ISI) network in the region which is further weakening our national security and integrity by widening the communal division as well as weakening moderate Muslim ideals. The entire process is weakening the secular fabric of our civil society leading to further erosion of social harmony.

Policy Options

Policy solutions regarding illegal Bangladeshi migration depend on a set of existing conditions. It may change if existing condition change. But the existing conditions always depend upon some factors of social, political and economic developments and also bilateral relations and international understandings between the countries. The present scenario demands :

- Land purchasing by the illegal migrants must be stopped by enacting a legislation and also by declaring all such purchases as illegal. There should be a law for the detention of all those Bangladeshis specially those who have been living in the border areas for quite some time; to check vigorously the further settlement of alien population in the border region, and to take measures to shift the existing settlement; to safeguard against easy access to certain unintended benefits such as ration cards, inclusion in voter's list, admission to educational institutions, etc.
- A public awareness campaign at home and abroad explaining the gravity of the problems and its adverse political, economic and security implications for the region.
- To complete and strengthen barbed wire fencing along the Indo-Bangladesh border without further delay and to include area within 15–20 km stretch from border under the effective higher administrative control (it may be jointly with state governments) and the procedure (law system) of push-back for alien people/infiltrators/illegal migrants must be simplified for immediate action by the law enforcing authorities.
- Immediately to prepare a list of the illegal migrants. They should be treated according to the established norms and rules of UNHCR. Commissioning the services of the UNHCR and other credible international agencies in repatriating the illegal migrants. The problem has reached such a magnitude that the other options will be more complicated.
- To grant citizenship to the Hindus coming from Bangladesh since 1971 because they are victim of partition and religious persecution. It is very important for the Government of India to chalk out a plan for safeguarding the existing Hindus in Bangladesh for resisting further migration.

NOTES AND REFERENCES

1. *Kalantar,* West Bengal CPI Bengali daily, August 26, 1991. The aforesaid memorandum was written by Gobin Kanrar on behalf of the CPI State Committee to the Chief Minister Mr. Jyoti Basu after visiting Khanpur (West Dinajpur).
2. A recent survey (October, 2002) conducted by Mihir Sinha Ray in the border districts of West Bengal on "Cross border migration from Bangladesh to West Bengal" sponsored by Maulana Abul Kalam Azad Institute of Asian Studies, Kolkata.
3. *Ibid.*
4. A statement was given by Minister of State for Home Affairs Mr. P.M. Syeed on Unstarred Question No. 2365, 17th August, 1995, Lok Sabha, Government of India.

18

Illegal Migration from Bangladesh to Tripura

ARUNODAYA SAHA

Tripura is a small State, one of the smallest in India. With only 10,000 sq. kms. area and 864 km. of international boundary along with Bangladesh and engulfed by Bangladesh from three sides. It is obvious that there will be some sort of influx of population across the border. I have with me the decadal variations of population of Tripura as well as that of Bangladesh. Tripura's decadal population variation, during 1981–91 was 34.30 and the latest during 1991–2001 is only 15.73, which is less than half of the former one. The decadal growth rate for the State of Tripura since 1951 to 2001 was 78, 36, 31, 34 and 16 respectively. So there is a regular falling trend of decadal rate of growth, but only with a little aberration in the year 1981–91. So it requires some sort of explanation. There is an overall fall but here we find a surprise. And it is due to Chakma refugees staying in Tripura for ten years since 1986. You might be knowing that 60 thousand Chakma refugees were given shelter in the South District. It is reflected here only. During 1951–61, it was quite high (78), but presently it is only 15.73. So I have one explanation to give. During that period, since Independence, there was lot of influx and the decadal growth rate of that decade had two parts, one, natural rate of growth and two, unnatural rate of growth. The natural rate of growth is okay, but due to influx that component was quite big. But over the years it is tending to be zero. So now I believe that it is only the natural rate of growth of population which is reflected in that.

Again, as you know, we have four districts—South District is entirely within Bangladesh, having almost 400 km international border with Bangladesh. South District is vulnerable in that sense.

But interestingly, this latest statistics show that decadal growth rate in that district in 1951–61 was 90 and now it is only 6. So it has gone down and down. But here in 1986, there is an aberration. In that period, as I told you, due to the influx of Chakma refugees, it was 14. So forgetting about this, or streamlining this trend, we can come to the conclusion that we have a falling tendency of rate of growth of population in Tripura.

Now what about Bangladesh? I have statistics with me and interestingly, Bangladesh has also registered a regular falling trend of population over there. Earlier, during 1981–91, the Bangladesh rate of grwoth of population was 20 and in this decade it is 14.80, less than India's rate of growth of population, and it reflects in other indicators also. There we find that the family size was quite big in Bangladesh but right now it is less than 5—it is 4.8. So if as a demographer we scrutinise this data, we find that there is a regular falling trend in the rate of growth of population in Tripura, as well as in Bangladesh. I have checked with other results. We have some border sub-divisions adjoining Bangladesh. I mean we have West Tripura, South Tripura and North Tripura having border with Mizoram. So in that part we have Brahminbaria, Comilla, Feni, Khagrachari, Chittagong, Habibgunj and Maulvi Bazar in Bangladesh. These are the sub-divisions or the smaller kind of units. They are having a common border with us and there interestingly we find that though the overall population of Bangladesh is registering a decline, there, I do not know how to match these figures, the family size figures are quite big, bigger than the national average of Bangladesh—5.4, 5.5, 5.6 and 5.7. The nuclear family must be 2+2 or 3, but it is higher. I am not going to make any comment, but on examining the figures one could conclude that there is no evidence that there is a big or substantial influx of population from Bangladesh to Tripura in the last decade. It is a very strong comment to make, but I am going to talk about that later.

In our local census also, we see that there is a sharp fall in the rate of growth of population in Tripura. It is even lower than the Kerala's rate of growth of population interestingly. Kerala is a role model of Indian States. Even then South Tripura has earned the distinction of being the lowest, even lower than the Kerala's rate also. How come? Here I want to put my own observations. It is a fact that there is no overall permanent migration from Bangladesh to

Tripura as we experienced in the sixties and seventies. But one thing is quite open, in fact wide open. Everyday in the morning, you can see hundreds of thousands coming into Tripura, they work for the whole day and go back after sunset. There is no border for all practical purposes. They are preferred, and as Dr. Madhab said, they are hard working, they are productive and they come. Agartala is just a stone's throw away from Bangladesh. In the morning you will see a lot of daily workers, rickshaw pullers coming. Today our population is around 32 lakhs. For all practical purposes, our Government claims to be 40 lakhs. Why? Because there is this floating population, they come, enjoy our civic amenities, they get treated in our hospitals. It came up in the newspapers (probably in Sentinel also). When doctors were asked, "Why do you treat Bangladeshi people when we are deficit in all medical facilities?" A doctor was quoted to have said, "To me, nationality does not make any difference. I don't care which nationality he belongs to, a pateint is a patient." In GB Hospital, in other district hospitals, a lot of people are coming, getting the best treatment and going back. And as compared to Bangladesh we have better medical facilities today. Not only that, other civic amenities, they come and they enjoy and they are not paying anything for that. That is a point of serious concern.

If we look into the scenario of Tripura's demographic pattern since Independence, or since 1901, there are two forces working behind this dynamics. One is the push factor and the other is the pull factor. We had a long, long history of royal dynasty in Tripura till its merger with India. During the King's regime, there was the pull factor, the King pulled resources, intellectual/elite people to come to help run Tripura's administration. A lot of Bengali intellectuals came, as you know Rabindranath Tagore also helped Tripura's King by sending his son-in-law, Ramani Mohan Chatterjee. Anyway, Dhaka and Vikrampur were the hub of intellectuals those days. The King gave them incentives to come, settle in Tripura and help run the Tripura's administration. That was the pull factor from our side. Then after Independence there was the push factor. From time to time, due to sporadic ethnic strifes, religious riots and all that, people are threatened to leave Bangladesh. But what worries us more is the floating population. Everyday they come and go back and they are not even quantifiable. They mix with us, they work with us and we prefer them to come. So this is the scenario.

Now I do not want to lengthen my discussion, but as a student of Economics, I have one or two observations to make here. Why do people come as a floating population or as permanent migrants from one place to another place? My hunch is this, my perception is this that it is the level of development. Tripura's level of development is higher than that of Bangladesh. So obviously people will be attracted to come to this side. As long as they have a lower level of development there, they will be rather lured to come. Water always goes down, we cannot stop it. So if we want to stop it, and we need to stop it, since with its limited resources, Tripura cannot afford to have this influx of people to come and stake claim to our civic amenities. There must be some monitoring management of resources most judiciously—first for us, then for others. I do not have any reservation or objection to that. But some theoretical suggestions I have to offer here.

One, we wish Bangladesh should be developed. We expect that there will be no flow of population from Bangladesh to Tripura in the near future. Second, is highly theoretical, if they cannot develop, we have a responsibility to help build their economy. I do not know in what way, but if we do that there will be no influx from that side to this side. This is a theoretical discussion. But if this is not taken care of, then what will happen? This perennial problem will continue. So we should find some economic solutions in the form of helping develop their economy or see that they should develop themselves. Otherwise it will continue to occur.

To sum up, when I say we should help develop their economy, it is something which is very hard to accept. Because when we cannot develop ourselves, how come we will be able to do this job for them? Yes, under compulsion we sometimes do that. I am giving one example. Say, I am going to construct a beautiful cottage for myself. My neighbour is a poor man who cannot afford to do like me. And he cannot afford to have a sanitary latrine, so bad smell comes and my life is made miserable. What do we do then? Under compulsion we give him some money, we bribe him so that he can convert this one to the better hygienic one and by doing this I make my life comfortable. So economic compulsions require us to do this job. Yes, I know we are deficit in resources ourselves, even then we should think about this.

19

Problems of Immigration in India's North-East: Aspects of Conflict Resolution

R. GOPALAKRISHNAN AND C. JOSHUA THOMAS

Scale, extent and scope of immigration in India's North-East is well documented. Various fora including non-governmental organisations, student bodies, administrators, bureaucrats and political parties, have articulated the consequences of this. Suffice it to say here that immigration into the North-Eastern region has been a continuous process. It has involved variety of elements that are from the Gangetic delta, from Burma/Myanmar and other parts of the country. These elements embraced variety of identities. This facilitated their gradual absorption in the region's economy and society. The latter, over a period of time, became politically important, as they began increasingly to encroach upon strategic and economic security and stability of the North-East.

Of course, the motive and reason might be different at different times. Prior to British annexation of the region, immigration followed normal pattern and did not assume the alarming proportions that it subsequently became, as in the late early twentieth century, when Mullen, in his Census Report, highlighted for the first time the consequences of this unhindered movement of population from the Gangetic delta to the North-East.

Impacts of Burmese incursions in the region were in the form of devastation of the economy and decimination of population. In order to make the region politico-administratively stable and economically viable, the Colonial power imported labour, personnel and technology. These provided necessary momentum for population from surrounding very high-density regions to move into the North-East. During the Colonial Rule, part of this movement consisted of labourers, technicians, clerks etc. With the gradual expansion and development of the tea and later oil industries, continuous movement of population catered to the requirements of ancillary industries.

All these movements of population occurred in the British India. But the equations were transformed with the separation of Burma from India in 1935 and partition of the Subcontinent in 1947. Post-1947 period saw politico-administrative stabilisation and development of the North-East. These efforts were hindered by growing political instability expressed initially as movements for political, eventually culminated in movements against immigrants. There were significant cross-border movement of population at the time of partition (from Delta to the North-East). This movement continued well—after 1947. Presence of enclaves on either side of the border with Bangladesh did not help either. Political situations in the regional geopolitical environment saw sizeable movements of Tibetan population into the region, just like the movements of Chins from the eastern frontiers and Chakmas from the Chittagong Hill Tracts in erstwhile East-Pakistan, now Bangladesh. Moreover, political situation within the region resulted in notable population displacements. As noted earlier, all these human movements included population elements that possessed multiple identities. They were forced to move initially by economic compulsions and subsequently by political factors. Their impact on the society of the receiving regions was profound and elicited responses that ranged from purely humanitarian considerations to threats to economic and political security of the region.

North-East has been a region of economic opportunities. Development initiatives have progressed in fits and starts. These were adequate for the regional population to aim for progressively developing social welfare facilities. These indicated the latent economic potential of the region. The scope of these facilities was continuously undermined and eroded by illegal influx of population from the adjoining countries.

In addition to these, the region became the gateways for migrants who were able to use their multiple identities to go deeper into the heartland in search of economic and social security along-with associated political fall outs. These have the region as beachhead to move for better pastures.

Causes: Some of the factors, that led to the large-scale immigration to the region, can be stated to include:

(a) British India imported substantial labour for tea plantation and other associated activities. This was further encouraged by the fact that local people were either unwilling to work in tea gardens and other economic enterprises initiated with Colonial encouragement at low wages and unhealthy climate or were reluctant to participate in the conomic activity sponsored by the administrators.

(b) The Colonial administrators found the local people inadequate to run their administration. Consequently, they encouraged people from the Gangetic delta to fill up the vacuum in the administrative sector.

(c) East-Bengal (later known as East-Pakistan and now Bangladesh), from where the massive immigration took place, was heavily populated area, characterised by difficult social and extremely poor economic conditions. Similar situation existed in the eastern frontiers, where the Chin population found it extremely difficult to maintain survival conditions and were compelled to migrate westwards or the Chakmas, in order to escape harsh political relations, moved east and north, crossing the international boundaries into India. These migrants were in constant search of better pastures. The latter was the North-East India, adjacent to the Gangetic delta. It was an area of low to low-medium density population, as compared to area to south across the frontier. It may be mentioned that in 1961, 51 million East Bengalis lived in in an area of 55,000 sq. miles, with population density of 925 persons per square mile, while in the North-East, fewer than 12 million people on 47,000 sq. miles with a density of 252 persons per square mile lived during the same period.

(d) In contrast to East Bengal, Assam was relatively less populated, had substantial fertile flood plains and vast forested vergin lands, Spate termed the extent of available cultural wasteland found in the North-East did not have any equivalent elsewhere in the habitable world. Apart from empty lands, there were substantial areas of forest reserves which attracted migrants from the East Bengal. Population movement was also facilitated by the contrasting land tenure. Of the two regions. East Bengal had (until shortly after 1947) a land holding system in which large number of tillers were tenants or under tenants to large landowners. North-East by contrast was a region of individual small landowner cultivators who paid revenue directly to the State or were governed by their respective traditional institutions.

(e) The political factors were also responsible for encouraging migration from East Bengal to Assam. It was during the pre-partition days when a conscious effort was made to include Assam and its adjacent areas as a part of Pakistan by political fora. The 1947 referendum held at Sylhet indicated the complexity and seriousness of this problem. Later, with the emergence of Bangladesh in 1971 in influx of immigrants increased to North-East India.

(f) Problems of immigration from the south were also due to the compulsions created by natural factors. Bangladesh has a growing population and high population density. Its social welfare measures and programmes are limited and constrained by resources. Consequently, it has prevented the movement into its territory of the co-ethnics from Myanmar or has retarded the return of Chakmas from India. Moreover, the Gangetic delta regularly succumbed to devastating floods and cyclones. This left sizeable population, largely rural in character, deprived of basic economic sustenance. The relief were inadequate and too far apart. This population either moved to adjacent urban nodes or across the border to almost all parts of India.

Immigration and Associated Effects:

(i) The impact of immigration, besides population growth, is many. It has led to innumerable socio-economic problems in the region. On the other hand, migrants have their own contribution in developing the region in various fields of agriculture, trade and commerce, tea plantation industry, jute production, livestock farming. The development in all the above fields was possible with the help of migrants. Their services in facilitative, vocational, utilitarian and constructional enterprises have been of immense value towards the economic growth of the State. But the immigrants who came in the recent time, particularly after independence have created more socio-economic problems than their contribution. The number of immigrants is constantly increasing and if their influx at the present rate continues, the identity of the homeland of Assamese people may be lost in the near future. Because of their presence the local people feel uncertain of their future for they think that their language, culture and economic opportunities are being encroached upon. Such attitude of indigenous people is a result of historical factors. The records show that Bengali culture and langauge was imposed upon the indigenous people and controversy raised upon. The Assamese people have the obvious fear which had a root in the history of the region.

(ii) The demands of tea labour community, and immigrants for more representation to the legislature and other policy-making bodies of the State on the basis of their population strength, have generated reactions among the natives. The popular response was that more representation by the member of the immigrant community would result in shifting of legislative power. In addition, the growth of exclusive immigrants settlements in the form of Cultural Islands and outposts throughout the region is being a cause of great concern as these have far-reaching consequences on the socio-economic, culturo-political life of the people of the region.

(iii) Except for the minor conflicts the socio-cultural and economic interaction between the immigrants and the indigenous people has been so far cordial. But the continuous addition of thousands of illegal immigrant since the recent years, is now adding a new dimension to the problem. For example, the earlier immigrants of Bangladesh origin who have created extensive pockets are harbouring illegal immigrants by providing physical and social shelter to them. Once inside the State, these illegal immigrants get settled and mingle with the earlier settlers from the same origin, it becomes difficult to detect them. These are the places where conflicts are reported to have taken place frequently resulting in communal disturbances and imbalance.

(iv) The most significant effect in recent past was observed as the evidence of increasing number of militant organisations, with a sizeable number formed by the immigrants as well came to light. These suggest the existence of a plethora of fundamentalist militant groups in the North-East. Though these groups are mainly based in Assam, yet they have their tentacles reaching out to Nagaland, Mizoram, Meghalaya, Manipur and other neighbouring States.

(v) The aim and objectives of these groups ranges from countering Hindu Fundamentalist organisations like R.S.S. and the VHP, to defending immigrant settlers and infiltrators from attacks by indigenous tribal groups like the Bodo Security Force (Bd.S.F.) and Mizo Zirlai Pawl (MZP), to, most ominously, carving out a sovereign republics from the territory of North-Eastern Region of India. All these groups are actively aided and supported by external agencies, Pakistan's Inter Service Intelligence Directorate, commonly known by its initials I.S.I., and Bangladesh. In Bangladesh these groups take logistic support from the Chattra Sibir, the student youth wing of the Jamaat-e-Islami. Reports indicate that these groups have also made contact with other global and regional fundamentalist organisations.

From the various newspaper reports, one can significantly infer that the I.S.I. has set up training camps for the fundamentalist militant groups at Madhupur on the Mymenshingh Dhaka road in Sylhet district. Ershadnagar in Rongpur district and at Akyab in Cox's bazar. The training course is normally of three months duration beginning with a month of indoctrination and motivation followed by two months of weapons and tactics instruction. This was known through confessional statements made by Muslim militants arrested by Indian Security Forces. The militant groups have placed agents all along the India Bangladesh border in the Barak valley and Dhubri district of Assam and Khasi and Garo Hills of Meghalaya. The duty of agent is to assist in infiltration and ex-filtration of cadres. Trained cadres have also been placed at various immigrant Muslim dominated areas of Assam like Dhubri, Bongaigaon, Mancachar, Barpeta, Mangaldoi, Nagaon, Hojai, Cachar and Karimganj. The above analysis suggest that the possible threat to the federal structure could be from the growth of Muslim fundamentalists and activities of I.S.I. This must be viewed as most serious implication of Immigration of Bangladeshis.

Global Parallels and Suggestions:

(a) Demography is density, population movements are the motor of history. it is on some of these premises that the German geographer Fredrich Ratzel, developed his Law of the Nations. Of particular concern to us is his Seventh Law. He states in unambiguous terms that a people with dynamic and vibrant culture have the tendency to extend up to the natural limits, as defined by the geographical features. History offers innumerable instances and H.G. Wells has treated this aspect in an explicit manner in his Study of History. Likewise, one can draw relevant inferences from these instances of large-scale transnational movements on the peopling of the various regions of the World. Thus, one can conclude that in past, differential growth rates, varying economic conditions and political circumstances, have produced massive migrations, be it Greeks, Jews, Norse, Turks, Russians, Chinese, and so on. In few of these instances, migrations have brought about violent changes, while on the whole it has been a peaceful invasion.

(b) Mass movements have transformed global relationships. Most of these transactions emanated from Europe. Export of people coincided with the rise of the West. Subsequent movements in the Twentieth Century drastically altered the political, social and economic environments of the States. In the 1990s, it was variously estimated that international migrants amounted to about 100 million, of which refugees roughly accounted for 19 million. The number of illegal migrants was estimated at a minimum figure of 10 million.

(c) Salient demographic movements in the second half of the last century was partially attributed to decolonisation, the establishment of new states, and state policies that encouraged or forced people to move. Yet, what was singularly consequential, were the level of modernisation and technological development. Access and availability of improved communication systems and network made migration easier and cheaper. This also ehnanced the incentives to pursue economic opportunities and maintain effective liaison with their respective source regions. In this regard, economic development provided remarkable parallel between developed and developing regions of the world: just as the economic growth of the stimulated emigration in the nineteenth century from the West, economic development of the post-1945 states stimulated emigration in the twentieth century. Myron Weiner aptly states that the migration becomes a self-reinforcing process. In other words, that once migration commences whatever may be the reason for the impetus, it induces further flows. The latter is reinforced by information on land and opportunities available in the receiving end.

(d) Till the closing decades of the last century, the West reflected its concerns over nuclear proliferation, consistently supported democracy and human rights all over. Their views on immigration were often ambivalent and changed with the balance shifting significantly against them, but initially they encouraged immigration as it alleviated their chronic labour shortages. However, with their economies reflecting signs of depression and lack of buoyancy, as in the late 1980's and 1990's, increasing unemployment and overwhelmingly non-European character of the immigrants introduced sharp cleavages within their respective societies. This compelled these states to review and introduce changes in their perception and policies.

(e) The challenge is demographic. The societal responses were in the form of incidences of acts of violence against immigrant communities and individuals in the early 1990s. Such types of situation exist in the North-Eastern Region of India. The social and political fora opposing immigration were more or less a mirror image of social and political fora of source countries. Both were outsiders, denouncing a corrupt establishment and its parties, exploiting economic grievances particularly unemployment, making ethnic and religious appeals, and attacking foreign influences in their society. The concerned parties and establishments responded to these developments in similar fashion. For example, in Bangladesh establishments became more rigid in their orientations, symbols, policies and practices. In the West, mainstream parties adopted the rhetoric and promoted the measures of the right wing, anti-immigration parties.

(f) In the early 1990s European political leaders competed with each other to respond to anti-immigration sentiment, e.g., in France (Immigration must be totally stopped in 1990, zero immigration in 1993, and anti-immigration stances), Immigration was a major issue in the parliamentary elections of 1993 and apparently contributed to the victory of the conservative parties. This was also reflected in strengthening the existing laws and policies which as in the early 1990s when the French policy was changed to make it more difficult for the children of foreigners to become citizens, getting visas for families more difficult and so on. Illegal immigrants were deported and the powers of the police and other government authorities dealing with immigration were strengthened. In Germany, political leaders expressed concerns about immigration, and in its most important move, the government amended Article XVI of the German Constitution guaranteeing asylum to 'people persecuted on political grounds' and cut benefits to asylum seekers. Overall in the mid-1990s, Western European countries were moving inexorably toward reducing to a minimum, if not totally eliminating, immigration from non-European sources.

(g) The immigration issue came to the fore somewhat later in the United States but did not generate quite the same emotional intensity. The United States has always been a country of immigrants. It has developed highly successful processes for assimilating newcomers. The sources of American immigration were also more varied than in Europe, and thus the fear of being swamped by a single foreign groups was less nationally, although real in particular localities. Despite these factors, American public favoured reduced immigration. While economic concerns and economic conditions affect attitudes toward immigration, the steadily rising opposition in good times and bad suggests that culture, crime, and way of life were more important in this change of opinion.

(h) The West perceived immigration as a threat to their culture. Growing public opposition to immigration prompted a political reaction. Given the nature of the political system, anti-immigration publicists and interest groups became more numerous, more active, and more vocal. Much of the resentment focused on the illegal immigrants, and politicians responded. The strongest reaction was at the state and local levels, which bear most of the costs of the immigrants. These were in the areas of education, welfare, law enforcement, and other costs produced by illegal immigrants.

Conclusion

For the North-East, resolutions such as tough immigration controls, tightening rules governing political asylum, creation of Immigration and Naturalisation Services, strengthening the Border Patrol, and construction of physical barriers along the boundary, to name a few, are some of the measures that need to be thought for implementation. Societies in developing countries generally either do not want to assimilate immigrants or have great difficulty doing so. However, sustained substantial immigration is likely to produce countries divided into different communities that are in competition and conflict with each other. This outcome can be avoided in a way and to the extent that European Governments and peoples are willing to bear the costs of restricting such immigration. This include the direct fiscal costs of anti-immigration measures, the social costs of further alienating existing immigrant communities' and the potential long-term economic costs of labour shortages and lower rates of growth.

(20)

Bangladeshi Immigration: Are We Heading for Another Partition?

PRAKASH SINGH

One of the biggest problems facing the country and having a direct bearing on national security is that the continuing illegal immigration of Bangladeshis into India. Unfortunately, the problem has been dusted under the carpet by all the political parties even though it has very serious political, social, economic and security implications.

This process of migration had started well before the partition. Large number of cultivators, primarily Muslims, came to Assam from the Mymensingh district in 1930s and 1940s. They were encouraged by the Sadullah regime in Assam for the 'Grow More Food Campaign', though as Viceroy Lord Wavell said, Sadullah was more interested in "Grow more Muslims rather than Grow more Food". The availability of large tracts of cultivable fertile area in Assam was an incentive to the migration.

In the wake of partition, large number of Hindus crossed over to the States of West Bengal, Assam and Tripura. In due course, when the Pak Army was persecuting the Bengalis, a large number of Muslims also crossed the borders into India. With the liberation of Bangladesh in 1971, it was expected that the new regime would ensure communal harmony and tackle the social and economic problems of its teeming millions in a manner which would eliminate or at least reduce the factors contributing to migration. However, that did not happen and both Hindus and Muslims continue to pour into India in large numbers. The Muslims have been moving primarily for economic reasons and it is estimated that presently they constitute nearly seventy per cent of the infiltrants.

The factors, which have been encouraging the influx from Bangladesh side, are:

- steep rise in population with increasing pressure on land and mounting unemployment,
- recurrent natural disasters like floods and cyclones, uprooting large segments of humanity,
- better economic opportunities in India,
- religious persecution of Hindus and discrimination of tribals,
- Islamic interests encouraging expansion of territory,
- patronage extended by vested political groups in India,
- organised immigration by touts and anti-social elements, and
- porous and easily negotiable international borders.

The Bangladesh Government hardly makes any efforts to stop these exfiltrations. Perhaps, it is happy that it would have that many less persons to feed and take care of. A section of intellectuals in Bangladesh have even been legitimising the theory of *lebensraum*—living space for the people of Bangladesh. In early nineties, Sadeq Khan, a former diplomat, recorded the following views:

> "All projections, however, clearly indicate that by the next decade, that is to say by the first decade of the 21st century, Bangladesh will face a serious crisis of lebensraum ...there is no reason why regional and international cooperation could not be worked out to plan and execute population movements and settlements to avoid critical demographic pressure in pockets of high concentration... The natural trend of population overflow from Bangladesh is towards the sparsely populated lands in the South-East, in the Arakan side and of the North East in the Seven Sisters side of the Indian sub-continent."[1]

Lately, several leading thinkers, economists and former diplomats of Bangladesh have been articulating the idea of free movement of people across the international borders. Prof. Amena Mohsin of Dhaka University asserts that "migration is a normal and natural phenomenon and cannot be stopped, the need today is to evolve ways to legalise it"[2].

As result, waves of Bangladeshis continue to flood eastern India. It is interesting that, according to Sharifa Begum of the Bangladesh Institute of Development Studies in Dhaka, nearly 3.5 million people "disappeared" from East-Pakistan between 1951 and 1961, and that another 1.5 million possibly entered India between 1961 and 1974. Significantly, the Hindu population of Bangladesh has been steadily going down over the past decades and has dropped in terms of ratio from 20 per cent of the total population to less than 10 per cent.

The bulk of the Bangladeshi immigrants are in the States of West Bengal, Assam, Tripura, Bihar and Delhi. Baljit Rai, in his book *Demographic Aggression Against India* published in 1993, gave the following estimate of Bangladeshi infiltrator, state-wise:

West Bengal	40.0 lakhs
Assam	40.0 lakhs
Bihar	20.0 lakhs
Delhi	3.0 lakhs
Madhya Pradesh	3.0 lakhs
Bombay	1.5 lakhs
Uttar Pradesh	0.5 lakhs
Rajasthan	10.0 thousand
Total	1,08,10,000.0[3]

The Home Ministry's Working Group on Border Management had also estimated the total number of Bangladeshis in India to be about one crore about ten years back. The latest estimate has been provided by Madhav Godbole, who headed the Task Force on Border Management. In his report, submitted to the Government in August 2000, he has placed the figure at 1.5 crore with about 3 lakhs Bangladeshi nationals entering India illegally every year.

Assam

Assam's rate of population growth during 1901–51 was the second highest (137.80%) in the world exceeded only by Brazil (204%). The trend of high rate of population growth continued even after independence. Election Commissioner, S.L. Shakdher, sounded the alarm bell at a conference of Chief Electoral Officers of States in 1978, when he made the following observations:

> "In one case [Assam], the population in 1971 census recorded an increase as high as 34.98 per cent over 1961 census figures and this figure was attributed to the influx of very large number of persons from foreign countries. The influx has become a regular feature.... A stage would be reached when that state may have to reckon with the foreign nationals who may in all probability constitute a sizeable percentage if not the majority of population in the State."[4]

During the last twenty years (1971–1991), Assam's population has increased from about 15 million to about 23 million. Out of this, while the non-Muslim population grew at the rate 45.39 per cent, that of the Muslims rose at the rate of 77.42 per cent. during 1981–91, the three border districts of Dhubri (71%), Cachar (56%) and Karimganj (58%) recorded very high increase in Muslim population. Census was not held in Assam in 1981.

The All Assam Students Union (AASU) and the All Assam Gana Sangram Praishad (AAGSP) launched an agitation, which lasted from 1979 to 1985, over the large scale influx of foreigners in the State. The Assamese had become apprehensive that they would be overwhelmed by the sea of humanity from across the international borders. Rajiv Gandhi's initiative led to the signing of the Assam Accord on August 15, 1985 whereby it was agreed that for purposes of detection of foreigners January 1, 1966 shall be the base date and year, that those who came to Assam on or after that date and up to March 24, 1971 shall be detected and their names deleted from the electoral rolls, and that those who came on or after March 25 shall be detected and expelled in accordance with the law. The non-implementation of vital clauses of the Accord is a sore point with the Assamese. The Illegal Migrants' (Determination by Tribunal) Act, which was enacted to detect and deport the foreigners, proved quite ineffective in dealing with the problem. The IMDT Act took away the powers of issuing 'Quit India' notices, arrest, interrogation, etc. from the police and passed on the burden of proof also, unlike in the Foreigners' Act, to the police. An immigrant got so much time at various stages that he could conveniently disappear whenever he found that action was going to be taken against him. Detection and deportation under the Act therefore became an extremely slow process. The Government of Assam went to the Supreme Court for abrogation of the Act. The North-Eastern states also filed affidavits in the Apex Court in this context. The Supreme Court, on September 20, 1999, expressed concern over the unabated migration of Bangladeshi refugees to various North-Eastern states and asked the Union Government to make "honest and serious" attempts to stop this influx. A Division Bench comprising Chief Justice A.S. Anand, Justice Srinivasan and Justice R.C. Lahoti said that this influx of Bangladeshis was posing a "danger to the region's demography".

The Congress Government in Assam recently filed an affidavit in the Supreme Court that the Illegal Migrants (Determination by Tribunals) Act was not protecting the interests of Bangladeshis as perceived by the former AGP regime. It was a masterpiece of hypocrisy. The Mahanta Government, with all its faults, had taken a courageous stand on the issue. It had termed the Act as a discriminatory piece of legislation and demanded its repeal. And yet we have Tarun Gogoi's Congress government taking the stand that the IMDT Act protects genuine Indians and that it alone can held detect and deport real foreigners. The affidavit itself admits that so far only 1,494 persons declared illegal migrants by the Tribunals could be deported from the State. This amounts to a mere. 01 per cent of the total number of illegal Bangladeshi immigrants in the country. What greater proof is required that the IMDT Act is a toothless piece of legislation? The Task Force on Border Management has made an emphatic recommendation that the IMDT Act should be repealed and action against immigrants taken uniformly under the Foreigners Act.

West Bengal

The State of West Bengal has about 2,200 km. long border with Bangladesh. The entire stretch, except a small portion in the southern extremity, is flat without any natural obstacles and people on both sides live very close to the border. Cultivation extends right up to the zero line. According to the census figures, West Bengal recorded higher population growth than the national average during 1971–81 (23%) and 1981–91 (25%). During 1971–81, while the Hindu population grew by 21.37 per cent, Muslim population increased by 29.55 per cent, largely on account of the influx of Bangladeshis. The border districts particularly very high population growth rates. In Murshidabad, West Dinajpur, Darjeeling and Calcutta, it was over 30 per cent during the decade 1981–91. According to a study done by the Centre for the State and South-East Asia Studies, out of the 292 assembly constituencies of West Bengal, Bangladeshi immigrants can determine the poll outcome in 52 assembly constituencies while in another 100 constituencies they can significantly influence it.

Tripura

In Tripura, the percentage of tribal population has been steadily going downwards, as the following would show:

Year	*Population*	*Tribal Population*	*% of Tribals*
1941	5,13,010	2,56,991	53.16
1951	6,39,028	2,37,953	37.23
1961	11,42.005	3,60,070	31.50
1971	15,56,342	4,50,544	28.95
1981	20,53,058	5,83,920	28.44
1991	27,54,205	8,53,345	30.95

The tribals have thus been reduced from a majority to a minority in the State. This is the root cause of disaffection among the tribals. As observed by BG Verghese:

"Tripura is the Northeast's nightmare being a state whose demographic transformation has rendered its original inhabitants a minority in what was once proud tribal kingdom ruled by a succession of 183 Tripuri princes who held sway over a land that finds mention in the *Mahabharata* and *Ain-i-Akbari* and whose history is recorded over the centuries in the *Rajamala*, the state chronicle".[5]

The tribals are disaffected because the presence of Bangladeshis means increasing pressure on land. Culturally also, they have a feeling of being swamped. This explains their support to the National Liberation Front of Tripura (NLFT) and the All Tripura

Tiger Force (ATTF), insurgent groups which have been perpetrating acts of violence in the State. Most militants, according to Rabindra Debbarma, General Secretary of the Tripura Upajati Juba Samity (TUJS), are from "impoverished tribal families who have lost their land to Bengali migrants, giving rise to a sense of deprivation and injustice that fuels the present insurgency in Tripura"[6].

Actually, there are over thirty extremist groups currently operating in Tripura. In 1999 alone, there were over 300 violent incidents in the State in which 119 civilians and 34 security forces personnel were killed.

Other North-Eastern States

Nagaland has more than 10,000 Bangladeshis. They are mostly concentrated in and around Dimapur. A couple of thousand Bangladeshis have reached Manipur also. There is a sprinkling of Bangladeshis in Arunachal Pradesh and Mizoram also. Meghalaya has 443 km border with Bangladesh; it has therefore received a larger share of Bangladeshis (about 10,000). The seeds of Nellie are there over several parts of the north-east.

Punjab

While posted as inspector General, BSF, Punjab Frontier (1987–91), I dealt with the problem in a rather unconventional way. I found that a number of Bangladeshis who had travelled all the way from Bangladesh to Punjab wanted to cross over to, what they thought, was their El Dorado - Pakistan. The official instructions to the security forces were that they should be intercepted, handed over to the State Police, who would then make arrangements for their transportation back to Bangladesh. Though technically correct, I found the policy very unrealistic. Here were a body of people who wanted to go to Pakistan. Why should we not then let them go across? Besides, in actual practice, the Punjab Police was seldom taking them to the eastern borders for being handed over to Bangladesh authorities. We were told that the Punjab Police, which had its hands full with the law and order problems would just let off the Bangladeshis, who would have food at some *langer* in a Gurudwara and soon became a part of population mosaic of the country.

I discussed the problem in the Ministry of Home Affairs and sought their permission to facilitate the Bangladeshis wanting to go to Pakistan. The Pakistani Rangers were regularly pushing terrorists across the international border into Punjab. We could return their compliment by sending unarmed and harmless Bangladeshis at least. The MHA said that they could not give any such instruction in writing but were prepared to turn the Nelson's eye to my efforts in the direction. "what thou would'st highly, thou woud'st holily", in Shakespeare's words, appeared to be their guiding principle.

I thereupon decided that the Bangladeshis should be helped to go across in the larger national interests. Oral instructions were given to all the border outposts that henceforth they shall assist the Bangladeshis in going across. They could even be collected at the BSF posts and moved across in the darkness of night. The policy was quite successful. We did not keep any records for obvious reasons but several thousand Bangladeshis were shepherded across the Punjab border. Their entry caused great concern to the Pakistanis. They had not faced such heavy infiltrations so far. Suddenly they realised that something contrary to their calculations was happening. At the subsequent meetings I had with the Director General, Pakistan Rangers, they would always raise this point and wanted India to stop the movement of Bangladeshis. We would reply by saying that they should stop exporting terrorists to Punjab.

Later, I discussed the proposal with the Prime Minister (VP Singh) and suggested that train loads of Bangladeshis could be sent to the Punjab border and that it would be our responsibility to see that they reached their destination. The PM approved of it and asked me to see the Director, Intelligence Bureau (R P Joshi) in this regard. I saw the DIB and, on his request, submitted a detailed scheme, calling it *Operation Locusts*. The Army Chief (Gen. Rodrigues) was apprised of the scheme and he also endorsed it. I Was however disappointed that there was no follow up action from the government side. The *babus* in the government, it seems, developed cold feet in pursuing the scheme.

Threat to National Security

It is a matter of serious concern that the fundamentalist elements in Bangladesh have been propagating that the borders defined at the time of Partition are no longer relevant and need to be changed, taking into account the recent demographic changes. The Jamaat-e-Islami of Bangladesh has been talking of *Swadhin Muslim Bangabhumi* in India. TV Rajeswar, a former Director, Intelligence Bureau, has expressed his misgiving that "there is a distinct danger

try, speaking Bengali predominantly,

t of India in future".

bservations in his memoris *The White*

t, are also ominous:

ergence of Bangladesh—which we postulated—presented India with fierce long-term problems. For Bangladesh was in effect East Bengal, separated only by religion from India's most fractious and most separatist State, West Bengal. They shared language, tradition, culture, and above all, a volatile national character. Whether it turned nationalist or radical, Bangladesh would over time accentuate India's centrifugal tendencies. It might set a precedent for the creation of other Moslem states, carved this time out of India. Once it was independent, its Moslem heritage might eventually lead to a rapprochement with Pakistan."[7]

Lt. Gen. (Retd.) S.K. Sinha in a report to the President of India submitted in November 1998 gave a grim assessment:

> "As a result of population movement from Bangladesh, the spectre looms large of the indigenous people of Assam being reduced to a minority in their home state. There cultural survival will be in jeopardy, their political control will be weakened and their employment opportunities will be undermined. This silent and invidious demographic invasion of Assam may result in the loss of the geostrategically vital districts of Lower Assam [on the border with Bangladesh]. The influx of these illegal migrants is turning these districts into a Muslim majority region. It will then only be a matter of time when a demand for their merger with Bangladesh may be made. The rapid growth of international Islamic fundamentalism may provide the driving force for this demand.... Loss of Lower [the area close to the Bangladesh border] will severe the entire land mass of the North-East from

the rest of India and the rich natural resources of that region will be lost to the Nation."[8]

The Group of Ministers, in their Recommendations on the *National Security System* (February 2001), while taking care of Bangladesh's sensitivity in the matter, have yet stated that "the massive illegal immigration poses a grave danger to our security, social harmony and economic well-being".[9]

Suggestions

Sanjoy Hazarika, Senior Fellow, Centre for Policy Research is of the view that it would be impossible for any government to push back the very large number of Bangladeshis and that, therefore, the following measures be taken to encourage legal inflows develop a regulatory mechanism to monitor the traffic:

(a) all Indian nationals be issued Identity Cards,
(b) the illegal immigrants should not be given I-Cards or the right to vote,
(c) a general amnesty could be given to those who have come to India between, say 1971 and 1991, and they could be given citizenship provided they acknowledged their illegal status,
(d) a quota system could be announced for those coming from Bangladesh (and also Myanmar) and wanting to work in Assam, the North-East or other parts of India on work permits,
(e) work permits could be issued to about 25,000 persons in the first year, rising gradually to a maximum of 75,000 for Assam; similar quota could be fixed for other states depending on their need,
(f) permits shall be issued to groups of not less than 20 persons,
(g) the employers shall be responsible for the well-being and non-disappearance of his/her employees under the permit scheme.[10]

The suggestions appear quite down to earth and could be given a trial by the Union Government.

The following other measures merit consideration:

- There should be compulsory registration of all those living in India, the citizen, the non-citizens and the foreigners who come with valid documents.
- The citizen should be given multi-purpose identity card. The non-citizens should also be given identity card but these should be different in colour/design.
- The scheme should be implemented in three phases: area up to a depth of 50 kms. along the border immediately; the remaining areas of the border states in the second phase; and the rest of the country in the third phase.
- The IMDT Act should be repealed and the Foreigners Act should apply throughout the country.
- BSF strength along the Bangladesh border must conform to the sanctioned strength of the force (a lot of force was diverted to other operational areas) and, if necessary, augmented.
- The Border Security Fencing/Lighting wherever sanctioned, should be raised without any delay.
- BSF Water Wing should also be strengthened.
- The matter should be taken up with the Bangladesh government and they should be persuaded to accept the repatriation of Bangladeshis beyond a particular cut off year mutually acceptable to both the countries. A Joint Working Group comprising representatives of both the countries may be formed for the purpose.

The mater is much too serious to be deferred any longer. Considerations of national security must override that of political expediency.

REFERENCES

1. *Holiday*, Dhaka, October 18, 1991.
2. Wasbir Hussain, 'Demographic Invasion, Anxiety and Anger in India's Northeast', *Faultlines*, Vol. 7, p. 128.

3. Baljit Rai, *Demographic Aggression Against India* (1993), B.S. Publishers, Chandigarh, p. 175.
4. *Faultlines,* Vol. 7, p. 111.
5. B.G. Verghese, *India's Northeast Resurgents* (1997), Konark, New Delhi, p. 166.
6. *Pioneer*, Septmber 2, 2001.
7. TV Rajeswar, 'Creation of a New State', *Hindustan Times*, Feb. 9, 1996
8. *Faultlines*, Vol.7, pp. 114-115.
9. *Reforming the National Security System*, Recommendations of the Group of Ministers, Feb. 2001, p. 60.
10. Sanjoy Hazarika , 'India's North-East and The Problem of Migration : What Is To Be Done?', *Dialogue*, Vol. 1 No.3, pp. 17-19.

21

Illegal Migration from Bangladesh

N. CHANGKAKOTI

The Problem in Brief

Large scale migration of people from the over populated territories, earlier known as East Bengal before partition of our country into two Independent Nations—India and Pakistan and since 1971 known of Bangladesh, into Assam, West-Bengal and Tripura had started from the beginning of the last century. Such migration was not illegal till the creation of Pakistan in 1947. However, since then, entry of any one from these areas, which became parts of Pakistan and now Bangladesh, into any part of Independent India, either for permanent settlement or temporary stay without acquiring citizenship of our country or without valid passport and visa is illegal. But despite the legal retrictions, ceaseless influx of people clandestinely from erstwhile East-Pakistan/Bangladesh into contiguous States of India, particularly Assam, Tripura and Wast-Bangal and also to other parts of India through the Indian States abjacent to Bangladesh for permanent habitation has been continuing because of many deficiencies in the guarding of the Indo-Bangladesh border.

Such large-scale illegal infiltration has already reduced the indigenous people of Tripura into minority and is fast changing the demographic composition of more and more areas of Assam in their favour and is also aggraving the unemployment problem and tensions and conflicts over possession of unchanging land area, resulting in many agitations and law and order situations. Such people, can also become security risks as, their loyalty will remain suspect.

In the Preamble of the Illegal migrants (Determination by Tribunals) Act, 1983, (IMDT) Government of India have acknowledged that "a good number of Foreigners who migrated into India across the borders of the eastern and north-eastern regions of the country on and ofter the 25th day of March, 1971, have by talking advantage of the circumstances of such migration and their ethnic similarities and other connections with the people of India and without having in their pessession any authority so to do, illegally remained in India. "Taking into consideration the fact that a large number of such foreigners had illegally come over and settled in India before this Act was passed and illegal migration of such people into India, in a significant degree, is continuing even after passing of this Act, it can be comprehended by anyone that the total number of such illegal migrants in our country is considerable. On May 6,1997, the then Home Minister of India late Indrajit Gupta—said in the Lok Sabha that an estimated ten million foreigners were, then, illegally living in our country. Shri L.K. Advani, Deputy Prime Minister, recently disclosed that the estimated number of Foreign Nationals illegally staying in India is around 15 million. It needs hardly any emphasis that the problem has assumed such alarming proportion, mainly because of not paying timely and adequate attention to the writing on the wall by the Central Government and the Governments of the States, mostly affected by this problem.

The Solution

There are two aspects of the problem which need to be tackled simultaneously and vigorously without any loss of time as delay has only complicated and aggravated the problem. The two dimensions are (I) Prevention of fresh infiltration and (II) detection and expulsion of illegal migrants already in the country.

Prevention of Fresh Infiltration

(a) It is entirely the responsibility of the Central Government to adopt fool-proof measures all along the international border of India with Bangladesh to prevent fresh infiltration and reinfiltration of those Foreigners who had been expelled earlier. It is also necessary to point out that in clauses 9.1 and 9.2 of the Assam Accord signed between the Leaders of All Assam Students Union and All Assam Gana Sangram Parishad on the one side and Government of India on the other side, on August 1985, Govt. of India solemnly pledged that "the international border shall be made secure against future infiltration by erection of physical barriers like walls, barbed wire fencing and other obstacles at appropriate places. Patrolling by security forces on land and riverine routes all along the international border shall be setup. Besides the arrangements mentioned above and keeping in view security considerations, a road all along the international border shall be constructed so as to facilitate patrolling by security forces. Land between border and the road would be kept free from human habitation, wherever possible. Riverine patrolling along the international border would be intensified. All effective measures would be adopted to prevent infiltrators crossing or attempting to cross the international border."

But, unfortunately, Government of India have not so far displayed required degree of seriousness and sense of urgency to fulfil this promise and infiltration is continuing unabated. The coordination meeting of the Police Chiefs of the seven North-Eastern states and senior officers of different Central Police organisations posted in this region, held at Shillong in October-November,1993, had commented that Govt. of India had not paid the same attention to securing the India-Bangladesh border as in the case of India-Pakistan border. The Committee on Police Reforms for the State of Assam, while visiting the Assam-Bangladesh border along Karimganj District of Assam in February, 2002, found, to their dismay, that the border fencing at a number of places had been cut to facilitate illegal movement of poeple to and from our country and that the posts of Border Security force were more than three kilometers apart which made intensive patrolling difficult. These forces also did not have sufficient number of patrol boats with search light facility for intensive patrolling on reverine border areas.

Border Security Force, as its very name suggests, was raised by Govt. of India, for the specific role of guarding the India-Pakistan border including border of East-Pakistan/Bangladesh. But though manpower of this Force is not enough even to perfrom this primary role effectively, diversion of many contingents of this Force for internal law and order and security duties, has only facilitated infiltation from Bangladesh and also clandestine movement of anti-national and anti-social elements to indulge in illegal activities. No more valuable time should, therefore, be wasted to deploy this Force exclusively for the role for which it was raised and its manpower and other resources should be adequately increased to make it capable of performing this role effectively. Govt. of India should also take all other measures required on war footing, to fulfil its promise given in Clause 9 of Assam Accord within the shortest possible time as a lot of valuable time has already been lost. Towards this end, following suggestions are made:

(a) A high powered committee consisting of Home Ministry officials, BSF officials and representatives of the Governments of highly affected States like Assam, West-Bengal and Tripura should be constituted to survey the entire India-Bangladesh border and furnish concrete and comprehensive recommendations by March, 2003, for implementation by the Central Government.

(b) On the other hand, Govt. of India should put pressure on Government of Bangladesh to take effective measures to ensure that citizens of Bangladesh do not try to sneak into India through illegal routes when liberal visa facilities have been provided for them to visit any part of India. Govt. of India should also direct BSF to open fire, if necessary, on any Bangladeshi seen to cross to our side stealthily. Of course, the Force must strictly adhere to the principle of use of minimum force in such circumstances.

(c) State Governments of affected States should prohibit movement of all types of vehicles, boats etc., between sunset and sunrise within one kilometer from the border inside our territory, without specific permission of the Deputy Commissioner/Sub-Divisional Officer.

(d) Village defence parties in the bordering villages should be formed and these parties should be given required facilities and incentive for effective joint patrolling along with police personnel of border police stations as a second line of defence against fresh infiltration. Police stations covering border areas should also be increased and strengthened as necessary for the purpose.

(e) As almost all the illegal migrants from Bangladesh are cultivators, every legal measures should be taken to prevent them from occupying any land, either by purchase or encroachment, and earn their living with such land, so that such people feel dissuaded from coming over to our country in search of livelihood. It, therefore, follows that Govt. should take energetic step to remove all encrachments from all Forest land and all other Govt. land as most of such illegal migrants are occupying such land. It is pointed out that through clause 10 of Assam Accord, both Govt. of India and Govt. of Assam pledged as follows "It will be ensured that relevant laws for prevention of encroachment of Government lands and lands in tribal belts and blocks are strictly enforced and unauthorised encroachers evicted as laid down under such laws." In Clause 11 of the Assam Accord, Central Govt. and Assam Govt. also proposed to strictly enforce the relevant law restricting acquisition of immovable properly by Foreigners in Assam. Clause 160 (I) in chapter Ten under head "protection of backward classes" of Assam land and revenue Regulations, says that "Notwithstanding anything herein before contained, the (State) Government may adopt such measures as it deem fit for the protection of those classes, who on account of their primitive condition and lack of education or material disadvantages are incapable of looking after their welfare in so far as such welfare depends upon their having sufficient land for their maintenance," Clause 160 (2) says that "The State Government may, by notification in the Official Gazette, specify the classes of people whom it considers entitled to protection by such measures as aforesaid." In pursuance of this clause, Govt. of Assam attempted to protect land belonging to tribal people in the areas predominantly inhabited by them by creating some belts and blocks. But no effort was made to protect the land of all other backward classes of the State. According to our informantion, the total number of other backward classes and most other backward classes in Assam is 145 and these people together with the people for whom belts and blocks were already created, constitute more than seventy per cent of the total population of the State. It is, therefore, high time to include under chapter ten of Assam Land and Revenue Regulations, all backward classes in the list of protected classes for preservation of their land. All other affected states should also review their land regulations to prevent alienation of land to foreigners.

(f) Similarly relevant law restricting acquisition of immovable property by foreigners should be tightened as necessary and should be strictly enforced. On the other hand, our citizens should be conscious enough to be very careful to ascertain the nationality of people wanting to purchase their land.

(g) State Governments concerned should organise properly planned motivational campaigns, particularly in the bordering area, to deepen their patriotic feelings and to make them adequately aware of the detrimental effects on our country's security and economy if the illegal migrants remain in our country, so that they also play a positive role in not only preventing fresh infiltration, but also in the detection of the illegal migrants staying in India.

(h) There should also be an organised effort to dissuade the Govt. and Private Agencies. Contractors and also common people from giving employment to anyone and from engaging any skilled and unskilled labour before being sure that such persons are not illegal migrants.

Detection of Foreigners Illegal Staying in India

(a) Except in Assam, all Foreigners in other states come within the purview of the Foreigners Act, 1946 and the Foreigners (Tribunals) Order 1964. But in Assam, after signing of the Assam Accord referred to above, all persons who came to Assam prior to 01-01-1966, including those amongst them whose names appeared on the electoral rolls used in 1967 elections, were regularised and Foreigners Act, 1946 became applicable to only those Foreigners who came to Assam illegally after 01-01-1966 (inclusive) and upto 24th March 1971. Illegal Migrants coming and staying in Assam, on or after March 25, 1971, are required to be detected and expelled in accordance with the provisions of the Illegal Migrants (Determination by Tribunals) Act, 1983. It appears to be unfair to apply this Act only in Assam, thereby exhibiting lack of sufficient faith in the sense of justice and fairplay of Assam Government for all time to come, even if at one time some unscrupulous officials had harassed some Indian citizens on the excuse of detection of Foreigners. However, the constitutional validity of the Act is under examination of the Hon'ble Supreme Court of India and it is advisable to wait for the verdict creating bitterness through arguments and counter arguments for or against it. The committee on police reforms for the State of Assam has commented in its report that there is considerable scope for improving the tempo and quality of enquiries both under the IM(DT) Act, 1983 and Foreigners Act, 1946, as during more than 16 years from 1985 to November, 2001 only 52677 cases under IM (DT) Act, 1983 and 38033 cases under the Foreigners Act, 1946 could be sent to the Tribunals by the inquiry officers in Assam and till now only 10590 persons were declared as Illegal Migrants under the IM(DT) Act, 1983 and only 26026 persons were declared as Foreigners under Foreigners Act, 1946. In order to accelerate the tempo of detection and in order that inquiries are taken up correctly and no citizen feels harassed in connection with such inquiries, adequate number of inquiry teams should be constituted with selected police and Revenue officers. These officers should be thoroughly trained for about a fortnight or so about how the enquiries should be conducted, what documents should be checked etc.

(b) Visa regulations should be amended requiring Foreigners with valid documents, to deposit one copy of their photograph in the Passport check post through which they enter our country which can be returned at the time of their exit through the same PPCP, so that, in case, after entering into our country any one destroys the documents and does not return within the stipulated period, the photograph becomes helpful in locating him/her as such a person may also give false address about his/her stay in our country.

(c) As already decided by Govt. of India, photo-identity cards should be issued to all Indian citizens as urgently as possible, giving priority to the citizens inhabiting the States contiguous to Bangladesh.

(d) Intelligence machinery of the Police Departments of the affected States, particularly in the bordering districts should be geared up to be able to furnish imformation about such illegal migrants masquerading as Indian Citizens and also about those Indian Citizens who may be guilty of promoting and abetting such illegal migration and giving shelter to such Foreigners. These Indian Citizens should be severely dealt with as per law. On the other hand, liberal rewards should be awarded to those who do not in any way assist such infiltration and also furnish information about such illegal migrants and also their abettors and shelterers.

Conclusion

It is hightime to treat this problem of silent invasion by Bangladeshis as a national issue of great importance, needing immediate and serious attention of the Central and the State Governments and also people at large to leave no stone unturned to pervent fresh infiltration and identify and expel the illegal migrants. Otherwise, in not too distant a future, these infiltrators will not only become the arbiters of the destiny of the North Eastern region, but will also have a mojor say in the national politics.

22

The Problem of Illegal Immigration: Some Tentative Solutions

D.N. BEZBORUAH

Introduction

The problem of large-scale illegal immigration from former East-Pakistan and persent Bangladesh into Assam and the north-eastern States of India is well-known problem by now, though it is still not a well-understood problem. This large-scale immigration was actually encouraged by the Congress from the early sixties mainly as a means of consolidating its vote-banks with alien voters. Even as late as in 1983, the Congress pushed through a legislation in Parliament bringing in a separate immigration law for the State of Assam alone in order to ensure that the large number of illegal migrants from East-Pakistan/Bangladesh could not be deported. When the ramifications of the problem began to be better understood, the Congress, rather than own up the disservice it had done to the country, began to pretend very doggedly that there were no illegal immigrants from Bangladesh in Assam, and that all the 'so-called' Bangladeshis were, in fact, Indian citizens. But now, after the *Time* Magazine report of October 21, 2002 about the activities of the ISI and the al Qaeda in Bangladesh, and the recent reports of the Home Ministry putting the total number of illegal immigrants from Bangladesh illegally living in India at about 15 million, the pseudo-secular political parties of India that had insisted on considering the religion of the illegal migrants, have become far less vocal about defending the illegal migrants or pretending that all of them are Indian citizens. Even the 'secular' CPI(M), which had seen the Assam Movement against foreign nationals as nothing better than a "picnic" (in the words of Mr. Jyoti Basu) have begun to take a firm stand against the illegal migrants from Bangladesh who are all Bengali speaking. Even the earlier talk of a "humanitarian approach" to the illegal migrants is not heard any more these days. Many of the "secularists" have also begun to realise that what had been dismissed for decades as no more than a silent unarmed infiltration only for economic reasons, is no longer unarmed, and that there are sinister political and expansionist designs behind the large-scale infiltration, with the support of some Indian citizens as well.

What Needs to be Done

1. The Government must get out of the familiar practice of ruling by *fait accomplis* or making a virtue of them as in the case of the recent signing of the Bodoland Territorial Council Accord.
2. The Indian Parliament sabotaged the immigration law of the country (namely, the Foreigners Act of 1946) by enacting another immigration law for Assam alone, known as the Illegal Migrants (Determination by Tribunals) Act of 1983, called the IM(DT) Act for short. The IM(DT) Act suffers from the following infirmities: (a) It is a second immigration law for our country (applicable to just one State). No civilised country has two immigration laws. This will enable illegal migrants in one part of the country to move to the only State where the IM(DT) Act is in force, everytime there is a drive to identify and deport illegal migrants. (b) It is the only immigration law in the world that is kind to the illegal immigrant, and looks for ways to protect the illegal immigrant, rather than seeking to deport him. (c) It is the only immigration law of any civilized country where the onus of proving nationality is not on the illegal migrant, but on individual citizens. (d) It is the only immigration law that transfers the process of detection and deportation of the illegal immigrant from the Executive to the Judiciary—to retired judges functioning as the officers of tribunals. The IM (DT) Act has to be repealed before

any other step is initiated to commence the Herculean task of detecting and deporting illegal immgrants of Bangladesh, especially from Assam and the North-east.

3. There should be no difference between the norms followed in guarding India's western border and the eastern one between Bangladesh and India. If there are shoot-at-sight instructions to the BSF for the Indo-Pakistan border, there should be no difference for the Indo-Bangladesh border either. Likewise, if he western border is fenced all through, so must the eastern border be completely fenced, This is not to suggest that fencing the border will be a major solution to the problem. It will not, because of the long reverine stretches that cannot be fenced. Even so, this is a step that will make infiltration a bit more difficult. Any step that inhibits illegal infiltration even by a bit must be made use of. The BSF must completely give up its lax ways making the Indo-Bangladesh border a soft border. It must be turned into a hard border, as the borders of all civilised countries are. In the matter of immigration, there is no virtue in softness and laxity.
4. There has to be a multi-purpose photo-identity card for Indian nationals that must not be made available to the foreigner as ration cards and franchise has been available to the alien in the past—even in New Delhi—thanks to secular humanitarian souls like HKL Bhagat and Jagdish Tytler. If the Photo-identity cards benefit the foreigners and keep out the Indian nationals, we might as well not issue them.
5. The idea of issuing work permits to those foreigners who have already lived in India illegally for two decades or more does not make any sense. No violator of the immigration law is going to say now, " I have lived illegally in this country for 20 years. I now want a work permit." He knows how hazardous such a statement is going to be. It could be an open invitation to deportation. Those who have already spent two decades or more are already moving heaven and earth to get citizenship in the most irregular manner imaginable. By mooting the idea of work permits,

we are actually sending out the message that there is *lebensraum* (living space) for many more foreigners who would be applying for work permits.

6. We must give up all the high falutin' ideas about opening up the Indo-Bangladesh border for more trade. It will only be a way of making illegal immigration that much easier. The Indo-Bangladesh border must remain firmly closed until Bangladesh decides to put an end to its unfriendly activities against India, including support to the ISI and the al Qaeda.
7. It makes excellent sense to release to Bangladesh its due share of the Ganga waters, so that the development of that country is not affected. Any lack of development in Bangladesh is going to impel more Bangladeshis to migrate to India in search of a better life and slightly more living space.
8. There should be Economic boycott of the illegal migrants.
9. A return to the National Register of Citizens, 1951, to enable us to find out who is the Indian citizen and who is the progeny of the illegal migrant. The search-and-sort programme of computers can make the task of identification of aliens a much easier task than the Centre makes it out to be.
10. The complaints process before the tribunals under the provisions of the IM(DT) Act should be speeded up as long as the present immigration law continues to operate.

23

Global Processes and Local Concerns

Bangladeshi Migrants in Assam

ANUP SAIKIA

Introduction

Migration is a complex process driven by many factors. As a process migration has important effects on migrants, their areas of origin and destination and with the onset of globalisation, the process of migration is likely to get accentuated. Migrants are motivated to migrate by the "push" or "pull" factors of possible origin/destination areas and are attracted or tend to go—other things being equal—to areas where previous streams have proceeded wherein networks of their predecessors making the migration process easier. Networks are particularly important for illegal or undocumented migrations. While developed regions are coveted destinations for migrants and account for major shares of global migration flows, within developing areas as well smaller flows take place, based on variations in the levels of development. India's north east is one such area that has traditionally been an attractive destination for migrants from Bangladesh.

Immigration from Bangladesh initiated in the early part of the last century became illegal with the changed political boundaries of independent India. Since 1947, there have been dramatic changes in the scale and complexity and implications of migration. Generated by British policy illegal immigration from its demographically larger neighbour has become problematic for Assam and the other states of north-east India by virtue of its sheer volume.

The paper examines how two global processes—international migration and global warming—have important local impacts and how these are sought to be dealt with. The first section considers the genesis of immigration from Bangladesh into Assam, and reviews estimates regarding its present magnitude and state policy in tackling the problem. The next section looks at future implications and the impact of climate change on immigration.

Genesis

The first wave of Muslims that came to Assam were those which came from north India during 13th century and belonged to the Afghan stock. They were followed by other Muslims from north India and Bengal who came in the wake of several 17th century Mughal invasions of Assam. In course of time these migrants assimilated themselves with the local culture and developed close societal relations with Assamese Hindus (Singh,1987) . These early streams of Muslims are identified as the Assamese Muslims and can be easily distinguished from the later Muslim migrants from the erstwhile East Bengal (Singh,1987) that started in the last decades of the 19th century. This latter stream of migration continues till today and has been problematic for Assam and the other states of north-east India. The later 19th century stream of migration had its roots in colonial British policy (Phukan,1981).

In 1912 the Bengali Muslim district of Sylhet and the Bengali Hindu district of Cachar were added to the Assam province (Weiner,1988). This inclusion was prompted by the colonial notion that Assam was a part of Bengal (Barua,1999).These new boundaries led to the coming of a minority Muslim League Government led by Sir Mohammad Sadullah in 1937. The Sadullah Government followed a policy of encouraging Bengali Muslims from the erstwhile East Bengal (Verghese, *et al.* 1980); prompting the then Viceroy, Lord Wavell to observe that:

> "The chief political problem is the desire of the Muslim Ministers to increase this immigration into the uncultivated Government lands under the slogan of Grow more food but what they are really after is Grow more Muslims" (cited in Sinha,1998) .

The next two decades saw migration from Bangladesh (then East-Bengal) continue unfettered and unabated under the political patronage of Sir Sadullah, who except for a brief interlude governed the state till the close of World War II. The results of Sadullah's policy were to become apparent in the near future. Immigration from East-Bengal continued till 1947, the year of Independence of India and Pakistan. Till now Bengali Muslims had entered Assam. Hereafter, it was Bengali Hindus (the minority in East-Pakistan) that began to dominate the migrating flocks, till about 1971, after which again Muslims began dominating the migration, a trend that continues till the present day.

The initial benefits that immigrants from Bangladesh brought with them soon began to get overweighed by the disadvantage of their sheer numbers as is apparent from Chief Election Commissioner, S.L. Shakdher's observations in 1978:

> "I would like to refer to the alarming situation in some states, especially in the North-Eastern region wherefrom disturbing reports are coming regarding large scale inclusion of foreign nationals in the electoral rolls. In one case, the population in the 1971 census recorded an increase as high as 34.98 per cent over the 1961 figures and this increase was attributed to the flux of a very large number of persons from the neighbouring countries. The influx has become a regular feature... the increase that is likely to be recorded in the 1991 census would be more than 100 per cent over the 1961 census. In other words, a stage would be reached when the state may have to reckon with the foreign nationals who may, in all probability constitute a sizable percentage, if not the majority of the population in the state." (cited in Verghese, *et al.*, 1980)

A document called "Influx" produced by the public relations section of India's Ministry of External Affairs sought to establish that large scale immigration from East-Pakistan—now Bangladesh—had occurred to Assam (Baruah, 1999). This document related the rise of the Muslim population in those Indian states with a corresponding decline in the population of East-Pakistani districts. While the population of Pakistan as a whole increased by 23.7 per cent during 1951–61, the document pointed out, the population of East-Pakistan rose only by 20.9 per cent. As there was no scientific evidence to suggest that fertility in East-Pakistan was lower than in West-Pakistan, the "constant and successful pressure on the Hindu minority in East-Pakistan to migrate to India" and "infiltration by the Muslim population of East-Pakistan into the border Indian States of Assam, West Bengal and Tripura" accounted for the difference, the pamphlet stated (cited in Baruah, 1999).

Magnitude of Migration

In recent years several studies have analysed immigration and its impact on Assam and the other states of north-east India. Much of the available literature points to immigration being problematic for Assam and the North East (Verghese, *et al.,*1980; Goswami and Gogoi, 1984; Hazarika, 1992; Weiner, 1993; Taher, 1997; Saikia 2000) though certain studies hold that the illegal immigration issue has been exaggerated (Dass, 1983; Dasgupta, 1999) and that post-1971 migration from Bangladesh is more a myth than anything else and that "there is no need to generate hysteria about a culture-in-crisis in order to expel a few thousand 'illegal' migrants." (Dasgupta, 2000).

What is the magnitude of illegal immigration from Bangladesh? On the basis of Indian and Bangladesh documents one estimate holds that not less than one third of Assam's 22.38 million population are immigrants and their decendants and that 10–14 million Bangladeshi migrants were settled in India (Hazarika, 1992). Another estimate by a former Governor of Arunachal Pradesh and West Bengal holds that about 5 million illegal migrants from Bangladesh are settled in Assam (Rajeshwar, 1996). Central Home Ministry/Intelligence Bureau sources place Assam's alien population from Bangladesh at about 4 million. Another study estimates that "based on the 1951 growth rate, the State of Assam should have a population of about 15 million. It has more than 7 million extra, according to the latest (1991) census. The extra numbers can be accounted for by either immigrants and/or their descendants" (Hazarika, 1994). This would seem very plausible considering the estimates of 4 to 5 million made by intelligence sources being of reference only to the Bangladeshi immigrants and not to the descendants of such migrants.

A scholar from the Institute of Development Studies, Dhaka, points out that about 4.65 to 5 million migrated from Bangladesh between 1961–1974 (cited in Hazarika, 1994) and that there was no reason to believe that the phenomena of migration ceased after 1974. Though this estimate is very conservative compared to Indian estimates, this is a rare acceptance of emigration from Bangladesh. Generally, the stance of Bangladesh had been to simply deny that any immigration to India is taking place (Ghosh, 1985; Subrahnaryan, 1988), in stark contrast to what Indian Home Ministry sources estimate. Myron Weiner pointed out that had Assam's population increased at the same rate as the rest of India from 1901 to 1971, at a rate of 130 per cent, the net population would be 7.6 million rather than 15 million in 1971 and consequently the share of migrants and their descendants amounted to 7.4 million. (Weiner, 1988).

Going by such analysis, had Assam's population increased at the same rate as India from 1901 to 1991 at 254.99 per cent her population would be 8.33 million rather than 22.4 million in 1991, the share of migrants and their descendants amounting to 14.03 million. (Table 23.1).

Table 23.1 : Population Variation in India and Assam

(in %)

	Assam	*India*
1901–1911	16.99	5.75
1911–1921	20.48	–0.31
1921–1931	19.91	11.00
1931–1941	20.41	14.22
1941–1951	19.93	13.31
1951–1961	34.98	21.51
1961–1971	34.95	24.80
1971–1981	23.36	24.69
1981–1991	24.24	23.82
1991–2001	18.85	21.34

Source: Census of India, various years.

If however, Assam's population increased at the same rate as India (excluding Assam) from 1901 to 1991 as another study between 1901–1981 estimates (Goswami and Gogoi, 1984) then Assam's population at a rate of 250.43 per cent increase would be 8.23 million. As to how such estimates point to a purported "myth of Bangladeshi migration" (Dasgupta, 2000) is difficult to fathom.

Though such analysis is indicative of the migrant population in Assam, it is not useful in estimating the illegal immigration from Bangladesh. For this the rate of growth of Muslim population in Assam proves more useful, though this would ignore any non-Muslim immigrants from Bangladesh. It is apparent that growth rates of Muslim population in Assam has been far higher than the all-India aggregates (Table 23.2). Such high growth rates can be attributed only to illegal immigration from Bangladesh (Misra,1999). Fertility rates of the indigenous Assamese Muslims, who are educated, have high economic and income levels are in no way higher than Muslims across other parts of India. On the contrary it is likely, given their high literacy rates, that fertility rates of the indigenous Assamese Muslims are lower than those of Muslims residing in other states of India. Finally, since Muslims from other states of India are not unduly attracted to migrate to Assam, it establishes beyond reasonable doubt that behind the abnormal growth rate of Muslim population in Assam lies the Bangladeshi factor.

Table 23.2 : Proportion of Muslim Population in India and Assam

(in %)

	India	*Assam*
1911	22.39	16.23
1931	23.49	22.78
1951	9.91	24.68
1961	10.71	25.30
1971	11.21	24.56
1991	12.12	28.43

Source: Census of India, various years.

While the 1991 and 2001 censuses show low population growth rates in Assam, the religion-wise data of 1991 provides insights to the proportion of illegal migrants between 1981–91. Growth rates of Muslim population in Assam have been inordinately

Table 23.3 : Estimating Illegal Bangladeshis (1971–91)

District	*1971–91⁺ GR⁺ of Muslim population*	*1971–91⁺ GR⁺ of non-Muslim population*	*Estimated Muslim population*	*Enumerated Muslim population*	*Excess Muslim Bangladeshi population*
Dhubri	71.13	30.15	713970	938789	224819
Kokrajhar	100.83	71.84	132453	154801	22348
Bongaigaon	94.11	53.72	209377	264393	55016
Goalpara	86.23	31.17	236153	335275	99122
Barpeta	64.84	22.17	575841	776974	201133
Nalbari	92.78	41.24	148473	202653	54180
Kamrup	88.98	59.91	395633	467544	71911
Darrang	108.10	39.14	277689	415323	137634
Sonitpur	130.80	59.72	131389	189859	58470
Lakhimpur	108.39	50.08	78508	109010	30502
Dhemaji	427.74	105.22	2766	7114	4348
Marigaon	69.42	37.91	235928	289835	53907
Nagaon	81.91	31.46	645576	893322	247746
Golaghat	117.43	55.41	42069	58859	16790
Jorhat	48.04	32.21	33625	37651	4026
Sibsagar	59.01	37.32	59812	69260	9448
Dibrugarh	69.00	36.56	37827	46814	8987
Tinsukia	88.45	46.03	23321	30095	6774
Karbi Anglong	111.42	74.23	8588	10421	1833
N.C.Hills	409.92	95.59	1281	3340	2059
Karimganj	57.93	29.50	333490	406706	73216
Hailkandi	55.56	35.76	214704	246016	31312
Cachar	56.57	43.26	383528	419150	35622
					*1,451,203

Sources : (i) Census of India 1991: Assam State District Profile 1991. (1998)
(ii) Census of India 1991: Assam: Religion, Series 4, Part IV–B (ii). For base year Muslim and non-Muslim populations and growth rates.
⁺GR = growth rates.

high (Table 23.3) vis-a-vis the non-Muslim population and had the former increased on the basis of the latter's growth rates substantially lower increases in Muslim population would be recorded. This is a variation of an earlier estimate (Bhuyan, 1995) which used a uniform growth rate of 45 per cent to calculate excess

Muslim population; here in place of 45 per cent for the entire state, the district-wise growth rates of other-than-Muslim populations have been used to estimate natural increase and delineate that portion attributable to illegal Bangladeshi flows. It was estimated on the basis of the non-Muslim population growth rates of Assam that illegal Muslim migrants would be at least 1.46 million between 1971–1991. Calculating the quantum of illegal Hindu migrants from Bangladesh, using Census data, is not as straightforward, but it can be safely stated that they would push the total illegal Bangladeshi migrants well above the 1.46 million mark.

Using the figure estimated by other sources, the quantum of illegal Bangladeshi immigrants in Assam of 4 to 5 million, would mean that between 18 to 22 per cent of Assam's population comprises of illegal aliens. Few regions in the world have such a high proportion of its populace as illegal aliens. In fact "every society can receive immigrants to a threshold level. Once that threshold is passed and it has been in Bengal just as it was many years earlier in Assam— they the host regards the new settler not merely as an intruder but a threat to his peace of mind, political control and prosperity" (Hazarika, 2000).

Compare the situation of USA with Assam. The former is one of the largest recipients of immigrants in the world and had 3 million or more illegal migrants (Weiner and Munz, 1997) which makes it have about 1.2 per cent of its populace residing as illegal migrants. A far cry from 18–22 per cent of its population as in Assam's case. This situation is aggravated by the low technological levels and land carrying capacities in Assam compared to USA.

The problem of immigration from Bangladesh is over a century old. Only with India's independence did the migration become 'illegal.' While the fact remains that several States of India face a similar problem, such as West Bengal and Bihar, the larger base populations of these states in a way alleviates the intensity of the problem. In Tripura, another north-eastern State of India, the local population have been turned into a minority community over time by the sheer numbers of cross border migrants from Bangladesh. In 1947, 56 per cent of Tripura's population consisted of tribal (or indigenous) population. Today this stands at a quarter of the total (Narayan, H., 1997). Bengali Hindus had become 71 per cent by 1971 and by then political and administrative power had passed from the indigeneous tribal population to migrant Bengalis; transfer of land to the Bengali migrants proved to be the critical factor in deteriorating social relations and in the June 1980 riots hundreds lost their lives (Singh,1987). The tribals of Tripura, have today been reduced to numerical non-entities and are engaged in armed conflict against the migrants whom they see as the usurpers of their homelands. With political and administrative power in the hands of the latter, the tribals are engaged in a losing battle for survival.

The problem that Tripura faces, is the same that confronts the entire North East today, points out a former Indian High Commissioner to the United Kingdom (Nayar, K.; 1996). The perception in Assam, is that just as the tribals of Tripura were economically, politically and numerically marginalised, the same fate may befall them. A veritable "Tripurisation of Assam" in the coming decades cannot be ruled out (Saikia,1996). Unfortunately, such fears have been treated lackadaisically, perhaps due to political compulsions, both by Delhi and Dispur (Taher, 1997).

A recent estimate by the Group of Ministers (GoM) on reforming the national security system, that post-1971 illegal migration from Bangladesh into India is to the order of 15 million. This report highlights the intensity and magnitude of the problem of illegal immigration from Bangladesh. Unfortunately this report has been kept under wraps by the Government of India. The problem of undocumented illegal Bangladeshi migrants is a serious issue that has reached proportions that make it a national problem confronting the nation as a whole, a point made amply clear by the Governor of Assam in his report to the President of India (Sinha,1998).

Environmental Impact

A growing population places increasing pressure on the land from which the requirements such as food, fuel wood and timber are met from. As food requirements increase, even marginal lands need to be put under plough. Forest resources from which various minor products including fuel wood are derived are needed in incremental quantities. Assam's population boosted by illegal Bangladeshi immigrants—to the tune of 2.7 million between 1961–81 (Weiner,1993) and above 1.5 million between 1981–91 estimated on the basis on non-Muslim population growth rates—has put incremental pressure on land and forest resources.

Since the inception of Bangladeshi immigration the impact on environment was intricately linked with the magnitude of migration. Between 1930 and 1950 some 1,508,000 hectares were settled by immigrants mostly in the Brahmaputra Valley (Weiner,1988) and it led to the opening up of new areas, previously under dense jungles. Although depletion of forests occurred slowly in the face of limited accessibility, it also meant that government control of the twin scourges of expanding tea plantations established on cleared forest lands and the encroachment of immigrants peasants from present day Bangladesh on forest lands, were much more ineffective (Tucker, 1988).

A study estimated that 58 per cent of the annual fire wood requirement for a village population of 20 members was 3060 kg (Mishra and Ramakrishnan, 1982) and if 500 kg of fuel wood is considered as the average annual consumption by 20 individuals the consumption for a population of 19.58 million in the North East in 1971 would work out to be about 489×10^7 kg ; an alarming impact on the natural resources on this account alone (Ramakrishnan,1985). North-east India's illegal immigrant burden of 12 and Assam's illegal component of above 5 million have substantial environmental impacts.

Beyond fuel wood consumption, illegal migrants from Bangladesh are known to have encroached on forest margins. Although illegal migrants tend to inhabit the 'char' areas (riverine tracts that get inundated during the monsoon), on account of growing population pressure some proportion spills over encroaching on nearby forest areas. While it is true that illegal Bangladeshi migrants have damaged the geo-ecological conditions of *chars*, *beels* (a beel is an inland freshwater body) and *bathans* (grazing lands) of buffaloes (Das, 2001) the quantum of damage, however, is difficult to estimate in the absence of reliable data. It is also alleged that Bangladesh migrants are engaged in illegal feeling of timber and timber smuggling.

The increasing population pressure triggered by Bangladeshi immigrants has been one agent, among others, that has aggravated deforestation in the north-east. Though the region accounts for under 8 per cent of the country's geographical area and contains more than a quarter of it's forest cover (Saikia, 1998) in terms of forest loss this is one of the critical areas in the country (FSI, 1995). Without illegal migrants the population of the region would have been 12 million less than the present 38.4 million and pressure on land and forests would have substantially less.

Socio-economic and Political Impact

The economy of the north-east, including Assam, is rooted in its colonial legacy. Precious little exists outside of tea, petroleum and forest resource utilisation. Agriculture is the predominant means of livelihood for the bulk of the working population; surplus, however, is nominal. Illegal migration from Bangladesh translates to a reduced share of an already limited cake. A flow of Bangladeshis seeking land and employment (Weiner, 1993) must be seen in this context.

Land, likewise, is limited and the illegal immigrant's preference to initially settle in the riverine tracts notwithstanding, the migrants have slowly apportioned a slice of the economic cake and with this, land. This has occasionlly caused alienation of tribal lands by Bangladeshis. At times this has led to ethnic conflict and in 1983 at a quiet little town called Nellie in Assam's Marigaon district, tribals, dispossessed of their lands, slaughtered between 1200 (Hussain, 2000) to 1753 (Hazarika, 2000) migrants from Bangladesh.

Although there exists, at least on paper, some legislation to prevent tribal land alienation, such legislation has proved ineffective (Singh, 1987). Nonetheless one price of legislation, the Inner Line Permit (ILP) that operates in Nagaland, Arunachal Pradesh and Mizoram has kept the problem of tribals being dispossessed of their land down to a minimum.

In other areas, no such mechanisms exist and land alienation by illegal aliens who are able to buy lands at rates higher than prevailing market prices goes on unabated. As to how migrants are able to offer substantially higher prices is not known and the allegation, that migrant settlement areas are safe dens for terrorists supported by the Inter Services Intelligence (ISI) of Pakistan, made not be as untrue as it is made out to be. It is alleged that such migrant settlements are well funded by the ISI.

Far more significant is the perceived threat of being outnumbered and outmanoeuvred by the immigrants. Since immigration from Bangladesh is an unending phenomena their numbers in Assam and other states are continually on the rise. The perception is that in the near future, a "tripurisation of Assam" is imminent (Saikia, 1996) and other states of the north-east might also end up meeting Tripura's fate.

The perception that unending immigrants from across the border will ultimately marginalise the original inhabitants haunts the north-east. There is widespread apprehension in Assam and the other states of the region that in the near future political power will be taken from them by the migrants (Singh, 1987). Stemming from unabated immigration, the immigrant population is slowly but surely playing an increasingly important factor in state politics. A secret intelligence report calculated that the ethnic Assamese were a minority in as many as 85 of the state's 126 constituencies (cited in Baruah, 1999) while the GoM report states that Bangladeshi migrants were in a position to influence the results of elections in a large number of constituencies in the North-East including 32 constituencies in Assam (*The Assam Tribune,* 24 May, 2001).

Additionally, immigrant strongholds and settlement pockets are used by terrorists backed by the ISI of Pakistan to engage in anti-state activities. Arms, ammunition, narcotics and counterfeit currency in addition to terrorist acts are being employed to destabilise the north-east. Unfortunately the Bangladeshi immigration issue is often viewed as being chauvinistic and anti-national or as a report by the Governor of Assam points out, it is viewed "as a regional matter affecting only the people of Assam. Its more dangerous dimension of greatly undermining our national security, is ignored" (Sinha, 1998). Large-scale illegal migration from Bangladesh into India's north-east poses a serious threat to regional security, Indian Home Minister L.K. Advani stated at Sualkuchi, Assam at an election rally on April 28th, 2001 and the after effects of the September 11 New York bombing may pose further threats to national/regional security.

Though illegal migration from Bangladesh is a serious problem, if one is to go by Census 2001 data, Assam' s growth rates during 1991–2001 (18.81 per cent) being lower than the all India rates (21.34 per cent) would point to illegal Bangladeshi migration being tripe and baseless: however, what the 2001 census data cannot explain is how the Muslim population in Assam has risen (both in terms of absolute increase as well as in terms of proportion of Muslim population to total population) during the 1971–1991 period (Table 23.2). Such an incompatibility of census 1991 and census 2001 data raises questions relating to the authenticity of census data and it appears that the census data has been watered down. Until the Religion Tables of the 2001 census are released, the issue of abnormally high growth rates of Muslims in Assam will remain in suspended animation.

Finally, the trend of illegal migrants turning certain districts of Assam into a Muslim majority region is well in motion. It may be only a matter of time before a demand for a merger with Bangladesh is made (Sinha, 1998) and Bangladesh would welcome such a move considering that its leaders and intellectuals have postulated Assam and the other States of the North-East as the most logical 'lebensraum' for Bangladesh's growing numbers (Borpujari, 1995; Shourie, 1997; Sinha, 1998).

State Policy

While the Foreigner's Act, 1946 (Act 31 of 1946) operates in the whole of India, in Assam it is the Illegal Migration (Determination by Tribunals) Act 1983 (IMDT) that is in force for detection of illegal migrants. Under the Act an illegal migrant is one who:

"(i) has entered into India on or after the 25th day of March, 1971,

(ii) is a foreigner,

(iii) has entered into India without being in possession of a valid passport or other travel document or any other lawful authority in that behalf." (IMDT, 1983).

Under the Act, detection and deportation of illegals would take place under the supervision of tribunals set up by the Central Government. Under the provisions of this Act, the onus of proving the citizenship credentials of a person in question lies with the complainant and the police, not on the accused. Under the Foreigners

Act, prevailing in the rest of the country, the onus in understandably on the accused. The motive of passing such an Act, that contravenes the spirit of the Indian Evidence Act in which the burden of proof lies with the accused (Reddy, 1996), is indeed questionable. There are a few contentested conditionalites in this Act. For instance, the complainant must reside within the jurisdiction of the same police station as the accused and the former must pay a fee to get his application processed; the applicant must get two persons to provide affidavits supporting the application. To cap it all "if the application is found frivolous or vexatious" the Central Government may not accept it.

This Discriminatory Act, that remains in force only to Assam, was passed in Parliament as a special act at a time when Assam was under Presidents Rule and under turmoil (Reddy, 1996) and the Act could not be contested. Even years after it was passed, its failure in serving the purpose for which it was enacted notwithstanding, successive parliaments governed by political compulsions, never considered amending, modifying or scrapping it altogether.

The track record of the Act is hardly anything to write home about and portrays its cumbersomeness. Between 1983–1994, out of 288,000 suspected aliens in Assam only 1219 illegal migrants could be identified (Reddy, 1996) an accomplishment that must be seen in the light of 4 million illegal migrants residing in Assam according to Home Ministry/Intelligence Bureau sources (Sinha, 1998).

This piece of legislation has merely had the effect of delaying and obstructing the process of action against illegal migrants in Assam (Reddy, 1996) and has primarily served the interests of the illegal migrants (Sinha, 1998), yet due to lack of political will and the growing clout of Bangladeshi migrant votes in Assam as well as in New Delhi, the Act continues to remain in force. Not that any other legislation is successful in the rest of India, which by an earlier Union Home Minister's admission, had in 1997, 10 million illegal migrants (Tribune, 1997).

While the IMDT Act looked into detection of illegal migrants, the Assam Accord, 1985 legalised all immigrants who had entered India prior to 25th March, 1971 and only those who entered after this date were to be detected by the IMDT Act and eventually expelled. In over a decade and a half barely a few thousand illegals were identified, inspite of 4 million illegals residing in the State, by the Home Ministers admission, and our estimates indicating a figure well above 4 million. To make matters worse the illegal immigration issue has not been taken up at the bilateral level with Bangladesh (Bose, 1997). The Census of India, 1991 managed to show Assam's growth rates being less than that for the rest of the country raising questions of its authenticity (Reddy, 1996); though the 1991 census did indicate abnormally high growth of Muslim population in Assam. The 2001 census has followed the trend set by the previous census and seems to be a watered down figure meant to assuage public sentiments.

To complement legislation, border fencing between Assam and Bangladesh along the lines of the Punjab-Pakistan border has been carried out. However, the pace of progress in fencing has been lethargic. Though the decision to fence the border was taken in 1985, actual fencing started only 7 years later and 15 years later it now remains half done. Compared to this fencing in the Punjab sector was completed in 3 years flat, reflecting the extremely lethargic pace of work in Assam. Moreover the quality of fencing in Assam in terms of elevation, frequency of observation towers, lighting (which is absent) and density of troops guarding the border is a poor cousin that in the Punjab sector (Sinha, 1996).

The tardy progress of fencing coupled with the cumbersome and time taking nature of legislation operating have allowed illegal migrants to continue entering Assam and.its sister states in the north-east. Given the nature of illegal migration, wherein illegals constantly expand and strengthen social networks between their origin countries and destination areas and such networks inject a self perpetuating dynamism into illegal flows (Hugo, 1995) illegal migration can only continue if not accentuate in coming years. With state policy being emminently unsuccessful in tackling the problem the observation that "the great increase in illegal migration in the Asian region is being implicitly supported if not encouraged by governments at origin and destination through poor policing and little investment in detection of illegals" (Hugo, 1995) might be true in the context of Assam and the other States of north-east India.

There is the option of legalising post-1971 illegals. Various countries have taken this route. USA legalised about 3 million aliens between 1987–89, a series of Italian policies in the 1980s and early '90s and French policies legalised large numbers of illegals (Miller, 1995). Once legalised aliens are conferred citizenship and issued necessary documents, detection of future immigrants could be easier. Such an option must, of necessity, be carefully analysed beforehand, as it is fraught with risks and if manipulated could do more damage than good.

Implications of Global Warming, Sea-Level Rise

Bangladesh, with an estimated population of 127,117,967 in July 1999 (CIA, 1999), is one of the most densely populated countries in the world. Many people are landless and forced to live on and cultivate flood-prone land; have limited access to potable water; water-borne diseases are prevalent and intermittent water shortages occur because of falling water tables in the northern and central parts of the country. It faces problems of soil degradation; deforestation and severe overpopulation (CIA, 1999). Despite sustained domestic and international efforts to improve economic and demographic prospects Bangladesh remains one of the world's poorest, most densely populated, and least developed nations (CIA, 1999).

Despite recent fertility reductions, its annual population growth rate is about 2.17 per cent. Studies conducted in the early 1960s indicated a Total Fertility Rate (TFR) of 7 children per woman. Such high fertility is declining but, according to the report of the Bangladesh Fertility Survey (BFS) conducted in 1989, TFR was 5 which is still quite high by any standard. Thus, the fertility conditions prevailing in the country should be the core concern of national policies and programmes (Islam and Islam, 1993) and though fertility rates are declining, it is still far from achieving its ultimate goals (Paul, 1997). The population of Bangladesh which was 115.6 millions in 1990 is expected to grow to 243.9, 212.0, 204.2 million in the year 2020 according to the high, medium and low variant projections respectively (Biswas and Paul, 1996).

The least developed among countries of the third world Bangladesh is characterised by a continued low level of socio-economic development, low literacy and high infant mortality, low status of women and a predominantly agrarian economy (Amin, *et al.,* 1993). Social and economic institutions are characterised by labour-intensive technology, low productivity, patriarchy, son preference, low female status, male dominance, children valued for labour and old-age insecurity are factors behind its high fertility (Amin, *et al.,* 1993).

The prevailing conditions in Bangladesh serve as push factors and migrants are attracted by the relatively better conditions in north-east India and other states. Considering the economic standing of Bangladesh, illegal immigration is likely to intensify in coming years, and with this the magnitude of problems in Assam.

It has been asserted that migration policies will have to become more concerned with the protection of the rights of the migrants and with the problems of vulnerable migrant groups, including asylum seekers, refugees, migrants exposed to serious exploitation and those affected by degradation, by natural and technological disasters and by armed conflicts (Mertens, 1994). This statement in a way reflects the general trend in literature on migration to look into the problems faced by migrants and migrant communities. Assam is piquantly placed in this regard: rather than the migrants, it the population of the receiving region that finds itself on the short end of the stick on account of the sheer numbers of migrants from Bangladesh.

What does the future for the north-east look like in terms of illegal immigrants from Bangladesh? The answer to this lies in an unlikely phenomenon: climate change. Future global warming could raise sea level by expanding ocean water, melting mountain glaciers, and eventually, causing polar ice sheets in Greenland and Antarctica to melt or slide into the oceans (Titus, 1990).

Global warming brought on by climate change would lead to sea level rise and submerge large coastal areas, deltas and islands the world over. Bangladesh incidentally would be one of the worst affected countries, straddling as it does the Ganga-Brahmaputra delta, and 17 per cent of her total area would get submerged by a 1 metre sea level rise (Titus, 1990; see Fig. 1). According to another study (cited in Gommes, *et al.,* 1998) the majority of the people that would be affected under the worst scenario, i.e., a 1 metre sea level rise, live in China (72 million) and in Bangladesh (71 million). Another study tends to corroborate such an estimate, and points out that a 1-m sea-level rise would have significant impacts in coastal and deltaic areas and would affect 6 million people in Egypt, with 12 per cent to 15 per cent of agricultural land lost. In Bangladesh, 13 million people would be directly affected and it would lose 16 per cent of its rice lands (Nicholls and Leatherman, 1995). No less than "tens of millions" of people in Bangladesh would be displaced by a 1-m sea-level rise (Watson *et al.,* 1998). Large areas of Bangladesh would be submerged by rising sea levels (Fig 23.1).

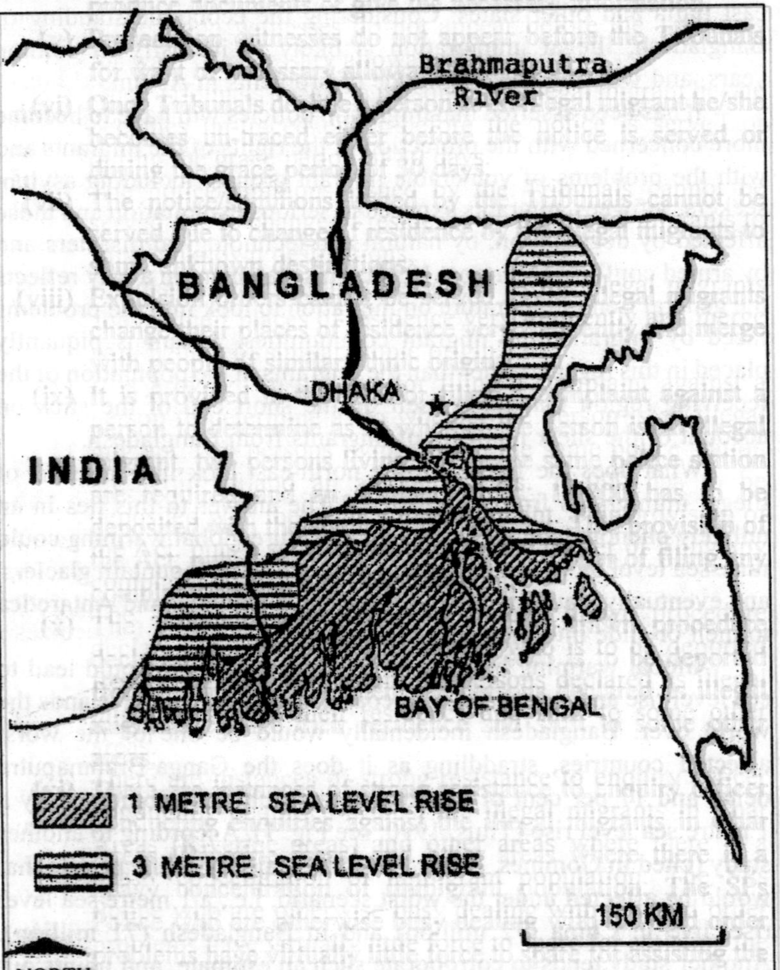

Fig. 23.1: Loss of Land due to Future Sea Level Rise in Bangladesh (After Titus, 1990).

Deltas would be areas very vulnerable to sea-level rise and deltas like the Ganges—Brahmaputra (in Bangladesh), as distinct from deltas in closed seas like the Nile or the Danube, face a much more complex set of problems as Gommes, *et al.*, (1998) point out:

> "as they are the areas where sea and land most closely interact: their average elevation is usually very low, to the extent that tidal effects can be felt for several tens of km, and in some cases hundreds, inland. This land/sea interaction results in very complex agricultural systems, where irrigation and rain-fed agriculture may be practised in alternate seasons, with attention to irrigation water quality (salinity) and to the washing out of salts by rains before planting crops. Although much of this production is for export, a disaster in the deltas would have profound effects on the whole country. This indicates a fragile situation *in which any major disturbance would result in economic and possibly political shock waves well beyond the delta proper*."(emphasis added)

In such a situation:

> "... major disasters or changes in deltas and small islands could have repercussions over large areas. Given the populations potentially involved, this is more likely to seriously affect the major deltas, such as the Ganges-Brahmaputra, Mekong and Nile ..... a likely scenario could be outmigration when disasters due to sea-level rise reach levels or frequencies considered unacceptable" (Gommes *et al.*, 1998).

While climate change led sea-level changes to the tune of close to a metre is the "worst case" scenario, global mean sea-level is expected to rise 95 cm by the year 2100, with large local differences due to tides, wind and atmospheric pressure patterns, changes in ocean circulation, vertical movements of continents etc., a recent estimate by the IPCC Working Group III's Special Report on Emission Scenarios places the most likely quantum of sea level rise between 1990 to 2100 in the range from 8 to 88 cm (Anon, 2001). In such a case the affected population in Bangladesh is likely to be under the estimates of approximately 70 million.

Until five years ago, the effects of sea level rise were uncertain. Scientific consensus, during that time, was that global warming should cause global sea level to rise; the rate of sea level rise was however uncertain (Warrick, *et al.*, 1996). The fact remained that global warming from increasing atmospheric concentrations of greenhouse gases would cause global warming. In turn, global warming should cause sea level rise by expanding the oceans, increasing the melt rates of ice sheets and glaciers and also affect the frequency and intensity of cyclones, storm surges and hence—in the case of the Bay of Bengal—coastal flooding (Warrick, *et al.*, 1996). The uncertainty of reports and studies appearing a few years ago, have now been settled, for the time being by the IPCC Working Group III's 2001 Report.

Nonetheless considering that in addition to the direct effect of sea-level change, there are a whole set of indirect effects, that would be no less important, the impact on north-east could be very substantial:

> "More than direct land loss due to seas rising, indirect factors are generally listed as the main difficulties associated with sea-level rise. These include erosion patterns and damage to coastal infrastructure, salinisation of wells, sub-optimal functioning of the sewerage systems of coastal cities with resulting health impacts, loss of littoral ecosystems and loss of biotic resources" (Gommes, *et al.*, 1998).

Although annual protection costs for many nations are relatively modest, about 0.1 per cent of Gross Domestic Product (GDP), in the case of small developing countries these could be as high as 5 per cent of GDP.

Climate change led problems would compound Bangladesh's existing environmental problems which include chemical degradation including salinisation, loss of soil fertility (nutrients and organic matter) and pollution and deforestation caused land degradation and are already very severe (Marcoux, 1996). If absolute annual losses continue, the forests of Bangladesh would be entirely gone by 2011 (Marcoux, 1996).

Bangladesh, like other countries of South Asia, faces problems interfacing population pressure and agricultural activities that cause land degradation. These include shifting cultivation without adequate fallow periods, absence of soil conservation measures, cultivation of fragile and marginal lands, unbalanced fertiliser use and a host of problems arising from faulty management of irrigation (Marcoux, 1996).

Given such a scenario, for a developing country like Bangladesh, the added impacts of rising sea levels would be beyond its capability to handle, given the limited availability of capital for investment. Additionally, since Bangladesh's economy is heavily dependant on agriculture and is hardly diversified at all, the effects of sea-level rise are likely to be that much more severe. In general a more diversified economy is less likely to be subject to the vagaries of climate, in Bangladesh's case while economic development has extended and diversified employment opportunities to an extent, it has not kept pace with population growth, especially in rural areas (Ericksen, Ahmad and Chowdhury, 1996). Bangladesh's problems are compounded by a skewed and highly uneven distribution of wealth and income aggravated by 'bad planning, managerial deficiency and corruption' (Ericksen, Ahmad and Chowdhury, 1996). The position of Bangladesh is precarious and with the spectre of sea level induced effects looming large an exodus of migrants to nearby areas seems imminent.

The concept of replacement migration (Anon, 2000) could change the course of immigration as problematic in the north-east, if developed countries were to seek migrants from Bangladesh; however considering that migrants from Bangladesh are relatively unskilled, untrained and almost illiterate (Islam, 1995), it remains to be seen whether they will be wanted by developing countries. Until then with the spectre of sea-level rise looming large, ecological refugees from Bangladesh, could be banging on the doors of north east as also other regions of India.

Conclusion

Uncontrolled illegal migrants can be problematic in the most situations. The issues get compounded when the receiving areas consist of relatively small numerical entities, as with the population groups in Assam and north-east India. Even within Bangladesh, erosion and flood affected displacees are not welcomed at their new places of settlement as the local people feel threatened due to limited resources and opportunities available in such areas (Huq-Hussain, 1995). Such feelings for migrants get compounded across the international border and Bangladeshi illegal immigrants by their sheer volume have created a plethora of problems in Assam.

Unfortunately state policy remains lethargic in tackling the problem and Bangladeshi illegal immigrants continue to pour in. The masses in the north-east are faced with a constant flux of migration, legal as well as illegal (Bose, 1997). The illegal migrants issue in Assam 'continues to fester' (Weiner, 1993) in the absence of political will from successive State and Union Governments. In the near future climate change is likely to generate a fresh stream of ecological refugees from Bangladesh and in the absence of suitable legal policy, the situation will virtually go beyond control.

REFERENCES

Amin, R., Chowdhury, J., Ahmed, A.U., Hill, R.B. and Kabir, M., (1993): Reproductive Change in Bangladesh: Evidence from Recent Data, *Asia-Pacific Population Journal* 8 (4): 39–58.

Anonymous (2000): The UN Population Division on Replacement Migration. *Population and Development Review*, 26 (2) : 413–418.

Anonymous (2001): Global Warming : New Scenarios from the Inter-governmental Panel on Climate Change. *Population and Development Review*, 27(1): 203–208.

Baruah, Sanjib (1999): India against itself : Assam and the Politics of Nationality, Pennsylvania University Press, Philadelphia.

Bhuyan, J.C. (1995): Religious Composition in Assam. *North-East Times*. 10th, 11th and 12th August. Guwahati.

Biswas, S. C. and Paul, J. C.(1996): Population Projection and Fertility for Bangladesh, 2020. *The Journal of Family Welfare* 42 (4) 45–50.

Bose, Ashish (1997): National Intergration in a Fragmented Society: Role of Population Stabilisation, *Vanchan* VIII (1): 49–54.

CIA (1999): The World Factbook, 1999. http://www.odci.gov/cia/publications/factbook Forest Survey of India (1995) *State of Forest Report 1995*, FSI, Dehradun.

Gommes, R., du Guerny, J., Nachtergaele, F., and Brinkman, R. (1998): Potential Impacts of Sea-level Rise on Populations and Agriculture, FAO, Rome.

Das, Manamohan (2001): Dimensions of Muslim immigration in Assam, *The North-East Times*, Guwahati, 24th, 25th and 26th February.

Dasgupta, Anindita (1999): Thinking With the Head: Foreign Nationals in Assam, *The Daily Star*, Dacca, Vol. 2 (252), 06 May.

Dasgupta, Anindita (2000): Political myth-making in post-colonial Assam. *Himal*, 13 (8) :14–23.

Dass, S.K. (1983): Immigration and Demographic Transformation of Assam, 1891–1981. *Economic and Political Weekly*, May 10 : 850–859.

Ericksen, N.J., Ahmad Q.K. and Chowdhury, A.R. (1996): Socio-economic implications of climate change for Bangladesh, pp. 205–87, in R.A.Warrick and Q.A.Ahmad (eds.). The Implications of Climate Change and Sea Level Rise for Bangladesh. Kluwer Academic Publishers : Dortrecht, Boston and London.

Ghosh, P.S. (1985): Ethnic and Religious Conflicts in South Asia, *Conflict Studies*, 178: 1–9.

Goswami, A. and Gogoi, J. (1984): Migration and Demographic Transformation of Assam, 1901–1971, pp.60–80, in B.L.Abbi (ed) Northeast Region: Problems and Prospects of Development, CRRID, Chandigarh.

Hazarika, S. (1992): Bangladeshisation of India, *The Telegraph*, 06 February, Calcutta.

Hazarika, S. (1993): Bangladesh and Assam: Land Pressures, Migration and Ethnic Conflict. Peace and Conflict Studies Programme, University of Toronto and the American Academy of Arts and Sciences, Cambridge.

Hazarika, S. (1994): Strangers of the mist, Viking Publishers, New Delhi.

Hazarika, S. (2000): Rites of Passage: Border Crossings, Imagined Homelands, India's east and Bangladesh. Penguin Books India (P) Ltd., New Delhi.

Hazarika, S. (2000) Migrant Issue: Ad Hoc Measures Will Not Do. The Statesman, 1 May, New Delhi.

Hugo, Graeme (1995): Illegal International Migration in Asia, pp. 397–402 in Robin Cohen (ed.). The Cambridge Survey of World Migration, Cambridge University Press, Cambridge.

Huq-Hussain, Shahnaz (1995): The Human Response to Environmental Dynamics in Bangladesh, pp.187–196, in G.P.Chapman and M.Thompson (eds.) Water and the quest for sustainable development in the Ganges Valley, Mansell, London.

Hussain, Monirul (2000): State, Identity Movements and Internal Displacement in the North-East. *Economic and Political Weekly*, December 16, 4519–4523.

I.M.D.T. (1983): The Illegal Migration (determination by tribunals) Act 1983, Gazette of India, Extraordinary, Part II, Section 1, 26th December.

Islam, M. N. and Islam, M. M. (1993): Biological and Behavioural Determinants of Fertility in Bangladesh: 1975–1989. *Asia-Pacific Population Journal* 8(1): 3–18.

Islam, Muinul (1995): Bangladeshi Migration: An Impact Study, pp.36–366, in Robin Cohen (ed.). The Cambridge Survey of World Migration, Cambridge University Press, Cambridge.

Marcoux, Alain (1996): Population Change-natural Resources-environment linkages in Central and South Asia, FAO Population Programme Service, Rome.

Mertens, Walter (1994): IUSSP Policy and Research Paper N°1. The Context of IUSSP Contribution to the International Conference on Population and Development, International Union for the Scientific Study of Population, Liège, Belgium.

Miller, M.J. (1995): Illegal Migration, pp. 537–540, in Robin Cohen (ed.). The Cambridge Survey of World Migration, Cambridge University Press, Cambridge.

Mishra, B. K. and Ramakrishnan, P.S. (1982): Energy flow through a village eco-system with slash and burn agriculture in north-eastern India. *Agricultural Systems,* 9, 57–72.

Misra, U. (1999): Immigration and Identity Transformation in Assam. *Economic and Political Weekly,* XXXIV, (21): 1264–71.

Narayan, H. (1997): Tribal Tribulation in Tripura, *The Statesman*, New Delhi : 20 March.

Nayar, Kuldip (1996): The north-east's dilemma, *The Eastern Clarion*, Jorhat : 20 March.

Nicholls, R.J., and S.P. Leatherman, (1995): 'Global sea-level rise.' pp. 92–123 in K.M. Strzepek and J.B. Smith (Eds), As Climate Changes: International Impacts and Implications. Cambridge Univ. Press, Cambridge.

Paul, B.K. (1997): Changes in Reproductive Behaviour in Bangladesh, *The Geographical Review* 87 (1): 100–104.

Phukan, Girin (1981): Foreign National Issue (1979–81) in Assam: A Colonial Legacy. *Man and Development.* 3 (4): 156–169.

Rajeshwar, T.V. (1996): Migration or Invasion? *The Hindustan Times*, 7th February, New Delhi.

Ramakrishnan, P.S. (1985): Tribal man in the humid tropics of the north-east, *Man In India* 65 (1): 1–32.

Reddy, P.S. (1996): Revision of Electoral rolls in Assam: A Case of Continuing Controversy, *Gauhati University Journal of Arts* XXXVIII : 49–60.

Saikia, A. (1996): Tripurisation of Assam, The Assam Tribune, Guwahati :15 May.

Saikia, A. (1998): Population, Shifting Cultivation and Sustainibility : The Changing Context of north-east India, *Development* 41 (3): 97–100.

Saikia, A. (2000): The Bangladeshi Migration Triggered Population in North-east India: Present Impact and Future Implications. Paper presented at the 29th International Geographical Congress, 13th–18th August.: Seoul.

Shourie, Arun (1997): A secular agenda, Harper Collins, New Delhi.

Singh, B.P. (1987): North-east India: Demography, Culture and Identity Crisis. *Modern Asian Studies* 21 (2): 257–282.

Sinha, S.K. (1998): Report on Illegal Migration into Assam, Submitted to the President of India by the Governor of Assam, Guwahati : Raj Bhawan.

Subrahmanyam, K. (1988): India's Security : The north and north-east Dimension, *Conflict Studies*, 215 : 1–25.

Taher, Mohammed (1997): Ethnic Situation in North-East India : A Geographical Perspective. *North Eastern Geographer*, 28 (1 & 2) 1–15.

The Assam Tribune (2001): 24 May, Guwahati.

The Tribune (1997): 07 May, Chandigarh.

Titus, G.J. (1990): Greenhouse effect, sea level rise, and land use. *Land Use Policy*, 7, 2, 138–53.

Tucker, R.P. (1988): The Depletion of India's Forests Under British Imperialism: Planters, Foresters, and Peasants in Assam and Kerala, pp. 118–140 in D. Worster (ed.). *The ends of the earth : perspectives on modern environmental history.* Cambridge University Press, Cambridge.

Verghese, B.G., Ahmed, B., Deshpande, G., Desai, N., Upadhyaya, R. (1980): Situation in Assam, Gandhi Peace Foundation, New Delhi (mimeo).

Warrick, R.A., Azizul Hoq Bhuiya, A.K., Mitchell, W.M., Murty,T.S. and Rasheed, K.B.S.(1996): Sea level changes in the Bay of Bengal. pp. 97–135 in R.A.Warrick and Q.A.Ahmad (eds.). The Implications of Climate Change and Sea Level Rise for Bangladesh. Kluwer Academic Publishers: Dortrecht, Boston and London.

Watson, Robert T., Zinyowera, Marufu C, Moss, Richard H. and Dokken, David J (Eds.) (1997): The Regional Impacts of Climate Change: An Assessment of Vulnerability A special Report of IPCC Working Group II, Intergovernmental Panel on Climate Change.

Weiner, Myron. (1978): Sons of the Soil: Migration and Ethnic Conflict in India, Princeton University Press (1988 Reprint, Oxford University Press, New Delhi).

Weiner, Myron (1993): Rejected Peoples and Unwanted Migrants in South Asia. *Economic and Political Weekly*, August 21: 1737–1746.

Weiner, Myron. and Munz, Rainer (1997): Migrants, Refugees and Foreign Policy : Prevention and Intervention Strategies, *Third World Quarterly* 18(1): 25–51.

Annexures

Annexure I

Seminar News and Recommendations

A two-day National Seminar on "Illegal Migration from Bangladesh" was organised by Astha Bharati in association with the Centre for North-East Studies and Policy Research (C-NES) in New Delhi on 27 and 28 November, 2001. It drew senior scholars, former top officials, media specialists, non-government groups and others from the North-East and other parts of the country. Participants included members of Parliament Arun Sarma and S. Bwasumatari from Assam; K.P.S. Gill, former Director General of Punjab Police; Prakash Singh, former Director-General, Border Security Force; Mr. Naresh Chandra, former Indian Ambassador to the United States; Shri N.N. Vohra, former Home Secretary, Government of India, North-East specialist and writer Sanjoy Hazarika, Shri D.N. Bezboruah, Editor, Sentinel, Guwahati, Prof. J.K. Roy, Centenary Professor, International Relations (Retd.), Calcutta University, Prof. Udayan Mishra of Dibrugarh University and Prof. Arunadoy Saha of Tripura University.

There were six working sessions of the seminar. Dr. Kumar Suresh Singh chaired the first session. Shri Sanjoy Hazarika spoke on "Problem and Long-term Perspective." The theme of the paper of Professor Jayant Kumar Ray was on 'Illegal Migration from East-Bengal/East-Pakistan/Bangladesh. Shri J.C. Bhuyan presented his paper on "Migration and Demographic Change in NE Region." Shri R.P. Joshi, former Director, Intelligence Bureau chaired the second session. Shri K.P.S. Gill deliberated on "Migration and National Security." Professor J.K. Ray chaired the third session. The resource persons were Shri N.N. Vohra, former Home Secretary, Govt. of India, Prakash Singh, DG, BSF, and Shri O.K. Pandey from Sahara TV. Shri Prakash Singh presented his paper on "Management of India's North-Eastern Borders" and Shri Pandey on "Migration and New Wave of Terrorism."

Shri D.N. Bezboruah, Professor Arunodaya Saha and Professor Udayan Mishra chaired other three sessions of the seminar. Professor Udayan Mishra deliberated on the "Historical Aspect" and Dr. Jayant Madhab, Dr. Arun Kumar Sarma, MP, and Professor Arunodaya Saha on "Migration and Economy" in the fourth session. Shri D.N. Bezboruah deliberated in the fifth session. The paper of Shri Charles Chasie, a journalist from Nagaland was distributed to the participants in his absentia. Dr. Arun K. Sarma, MP deliberated on "Migration and Electoral Politics" and Dr. Anup Saikia on Global Processes and Local Concerns: "Bangladeshi Migrants in Assam" in the sixth session. Shri Naresh Chandra gave the valedictory address. Dr. Jayant Madhab chaired the session.

The participants, among others, included noted Gandhian Shri Natwar Thakkar, Mrs. Manorama Dewan of Press Asia International, Professor Devendra Kaushik (Chairman, EC) and Dr. Mahavir Singh (Director) of Maulana Azad Institute of Asian Studies, Kolkata, Professor Warikoo and Dr. L.C. Kumar from JNU, Ms. Zolhanpari Hrahsel, Shri Kalyan Baruah of Assam Tribune, Shri Binod Kumar, IAS, Joint Director, Shri R.C. Jain, IAS (Retd.), former Secretary, Government of India, Dr. Suresh Sharma, Senior Fellow, CSDS, Shri S.P. Rai, Indian Postal Service (Retd.), Shri K.K. Mitra, ex-IRS, Dr. Bachchan Kumar of Indira Gandhi National Centre for Arts and Shri D.C. Pathak.

The seminar recommended a set of far-reaching changes in Government policy, including the setting up of a National Immigration Commission, the inclusion of the issue on the platform of all political parties and a regulatory mechanism to tackle the problem, including multi-purpose, coloured identity cards and work permits.

The following are the main recommendations of the seminar, which noted that according to the Central Government, there are not less than 1.5 crore Bangladeshis illegally resident in the country:

- Illegal migration from Bangladesh must be recognised as a national problem and not a regional issue. The Central and State Governments must not underplay the gravity of the threat posed to national security.

- All political parties should put the issue of illegal migration and their view on ways to tackle it on their agenda.
- The Central Government should appoint a National Immigration Commission to frame a National Migration Policy and a National Refugee Policy. The Commission should examine ways of strengthening the Foreigners Act, 1946, as well as feasibility of Identity Cards for both citizens and non-citizens and Work Permits for migrants.
- The Foreigners Act, 1946, should be made applicable to the whole country, including Assam.
- The discriminatory Illegal Migrants Determination by Tribunal Act of 1983 should be repealed.
- Preventive measures should be taken urgently to curb further illegal migration. The existing Border Security Force posts and the BSF water wing should be strengthened and border fencing, patrolling and lighting should be improved. A vigorous campaign against aliens should continue throughout the year.
- The work of deletion of the aliens' names from the Voters' List and their disenfranchisement throughout the country should be speeded up.
- The Central Government should explore the feasibility of issuing work permits as a mechanism to regulate illegal migration.
- The National Register of Citizens of 1951 should be reviewed, computerised and updated. The process of updating the NRC should be done regularly and citizen registration should be made compulsory by law.
- Citizens and non-citizens should be issued different colour identity cards. Citizens should receive multi-purpose ID cards.
- The Godbole Committee report on border management should be made public.
- The protection of the land and political rights of the original inhabitants of the North-East, in particular, should be assured by the Constitution. Reservations should be made in state legislatures in those regions, especially the North-East, where the illegal influx is posing a demographic threat

to the stability of the political structure. The basis for such reservations should be the updated NRC as well as the ethnic composition of the area and its geographic location.

- Criminal proceeding should be launched against those found harbouring illegal migrants as also against employers who engage such labourers in economic activities.
- Governments, non-government organisations and media should launch campaigns to educate the public about the dangers inherent in illegal influx.
- The Centre should improve the quality of existing fencing to the level of that existing on the Punjab-Pakistan border; the fencing on the entire Bangladesh border should be completed within two years.
- The Central Government must continue to respond diplomatically to the problems faced by religious minorities in Bangladesh.
- The Centre should encourage legal border trade with Bangladesh and persuade Dhaka to provide the North-East a transit route to West Bengal and to the sea through Chittagong port.
- The North-East MPs Forum will be requested to take up the issue of the repeal of the IMDT.

Annexure II

THEME PAPER
REPEAT SEMINAR ON "ILLEGAL MIGRATION FROM BANGLADESH-SOLUTIONS"
(FEB. 21-22, 2003 AT GUWAHATI)

A two-day National Seminar on "Illegal Migration from Bangladesh" was organised by Astha Bharati, Delhi in association with the Centre for North-East Studies and Policy Research (C-NES) in New Delhi on 27 and 28 November 2001. Senior scholars, members of parliament, former senior officials, media specialists, non-government groups and others from the North-East and other parts of the country attended the seminar. The recommendations of that seminar are attached as the appendix. Astha Bharati is organising a second seminar on the same theme in Guwahati (Venue—Hotel Brahmaputra Ashok) on February 21–22, 2003.

The Focus: The Guwahati seminar shall focus on the ways and means of finding solutions to the problem. While there may be a dispute on actual number of Bangladeshi illegal immigrants in Assam, West Bengal and elsewhere in the country, as well as on the numbers still coming in currently; there is no dispute that the problem is a serious one and it is a national problem. In brief, the dimensions of the problem may be contested, but not the problem.

The seminar wishes to keep clear of the controversies and concentrate on *positive and practical steps* towards the following:

(a) to prevent future migration;
(b) to contain the problem;
(c) to identify and deal with the illegal migration in the country as a whole;
(d) identification and deportation of post-1971 illegal migration in Assam;
(e) to deal with the problem of discriminatory laws of identification and deportation.

The approach to the above-mentioned formulation is based on the following premises:

(a) It is now a national problem and not a problem confined to Assam and West Bengal only;
(b) It is not a communal problem and any effort to make it a Hindu-Muslim issue is not only mischievous but directed towards confusing the issue;
(c) The recent developments in Bangladesh where Islamist terror groups are making their presence felt and Pakistan and ISI are reported playing greater role, the problem cannot but have security implications for the entire country, and particularly for the North-Eastern States and West Bengal;
(d) The problem has been politicised and confused due to short-sightedness of the Indian politicians/political parties; the aliens have settled in large number on our side of the border creating a demographic dimension. The borders have become dangerously porous; aliens gradually dominate more and more Assembly/Parliament constituencies as voter. They receive strength the weaknesses of the Indian politics.

Working Sessions: Broadly, the following themes shall be discussed in the working sessions of the seminar:

I. Border management and effective prevention of future migrations;
II. Proposed 'Citizens Registration' and 'National Identity Cards'; its implementation mode, ground-level difficulties; how to tackle the problem;
III. Maintenance of land and property records in all the districts of Assam, West Bengal and Tripura; restriction on land/property alienation to non-citizens; rules/restrictions with regard to employment and work.
IV. Steps to counter politicisation and communisation of the issue; launching 'People's Education'/Public opinion making' programmes throughout the country to generate requisite pressure on the politicians/political parties to act

in national interest; other steps to achieve the objective; disfranchisement of the aliens.

V. Steps to discourage aliens from acquiring landed/immovable properly in India; confiscation of such properties acquired; other steps to make illegal immigration less attractive;

VI. IMDT Act, is weaknesses and the need to extend 'Indian Foreigners Act' to Assam; amendments, if necessary, to protect pre-1971 migrants and make identification of post-1971 migrants expedient and practical; people's education throughout the country about the discriminatory act;

VII. Deportation in the light of the refusal by Bangladesh to accept them.

VIII. Economic Development as a means to contain ethnic aspirations.

IX. Other related topics.

Annexure III

RECOMMENDATIONS
ASTHA BHARATI REPEAT SEMINAR ON "ILLEGAL MIGRATION FROM BANGLADESH"

A two day seminar on "Illegal Migration from Bangladesh" was organised in Guwahati on 21–22 February 2003. The Seminar was in continuation of the one, on the same theme, held earlier in Delhi on November 27-28, 2001. The Seminar drew senior scholars, former top officials, media specialists, non-governmental groups and others from the North-East, Delhi and Kolkata. The six working sessions of the Seminar were chaired by Dr. Jayanta Madhab, eminent development economist; Shri N. Changkakoti, Chief Vigilance Commissioner and former Director General, Assam; Shri H.N. Das, former Chief Secretary, Assam; Professor Imdad Hussain of North-Eastern Hill University, Shri Kamaleshwar Bora, former Vice-Chancellor, Dibrugarh University, and Shri Jatin Hazarika, former Home Commissioner, Assam. Dr. Jayant Madhab also chaired the concluding session in which recommendations of the Seminar were read and approved.

The Seminar started with a talk by Dr. Jayanta Madhab on the structure of the Seminar followed by the presentation of the theme paper and the background of the Seminar by the secretary. Presentations in the Seminar were made by Shri Prakash Singh, former Director General, BSF and former DGP, U.P. and Assam, Shri Nishi Nath Changkakoti, Professor N. Lokendra Singh of Manipur University, Shri J.N. Roy, Shri H.N. Das, Shri A.K. Jain, Joint Secretary, Ministry of Home Affairs, GOI, Shri D.N. Bezboruah, Editor, Sentinel, Dr. C.J. Thomas Dy. Director, ICSSR, NE Regional Centre (the paper was jointly prepared with Professor R. Gopalakrishnan of NEHU); Professor Gautam Chakma, Tripura University; Shri Bimal Pramanik, Director, Centre for Research in

Indo-Bangladesh Relations, Kolkata; eminent Gandhian, Shri Natawar Thakkar, Shri S.B. Medhi IAS (Retd.), Prof. Bazlur Rahman Barooah, Shri Pradip Phanjubam, Editor, Imphal Free Press, Shri J.C. Bhuyan, Dr. Anup Saikia, Dr. M.P. Bezbaruah, Shri H.K. Bhattacharyya, IPS (Retd.) Shri P.K. Bhattacharyya, Smt. Hema Kakoti, Smt. Arati Devi and others. Guwahati based eminent journalists from various national and regional newspapers and news-agencies attended the Seminar. The main focus of the Seminar was on finding ways and means to tackle the problem.

The discussions during the Seminar took cognisance of growing awareness in the country about the seriousness of the problem and its adverse implication for the country. The Seminar felt in a broad sense that the problem should be tackled in an organised and segmented manner to contain it immediately, prevent it, as far as possible, for the future, and rectify with due and legal action the social and demographic adverse impact of the illegal migrants who are already in the country.

Recommendations of the seminar, broadly cover these three aspects of the problem.

The Seminar also noted with satisfaction:

(i) that there is greater awareness about the seriousness of the problem of illegal migration in the country today and it is recognised as a national problem by the people of the country, the Central and State Governments and the political parties;

(ii) that urgent steps are contemplated towards preventing further infiltration as well as towards speedier detection and deportation of the aliens; and steps being taken towards speedier construction of better quality border fences by 2006; construction of the roads along the border to facilitate border patrolling as well as the economic development of the border areas, issue of multi-purpose identity cards to the citizens, enforcing the compulsory registration of the birth and death of the citizens, and review, updating and computerisation of the National Register of Citizens, etc.; and

(iii) that our foreign policy towards Bangladesh is showing the signs of moving towards realism.

In the light of the deliberations the Seminar recommends the following:

I. Border Management

- As the effective management of border is crucial to check illegal movement and migration, the Seminar recognises the need to look at the border along Bangladesh as a region and not as a line, and accordingly recommends that this region with a certain depth should be regarded, as a special zone. Within such a zone, administrative framework, development schemes, security measures appropriate to the conditions and requirements of the zone should be undertaken. The Seminar also recognises the utmost importance of monitoring the activities of anti-national groups within the zone.
- The seminar re-iterates that the existing Border Security Posts and the BSF water-wing should be strengthened; outposts should be made permanent if possible, border fencing, patrolling and lighting should be improved. Since the border has to be guarded at all time the minimum number of BSF personnel required to do that must be maintained, irrespective of requirement elsewhere, at all time.
- A high power committee consisting of Home Ministry officials, BSF officials and representatives of the States bordering Bangladesh should be constituted by the Govt. of India to survey the entire Indo-Bangladesh border and suggest concrete measures about requirement of BSF posts, manpower and other resources required by each post, number and location of floating posts on riverine areas, mechanised patrol boats for each such posts, distance between any two posts, fencing, border roads etc., so that illegal infiltration from across the border can be effectively prevented.
- Immediate steps should be taken to improve the quality of existing fencing to the level of that existing on the Punjab border. The entire fencing should be completed within two years.

- Steps should be taken to construct jeepable roads on entire Indo-Bangladesh border; and it is possible to do so within a year on the pattern of the same on Indo-Pak (Punjab) border.
- It was felt that proper, un-ambiguous, clear-cut directives to the agencies like BSF/police should be given to avoid vague/ unclear directives by the Central/State Government to these agencies.
- Seminar recommends that all boats in the border-zone under the jurisdiction of bordering Police stations should be registered so that their movements can be regulated. Plying of unregistered boats should be prohibited.

II. Dealing with those Already in the Country

- The Foreigners Act, 1946 should be made applicable to Assam and the discriminatory Illegal Migrants (Determination by Tribunal) Act of 1983 should be repealed without further delay. The Seminar also felt that the issue of the repeal of IMDT Act should be brought before the joint session of Parliament as an act of faith towards the people of Assam and the country as a whole.
- The detection and deportation work suffers due to lack of will on the part of the agencies responsible for the work. The Centre, if necessary, should intervene. The States must act and act speedily.
- The identification of the aliens should be based on National Register of Citizens (NRC). The land/home-stead pattas should be also helpful in the process. Financial help to Assam Government for updating NRC should be given.
- The work of deletion of the aliens' names from the Voters list and their disenfranchisement throughout the country should be speeded up.
- Steps should to taken up to update the land-records and to create it where ever lacking, such as in the *char* areas of Assam.
- Steps should be taken to prevent aliens from acquiring land and immovable property anywhere in the country. Appropriate steps should be taken to confiscate land and immovable property acquired by the illegal immigrants.

- Criminal proceeding should be launched against those found harbouring and employing illegal migrants.
- The forest and all government lands should be cleared of the encroachers. The Seminar also recommends the formation of the 'Task Force for protection of existing forests and wastelands.
- The Seminar recommends immediate steps to suitably amend Indian constitution to deprive the children of the illegal migrants of Indian citizenship.
- In order to freeze further illegal migration, pending verification, there is a need to issue multi-purpose identity cards of different colours to the citizens and those of doubtful categories.

III. Dealing with Bangladesh

- In the light of the demographic aggression on our country by Bangladesh; arrival of 20 million illegal aliens and large number of refugees; the "missing population" of Bangladesh as per its own census studies; its denial to accept its own citizens and even to accept their presence in India; the motivated claims/opinions of Bangladeshi intellectuals about "lebensraum"; their design and dream for greater Bangladesh; and continued unfriendly acts towards India such as harbouring Indian secessionists and terrorists, the Government of India should pursue a firm, and if necessary, coercive diplomacy towards that country and claim land proportionate to its population in India.
- Govt. of India has rightly started giving deterrent signals to the illegal migrants as well as to the Government of Bangladesh. The deterrent signals should be backed by effective, strong, continuous action. There may be need of even interventionist/economic pressure on Bangladesh to elicit response over our concerns.
- The Central Government must continue to respond diplomatically to the problems faced by religious minorities in Bangladesh and to protect their interest.
- India should help in the economic development of Bangladesh, if there is change in the attitude of that country towards India.

- The Centre should encourage legal border trade with Bangladesh if that country reciprocates. Dhaka may be persuaded to provide the North-East a transit route through West Bengal and to the sea through Chittagong port.
- The External Affairs Ministry should take urgent steps to resolve the problem of border with Bangladesh and also demarcate the disputed portion of Indo-Bangladesh border without any further delay.

IV. Miscellaneous

- Most importantly, the Seminar felt that there was a need to change the prevalent mindset of the Governments, political parties and individuals vis-à-vis the serious implications of the crisis. In order to achieve this objective, the seminar recommends that the concerned State Govt., NGOs and media should carry out effective public education programmes through books/booklets, citizen's guides etc., in English and Indian languages about the dangers inherent in the illegal influx to the country's security and economy. These publications should also emphasise that harbouring illegal migrants is a cognisable offence under the Foreigner Act, 1946.
- The Seminar also recommends that from security and general point of view it is essential to depoliticise and de-communalise the issue of illegal migration. The above mentioned mass-education and publicity programmes should also endeavour in this direction as well as to counter the confusion being created by pro-Bangladesh lobby on this issue. It will, to a large extent, discourage the vote-bank politics presently surrounding the issue.
- The seminar recommends the compilation of a Register of Villages like the NRC, to be captioned as National Register of Villages.
- The protection of the land and political rights of the original inhabitants of the North-East, in the areas threatened by the illegal influx, should be assured by the constitutional reservations. The basis for such measures should be the 1951 census.

Annexure IV

GROWTH OF VARIOUS RELIGIOUS COMMUNITIES IN ASSAM SINCE INDEPENDENCE

Religion	*1951 Population*	*1961 Population*	*Growth Rate*	*1971 Population*	*Growth Rate*	*1991 Population*	*Growth Rate*	*Increase Absolute*	*1951–91 Percentage*
(1)	*(2)*	*(3)*	*(4)*	*(5)*	*(6)*	*(7)*	*(8)*	*(9)*	*(10)*
1. Hindus	58,86,063 (66.65)	78,84,921 (66.41)	33.96	1,06,25,847 (71.04)	34.76	1,50,47,293 (67.13)	41.61	91,61,230	155.64
2. Muslims	19,95,936 (22.60)	27,65,509 (23.29)	38.56	35,94,006 (24.03)	29.96	63,73,204 (28.43)	77.33	43,77,268	219.30
3. Christians	4,87,331 (5.52)	7,64,553 (6.44)	56.89	6,67,151 (4.46)	–12.74	7,74,367 (3.32)	16.07	2,87,036	583.89
4. Sikhs	3,949 (0.04)	9,686 (0.08)	145.28	12,347 (0.08)	27.47	16,492 (0.07)	33.57	12,543	317.62
5. Buddhists	22,628 (0.26)	36,513 (0.31)	61.36	45,212 (0.30)	23.82	64,008 (0.29)	41.57	41,380	182.87
6. Jains	4,169 (0.05)	9,468 (0.08)	127.10	12,917 (0.09)	36.43	20,645 (0.09)	59.83	16,476	395.20
7. Others	4,30,656 (4.88)	4,02,122 (3.39)	–6.63	062	–99.98	1,38,230 (0.62)	0.61	–2,92,426	–67.90
8. Religion not stated	—	—	—	—	—	10,083 (0.05)	—	—	—

Figures in parenthesis are percentage to total population.
Source: Census of India, Asam, 1991.

Annexure V

POPULATION OF BANGLADESH BY RELIGIOUS GROUPS, 1901–1991

(Numbers in million)

Religion	1901	1911	1921	1931	1941	1951	1961	1971	1981	1991
Total	28.927	31.555	33.254	35.604	41.999	41.933	50.840	71.478	87.120	106.315
Muslim	19.113	21.202	22.646	24.731	29.509	32.227	40.890	61.039	75.487	93.881
Hindu	9.545	9.952	10.166	10.453	11.747	9.239	9.380	9.673	10.570	11.179
Buddhist	—	—	—	—	—	.319	.374	.439	.538	.623
Christian	—	—	—	0.61	.053	.107	.149	.216	.275	.346
Others	.269	.401	.442	.359	.690	.041	.047	.111	.250	.286

Annexure VI

NUMERICAL DISTRIBUTION AND PERCENTAGE VARIATION OF BANGLADESH POPULATION BY MAJOR RELIGIOUS COMMUNITIES 1901–1981

Census Year	Total population (000)	Muslim		Hindu		Buddhist		Christian		Others	
		Number (000)	Per cent Variation	Number (000)	Per cent Variation	Number (000)	Per cent Variation	Number (000)	Per cent Variation	Number (000)	Per cent Variation
1901	28927	19113	—	9545	—	—	—	—	—	269	—
1911	31555	21202	10.9	9952	4.3	—	—	—	—	401	49.1
1921	33254	22646	6.8	10166	2.2	—	—	—	—	442	10.2
1931	35604	24731	9.2	10453	2.8	—	—	61	—	359	–18.8
1941	41999	29509	19.3	11747	12.4	—	—	53	–13.1	690	92.2
1951	41933	32227	9.2	9239	–21.3	319	—	107	101.9	41	–94.1
1961	50840	40890	26.9	9380	1.5	374	17.2	149	39.3	47	14.6
1974	71478	61039	49.3	9673	3.1	439	17.4	216	45.0	111	136.2
1981	87120	75487	23.7	10870	9.3	538	22.6	275	27.3	250	125.2

Note: 1. Hindus in this and subsequent tables include both caste Hindus and Scheduled Caste.
... upto 1941 Buddhist and upto 1921 Christian communities are not available separately and as such these two communities have been included in 'Others'. Christian community is not available separately in the district of Sylhet in 1931 census and as such they have been included in 'Other'.
It may be noted that due to the rounding of the totals in thousands, slight difference from the actual figures may appear.

Annexure VII

DISTRICT-WISE PERCENTAGE DECADAL VARIATION IN POPULATION SINCE 1951 IN ASSAM

State/District	*1951–61*	*1961–71*	*1971–91*	*Average decadal growth*
ASSAM	34.98	34.95	53.26	26.63
1. Dhubri	27.62	40.51	56.57	28.28
2. Kokrajhar	46.34	54.30	76.78	38.39
3. Bongaigaon	60.51	40.29	64.64	32.32
4. Goalpara	37.22	45.88	54.12	27.06
5. Barpeta	32.62	35.81	43.02	21.51
6. Nalbari	49.62	42.02	49.27	24.63
7. Kamrup	37.73	38.80	65.72	32.86
8. Darrang	44.75	43.24	55.63	27.81
9. Sonitpur	35.82	27.62	57.14	28.57
10. Lakhimpur	50.46	43.39	56.29	28.14
11. Dhemaji	68.56	103.42	107.50	53.75
12. Marigaon	37.89	37.51	50.90	25.45
13. Nagaon	35.91	38.99	51.26	25.63
14. Golaghat	26.04	30.85	58.12	29.06
15. Jorhat	24.17	17.47	33.10	16.55
16. Sibsagar	23.36	19.45	38.76	19.38
17. Dibrugarh	31.55	22.93	37.78	18.89
18. Tinsukia	35.92	31.02	47.03	23.51
19. Karbi Anglong	79.21	68.28	74.72	37.36
20. North Cachar Hills	36.95	40.00	98.30	49.15
21. Karimganj	22.96	25.13	42.08	21.04
22. Hailakandi	27.23	23.61	45.94	22.97
23. Cachar	22.60	23.96	47.59	23.79

Source: Census of India, 1991.

Annexure VIII

DISTRICT-WISE POPULATION PERCENTAGES OF HINDUS AND MUSLIMS AND OTHER RELIGIONS IN ASSAM—1991

Name of District	*Hindus (percentage)*	*Muslims (percentage)*	*Other Religion (percentage)*	*Total population*
1	2	3	4	5
Dhubri	3,82,817 (28.72)	9,38,789 (70.45)	10,869 (0.83)	13,32,475
Kokrajhar	5,31,477 (66.37)	1,54,801 (19.33)	1,14,381 (14.30)	8,00,659
Bongaigaon	5,16,830 (64.00)	2,64,393 (32.74)	26,300 (3.26)	8,02,523
Goalpara	2,66,499 (39.88)	3,35,275 (50.18)	66,364 (9.94)	6,68,138
Barpeta	5,57,929 (40.26)	7,76,974 (56.07)	50,765 (3.67)	13,85,659
Nalbari	7,87,485 (77.47)	2,02,653 (19.93)	26,252 (2.60)	10,16,390
Kamrup	14,86,526 (74.32)	4,67,544 (23.37)	46,001 (2.31)	20,00,021
Darrang	7,86,332 (60.54)	4,15,323 (31.97)	97,205 (7.49)	12,98,860
Sonitpur	11,47,228 (80.19)	1,89,859 (11.11)	92,200 (6.48)	14,24,287
Lakhimpur	5,98,946 (79.69)	1,09,010 (14.50)	43,561 (5.81)	7,51,517
Dhemaji	4,49,492 (93.87)	7,114 (1.48)	22,224 (4.65)	4,78,810
Marigaon	3,48,989 (54.55)	7,89,835 (45.30)	858 (0.15)	6,39,682
Nagaon	9,79,395 (51.73)	8,93,372 (45.18)	20,454 (1.09)	18,93,171
Golaghat	7,13,131 (86.11)	58,859 (7.10)	56,106 (6.79)	8,28,096

(contd.)

Annexure VIII (contd.)

1	2	3	4	5
Jorhat	8,15,320 (93.58)	37,651 (4.32)	18,236 (3.00)	8,71,206
Sibsagar	8,10,445 (89.25)	69,260 (7.62)	28,278 (3.13)	9,07,983
Dibrugarh	9,51,763 (91.29)	46,814 (4.49)	43,880 (4.32)	10,42,45
Tinsukia	8,67,825 (90.18)	30,095 (3.12)	64,378 (6.70)	9,62,298
Karbi Anglong	5,62,102 (84.81)	10,421 (1.57)	90,200 (13.62)	6,62,72
North Cachar Hills	1,09,957 (72.91)	3,340 (2.21)	37,504 (24.88)	1,50,801
Karimganj	4,14,731 (50.14)	4,06,706 (49.17)	5,626 (0.69)	8,27,06
Hailakandi	1,96,269 (43.70)	7,46,016 (54.78)	6,763 (1.52)	4,49,049
Cachar	7,70,803 (63.42)	4,19,150 34.48)	25,432 (2.10)	12,15,381
ASSAM	1,50,47,293 (67.13)	6,73,204 (28.43)	9,93,825 (4.44)	2,24,15,154

Source: Census of India, Assam, 1991.

Annexure VIIIA

GROWTH OF MUSLIM POPULATION IN SOME BORDER DISTRICTS OF WEST BENGAL AND ASSAM DURING 1991–2001

District	*Percentage of Muslim Population*	
	1991 Census	*2001 Census*
West Bengal		
South 24 Paragana	29.9	33.2
North 24 Paragana	24.2	24.2
Nadia	24.9	25.4
Murshidabad	61.4	63.7
Malda	47.5	49.7
South Dinajpur	36.8	38.4
North Dinajpur	36.8	38.4
Jalpaiguri	10.0	10.8
Coch Bihar	23.4	24.2
Kolkata	17.7	20.3
Total	23.6	25.2
West Bengal		
Dhubari	70.4	74.3
Gowalpara	50.2	53.6
Hailakandi	54.8	57.6
Karimganj	49.2	52.3
Barpeta	56.1	59.4
Nagaon	47.2	51.0
Marigaon	46.0	47.6
Cachar	34.5	36.1
Darang	32.0	35.6

Percentage increase of Muslim and non-Muslim Population in some border districts of Assam between 1991 and 2001 censuses

Districts of Assam	*Increase of population (%)*		
	Muslims	*Non-Muslims*	*Total*
Dhubari	29.5	7.1	22.9
Gowalpara	31.7	14.4	23.0
Hailakandi	27.2	13.3	20.9
Karimganj	29.4	14.5	21.9
Cachar	24.6	16.0	18.9
Barpeta	25.8	10.0	18.9
Nagaon	32.1	11.3	22.2
Marigaon	27.2	16.3	21.2
Darang	26.9	9.6	15.8

Annexure IX

EXTRACTS FROM THE REPORT OF THE GENERAL SECTRETARIES OF THE CONGRESS (I) TO THE SEVENTH GENERAL CONFERENCE OF THE NORTH-EASTERN CO-ORDINATION COMMITTEE, GUWAHATI, 3rd JULY 1992

Part 3 : Migration: Secularism vs. Fundamentalism

Migration is a natural phenomenon in history. But during the last four and a half decades the population movements in the Indian sub-continent across the international borders have been anything but natural. In the Eastern region, the population movement across the borders in its unnatural form remains a disturbing fact of our social life with a threat that it may become even more disturbing in not too distant future.

2. The assumption that the partition would solve the Hindu-Muslim question and that, on both sides, Hindus and Muslims would be able to live in peace and unity, proved to be unreal. In the eastern sector, there could be virtually no exchange of population as in the western sector. The size of the population was too big for such a source.

3. With the gradual decline in the power of the Muslim League which had been playing the fundamentalist role and, with the growing resistance of the people of Eastern Bengal to attacks on their language and culture and to economic exploitation, the intensity and frequency of communal riots to evict the minorities declined. Progressive and secular forces among the Muslims came to the defence of the minorities. The movement for autonomy, although fanatically resisted by the fundamentalists, culminated in the liberation of East-Pakistan and the Republic of Bangladesh came into existence. India's moral and material support to the cause of the

revolution was based on yet another assumption that, in the new Republic, the remaining minority population would be able to live in dignity and peace. A secular atmosphere on both sides of the border would act as safety valves for sustained economic co-operation and ensure prosperity and growth and prevent migration of people from Eastern Bengal to India's Eastern region which, between 1947 and 1971 had to absorb, at a terrible cost, history's largest exodus. To remind ourselves, the religious minorities, which accounted for 29.7 per cent of population in the area comprising East-Pakistan (now Bangladesh) in 1947, were reduced to 14.6 per cent of the total population in 1974, the influx period being 1947–1971.

4. Quick on the heels of liberation, Bangladesh became a secular democratic Republic. All communal and religion based parties were banned. The four major fundamentalist parties affected by the ban were Jamat-e-Islam, Nisan-e-Islam, Pakistan Democratic Party and the Muslim League.

5. After the assassination of Sheikh Mujib in August 1975, Khondkar Mustaz Ahmed tried to lift the ban but did not succeed. At the social level, however, these parties were busy propagating their cause. Mosques were the focal points in this exercise. It was at this time that the fundamentalists scored their first victory. The unifying slogan of 'Joy Bangla' of Bengali nationalism was replaced by the slogan, 'Bangladesh Zindabad.' Similarly, the name 'Bangladesh Betar' was replaced by 'Radio Bangladesh.' These were very subtle and sophisticated moves, reminiscent of East-Pakistan days, away from 'Bengali Nationalism' to 'Bangladeshi Nationalism.'

6. On April 21, 1976, the first action of General Zia as President was to erase secularism from the Directive Principles of the Constitution. Ordinance and rules were passed to provide opportunities to the fundamentalist parties to function openly and legally.

7. Blessed by the military rule, the fundamentalists lost no time to entrench and emerge as a force. In 1979 elections, an alliance of pro-Pakistan and Islamic Fundamentalist forces, who had opposed the liberation of Bangladesh in 1971, won 20 seats in the Parliament. In 1986 elections, the Jamat got 10 seats while it had won only 6 seats in 1979 under the protective banner of Islamic Democratic League, (IDL). In the 1991 elections, the Jamat and their associates won

18 seats and occupied the second position in 24 constituencies. They polled 11.73 per cent of the total votes cast.

8. It is instructive to note that in the pre-liberation era the Jamat never gained as many seats. In 1970 elections, they failed even to open their account. Between 1979 and 1988 the persistent efforts of the fundamentalists to wean away people from secularism, socialism and democracy in favour of the Islamic ethos continued unabated. It was essential to get the students' support because of the revolutionary role they had been playing. It was also essential that the Constitution be made Islamic sealing the path of progressive forces. In 1979, just on the eve of the general elections, Lt. Col. Mustatizur Rahaman, the present Foreign Minister of Bangladesh, announced in a seminar inaugurated by the Ambassador of Saudi Arabia, 'The first and foremost concern of the new Parliament will be to enact laws based on the Quran and the Sunnah.'

9. To indoctrinate the youths in the cause of Islam, the Madrasah Education System was reformulated with much sophistication. It is today a parallel system recording faster rate of growth than that of the secular educational system. Science and other modern subjects have been introduced into the Madrasah syllabi so that the Madrasah students can go to technical lines and occupy decision-making positions in society with an Islamic bent of mind. This is a unique phenomenon witnessed in Bangladesh today since the establishment of Calcutta Madrasah in 1971. In 1972–73, there were 7792 secondary schools as against 1351 Madrasahs. In 1989–90, there were 9822 secondary schools and 5766 Madrasahs. It is clear that the rates of increase in the number of teaching staff and the number of Madrasahs were far higher than those of secondary schools.

10. General Ershad, who seized power on March 24, 1982, continued the policies of the Zia regime and gave full support to Madrasah Education. He also took the stand that the question of State Religion for ten crore Muslims of the country should be settled: "We do not have a State Religion. I am waiting for that day when a decision will be taken in the matter and that decision will be incorporated in the Constitution" (5/2/1988). On 28th February, 1988, he again declared, "I am happy at the regeneration of Islam in the country, Bangladesh is a country of ten crores of Muslims with

the co-operation of the people, Islam will one day be established as the State Religion. We are real Muslims." In March 1988, he announced that the name of Bangladesh Red Cross would be changed to Bangladesh Red-Crescent Society.

11. To set at rest the apprehension of the minorities, he made a clever move to convince the Indian leaders that minorities would lose nothing as Islam would only be a State Religion on paper with no change in the ground realities. When faced with angry protests from his own youth leaders, he argued that when Indian leaders were convinced of the innocence of the move, why should they worry! In June 1988, Islam was declared the State Religion of Bangladesh. The fundamentalists, thus, acquired enough legitimacy and ground to continue with their other plans.

12. We are thus back to square one. Against this backdrop, it is easily understandable why migration of minorities (i.e., Hindus and Buddhists) continues unabated. With the steep fall in the numerical strength of the religious minorities, there is, however, a qualitative change in the causes of migration. Riots and killings have yielded place to other means of oppression. Minorities today find that they are seldom able to protect their faith, property and women. Reports of forced marriages and conversions have been pouring in. With the Muslim population growing at a faster rate, there is a rising pressure on land and minority properties are the obvious targets. Even temple lands are not being spared. Certain inequitous laws in force like the Vested Properties Act and the Enemy Property Act are handy weapons to deprive the minorities of their properties. Added to the atmosphere of general insecurity, there is the economic insecurity due to continuous shrinkage of job and other economic opportunities.

13. In this context, the story of the Chittagong Hill Tracts (CHT) is one of the most tragic episodes in recent history. Once inhabited by tribals, this beautiful land had been substantially captured by the Muslims. Between 1979 and 1984 the Government settled about 4 lakh Muslims in the CHT area. As there was no provision for the protection of ethnic minorities in the Bangladesh Constitution, the invasion from the neighbouring areas continued and led to clashes and protracted armed resistance by the major tribal group—the Chakmas. In this explosive situation, the regime sought

a military solution and thousands of refugees crossed over to India. In 1974, there were 5.08 lakh people in the CHT area. In 1981, the population increased to 5.80 lakh, a growth of 14.17 per cent. Against this, the Muslims in 1974 were 96,000 which increased to 1.88 lakhs in 1981, a growth rate as high as 95.83 per cent. All other tribal groups, except the Tripuris, recorded a negative growth varying between –5 per cent to –7.5 per cent. The threats to the ethnic identity and culture as well as their land were evident.

14. Under growing pressure of International opinion, the District Council Act was passed in 1989 to give autonomy to the region. In the CHT three District Councils were created. The District Councils were given powers excepting foreign affairs, finance, defence and the reserve forests which is 40 per cent of the total CHT land. A scrutiny of provisions of the Act would reveal that the Councils have got very little power to settle the vital issues affecting their secuirty as well as other economic rights including the right to land. Even in the representation to the Councils, the major tribe, Chakmas, have been deliberately cornered as they were the ones who fought for their rights. The militarisation of the Tracts by establishing three permanent garrisons in addition to 12 police stations has been designed to suppress any dissent. In this context, one wonders, how the Chakmas, now in Tripura camps, could ever return. In fact, the flow of the refugees remains steady as the oppression continues.

15. The arrival in Bangladesh of several lakhs of Rohingya Muslims from the Arakans of Myanmar has added a new dimension. The Jamat has been pressing for the settlement of Rohingyas in the CHT. Already clashes between the Jamat-led Rohingyas and the Buddhist tribals of the CHT have resulted in loss of lives. More refugees from the CHT are everyday heading up towards India.

16. The ongoing debate on the question of infiltration has not only generated much heat but is also bringing to light vital information:

16.1 Between 1971 and 1981, Bangladesh census records show a reduction of 39 lakhs in the minority population.

16.2 Between 1981–89, 36 lakh religious minorities were missing from that country.

16.3 In 1972, there were 7.5 lakh Bihari Muslims in the camps in Dacca. As a result of mediation by Saudi Arabia only 33,000 of them were accepted by Pakistan. At present, there are less than who lakh in the camps, where have the rest gone?

16.4 Bangladeshi Journalists met Bangladeshi Muslim families residing in Delhi, took their pictures and wrote about their life style in a Dacca Daily. According to them, there are about 1.5 lakh Bangladeshi Muslims in Delhi. According to other sources, the number will be more than 3.5 lakhs. Whatever be the number, they came from Bangladesh.

16.5 In July 1990, the Bangladeshi Muslims residing in West Bengal formed an organisation named 'Bangladesh Mohajir Sangstha.' On 12th February 1991, the spokesman of the above organisation told a Press Conference that there were one lakh Bangladeshi nationals in West Bengal at that time and many more are spread over in Delhi, Bombay and Ahmedabad whose total number would exceed 5 lakhs.

16.6 Shri M.M. Jacob, Union Minister of State for Home Affairs, said in Parliament in December 1991, in reply to a question, there there were one lakh Bangladeshi nationals in Delhi and 5.87 lakh in West Bengal.

16.7 Here we are speaking from records. About what is not recorded and what cannot be recorded, we have our own experience and observations to rely on. The economic stagnation of Bangladesh has compelled many Muslims, besides, minority groups, to come to India for earnings. There is also a floating population—comprising all communities—who come and go back with their earnings. In such a process, it is only natural that a part of it is settling down in our areas. We also accommodate them with no questions asked as we require cheap and scarce labour in construction and in farm and household work.

17. It is time to ponder, if Bangladeshis are infiltrating into Calcutta, Mumbai, Delhi, Ahmedabad etc., should be think that there

is no infiltration into Tripura which has a 867 km. border without any natural barriers and into Assam which has about 300 km. border with Bangladesh?

18. It would be interesting to note that a group of intellectuals in Dacca is seeking to legitimise the migration of Muslims into the adjoining areas of North-East region by invoking the theory of Lebensraum or living space. A number of Dacca dailies carried articles written on these lines by University Professors. They were not at all apologetic about the infiltration. People are sought to be inspired by the hope that one day the North-Eastern region will be added to Bangladesh giving it a natural boundary in place of the present one which throttles Bangladesh.

19. We do share the apprehension of the minorities that any talk about infiltration tends to make their life miserable as genuine citizens easily become the targets of harassment in the hands of certain vested interests operating as political groups and parties. The memory of a misconceived and misdirected movement against 'foreign nationals' is still too fresh in our mind. But the emerging trends in Bangladesh today and the increasing infiltrations have thrown a challenge to the minorities living in the region to take a wise and farsighted stand. To turn a blind eye or to oppose any such talk, using a forum in the name of a particular community, in a tone and temper that strengthen only the fundamentalist forces, will be the height of folly.

20. From the above we may infer,

20.1 There are infiltrations—though it is a difficult task to examine the precise number.

20.2 The infiltrations are not only by minorities of Bangladesh but also from the majority community—Muslims. In absolute terms, the number of Muslims crossing into India is likely to be much larger than that of non-Muslims.

20.3 An ideological support is given to the phenomenon by the Islamic Fundamentalists creating the vision of a larger Islamic country comprising Bangladesh and the entire North-East where its economic problems will be solved and security ensured.

20.4 There is a direct correlation between the *rise of fundamentalism and increase in influx.*

21. On the Indian side, the rise of the Hindu Fundamentalism can be traced to a number of factors:

(a) Islamic character of the neighbouring states.
(b) The Shah Bano case.
(c) The Babri Masjid controversy.
(d) The increasing infiltrations from Bangladesh.

22. This brand of fundamentalism scored significant success in 1989 and 1991 elections. In the North-East, we have a very strong secular tradition in spite of occasional disturbances caused mostly by exogenous factors. The fundamentalists never had a foot-hold either in North Bengal or Assam. But in the last elections they stormed the Barak valley and registered their presence elsewhere. Even in West Bengal they have secured 11.7 per cent of the votes cast though they could not win any Seat.

23. The BJP has introduced Vidya Bharati School system with Syllabi that include the Hinduised version of history. They have issued instructions to the RSS to open more and more schools all over India. Excepting the Hill States of the NE region Vidya Bharati Schools are there in all the States of India. The four States they are in power, this is being practised in full swing and the influence is bound to spread over. This is nothing but a systematic attempt to indoctrinate the youths to Hindu fundamentalism and is comparable to the spirit, aim and objects of Madrasah system of education in Bangladesh excepting the fact that in India it does not have any support or blessing of the Central Government or any encouragement from any provision of the Constitution.

24. The message is clear. Fundamentalist forces are working in both the countries and are constantly trying to gain in strength. If this is not checked now, and secular forces do not triumph to give a new shape to the destiny of Eastern Region, fundamentalists will fight fundamentalists and the battle can be unimaginably costly in all conceivable terms—human and otherwise. It is also clear that, just as the growth of fundamentalist forces in one country encourages its

growth in the other, the growth cannot be checked by unilateral efforts at one end alone. If secularism has to triumph in the Eastern part of the subcontinent we have to help and support the secular forces in Bangladesh also.

25. Unfortunately the Government of India appears to be suffering from a half-hearted approach or no approach to this challenging problem. The External Affairs Ministry has not done the job it should have done. The concerned desk has virtually been a non-functioning one. For years, the practice has been: if anything appears to be wrong there, ask Mr. so and so of West Bengal who is in the limelight at that time. The Desk is not asked to come forward with its findings. It is not realised that the problem is too deep for an active politician, however talented he is, to understand without the help of expert watchers. It is also not realised that the problem is not merely of West Bengal but of others as well.

26. History has taught us in the North-East that our very survival is dependent on the survival of secularism in the region and the virus of fundamentalism cannot be allowed to persist or spread. As Congressmen, we have an additional responsibility of upholding secularism as a cherished ideal and establishing it as a potent instrument for separating politics from religion and liberating men from religious gangsterism. The question is, will the nation fight a real battle for the victory of secularism in this part of the country? We ask this question because our fate hinges on the answer to it.

27. The subject calls for systematic research and projections of the available data and trends into the future to guide leaders in policy making. Let us not forget that we have made most of our experiments in the region to improve and stabilise its political and economic profiles and yet problems continue to multiply. Let us also caution ourselves and the nation on either side of the divide that the leaders have to rise to meet the challenge or 'they will be waylaid by history and time.' We beg of the Prime Minister to give his personal attention to this affair that calls for answers to India's Eastern Questions.

Our term of office has come to an end. We have great pleasure in placing on record our gratitude to the Chairman Shri P.A. Sangma with whom we have worked for three long years for his never-failing sympathy and love for us and the wisdom of his counsel with which

he has always guided us. We also thank all the Vice-Chairmen and all of you for your valuable co-operation and guidance.

JAI HIND

Sd/-		Sd/-
R.C. Chiten Jamir		*B.B. Dutta*
General Secretary		General Secretary
Nagaland		Tripura

Sd/-	Sd/-	Sd/-
D.D. Pugh	*H.K. Bora*	*Liansuama*
General Secretary	General Secretary	General Secretary
Meghalaya	Assam	Mizoram

Annexure X

INTERNAL NOTE PREPARED BY THE HOME MINISTRY, GOVERNMENT OF INDIA, IN MARCH 1992

Problem of Infiltration from Bangladesh

The illegal immigration from Bangladesh into the Eastern and North-eastern States and several other States in the country has become a serious problem. Immigration into border States such as Assam and West Bengal was taking place prior to the formation of Bangladesh but the magnitude of the problem has assumed serious dimensions as large-scale infiltration has changed the demographic landscape of the borders and affected Delhi, Rajasthan, Gujarat, Maharashtra etc.

2. According to the figures available (in 1987) with the Government of West Bengal, the total number of Bangladeshi infiltrants in that State was around 4.4 million. It should be near about five million today. In Assam, the estimated figure of infiltrants today in about 2–3 million. Tripura and Bihar are also seriously affected by infiltration from Bangladesh. The infiltrants are now spreading to newer areas like Manipur and Nagaland.

3. The influx, in certain cases, has changed the demographic character as illustrated above. Its serious religious and cultural dimensions are being increasingly felt in the States of West Bengal, Tripura ánd Bihar. It is observed that more and more Muslim immigrants are settling down in the Border areas. Accordingly, large stretches of the border in these States are becoming predominantly inhabited by Bangladeshi Muslims. The simmering communal tension in some of the Border areas is one of the manifestations of the effects of large-scale illegal migration of Bangladeshi nationals who have slowly displaced or dispossessed the local population, particularly those belonging to the Hindu community, in these areas.

4. The Hindu immigrants have been generally staying in shanties in miserable conditions in visible concentration in South

West Bengal districts. Details given in Appendix 'A'. The Muslim infiltrators have mostly fanned out to urban areas in other States most notably in Delhi, Rajasthan, Gujarat, Maharashtra etc. In the metropolitan cities of Delhi and Bombay not less than 4 to 5 lakhs Bangladeshi Muslims have been residing. A list of places in West Bengal and Bihar where Muslim infiltrators are living in concentration is given at Appendix 'B'.

Hindu Migration

5. In the first four decades of the current century, i.e., between 1901 and 1941, the Hindu population in East-Bengal declined from 33 per cent of the total population to 28 per cent. The next forty years between 1941 and 1981 witnessed a drastic fall in the Hindu population from 28 per cent to 12.1 per cent (i.e., a net decline of 16 per cent as against 5 per cent in the corresponding forty year period). The highest fall in Hindu population was recorded during the 1941–51 decade when it was reduced to 22 per cent of the total from 28 per cent, i.e., a net decline of 6 per cent, mainly due to massive migration to India in the wake of serious communal disturbances after the partition of India in 1947. In 1950 alone, after extensive communal riots in East-Pakistan, not less than one million Hindus migrated to India.

6. In the next decade, 1951–61, the Hindu population declined from 22 per cent of the total to 18.5 per cent, i.e., 3.5 per cent signifying a substantial drop in the rate of migration. The main reason for this fall in Hindu migration was the decimation of the Muslim League in the 1954 Provincial Assembly elections. Under the separate electorate system then prevalent in Pakistan, Hindus had 69 representatives in the Provincial Assembly. There were two Hindu Ministers from East-Pakistan in the Central Pak Cabinet and in East-Pakistan, the coalition governments of Abu Hossain Sarkar and Ataur Rahman Khan during 1954–58 had three and four Hindu Ministers respectively.

7. Substantial presence of Hindu representatives in the Provincial Assembly and their effective strength in the Provincial and Central Governments gave a strong voice to the minority in the affairs of the country. Many Hindu leaders of Bangladesh say that the Hindus and enjoyed maximum security and protection of their interests during this interregnum because of this political clout. The

flow of Hindu migration during these years was consequently the minimal.

8. The 1958–71 period was the worst for the Hindu community in East-Pakistan. During the martial regime under Ayub Khan, Hindus came under intense communal pressure and atrocities. In the absence of a parliamentary forum and accountability of the military junta, the minority community had no remedy against communal excesses. During and after the Indo-Pak War of 1965, anti-India and communal propaganda was intensified. Enactment of the Enemy Property Act and dispossession of Hindu owners of their immovable property under this law added a potent economic push factor for Hindu migration. The Hindu population declined by 5 per cent during this period from 18.5 per cent to 13.5 per cent of the total population.

9. While the Hinus who had migrated to India till 1964 were absorbed as Indian citizens, during the Liberation War in 1971, ten million people from East-Pakistan mostly took shelter in India. All these refugees including the Hindus, however, went back within a few months of liberation in the hope of getting a better deal under a secular, democratic set up. The Hindus, however, were soon in for a rude shock. The Enemy Property Act continued to be enforced, albeit under a different name, i.e., Vested and Non-Resident Property (Administration) Act of 1974 and the Hindus were persecuted in liberated Bangladesh.

10. The assassination of Sheikh Mujib in a military coup on August 15, 1975, heightened the sense of insecurity among the Hindus. Ziaur Rahman carried out Islamisation of the polity substituting secularism, which was one of the four cardinal principles of State policy, by Allah and incorporating the Quranic invocation "Bismillah-hi-Rahman-e-Rahim" in the Constitution. The ban on the communal parties was lifted and many leaders and cadres of these parties with records of Hindu-baiting were admitted to Zia's ruling BN party. Some of them were given key positions in the government and the party and its front organisations. This rendered the Hindus vulnerable to their machinations. In the 1974–81 period, Hindu population declined from 13.5 per cent to 12.1 per cent which is mainly attributable to the 1976–81 quinquenium.

11. The process of Islamisation, initiated by Ziaur Rahman, reached its high-water mark in June 1988 when Islam was declared

the State Religion of the country. This emboldened the communal forces further and the country witnessed wide-spread communal disturbances in 1989 and 1990 in reaction to developments over the Ram Janma Bhoomi-Babri Masjid controversy in India. Following large-scale destruction, desecration and damage inflicted on Hindu temples and religious institutions for four days between 30-10-90 and 2-11-90 by the then ruling Jatiya Party in an attempt to divert attention from the mass movement against the Ershad regime, clandestine migration by the Hindus to India went up.

12. Harassment of the Hindus after the 1991 Parliamentary elections by the ruling BNP and its ally, Jamaat-e-Islami, for allegedly voting for the Awami League, further heightened the insecurity of the minority community and contributed to their influx to India. Besides insecurity, lack of economic opportunities and discrimination in the fields of education and employment have been other powerful push factors behind the unabated flow of Hindu migration to India.

Changing Pattern of Immigration

13. In recent years, the pattern of illegal migration from Bangladesh has changed in that Muslims have been infiltrating in larger numbers. In fact, Muslim infiltrators including the so-called Behari Muslims, now far out-number the Hindu immigrants. Late last year, Shri Jyoti Basu, Chief Minister of West Bengal, revealed in the State Assembly that in the first six months of 1991, of the 39,055 Bangladeshis intercepted at the point of crossing the border, as amny as 28,000 were Muslims. The figures released by the BSF from time to time confirm this changed pattern of immigration.

Extent of Immigration

14. In the absence of a reliable comprehensive census, exact quantification of the extent of infiltration is not possible but the 1991 census data of both Bangladesh and Idnia throw significant light on its magnitude. The total population of Bangladesh was estimated in 1991 at 104.76 million, the annual growth rate being 2.02 per cent against 3.13 per cent during the decade 1974–81. The total population for 1991 was earlier projected by the Bangladesh Government between 112 and 114 million. The UNDP projection

was 116 million for 1990 and 117–118 million for 1991. The net shortfall, according to Bangladesh Government projection was between 7.24 and 9.24 million, and according to UNDP estimates it was between 12.24 and 14.24 million. Combined with others census statistics one can safely conclude that no less than 7 to 12 million people have infiltrated into India between 1981 and 1991.

Growth Rate in Border Districts

15. A comparison of growth rates in some contiguous border districts of the two countries would give an idea of the extent of infiltration.

Bangladesh	*India*
National growth rate 2.02%	National growth rate 2.35%
	(*West Bengal St. Avg. 3.45%)*
Greater Jessore 1.97%	North 24 Parganas 3.16%
Greater Khulna 1.58%	Maldah 2.6%
Greater Rajshahi 2.11%	Murshidabad 2.80%
Greater Rangpur 1.95%	Cooch Behar 2.18%
Greater Dinajpur 1.95%	West Dinajpur 3.25%
Greater Kushtia 2.015%	Nadia 2.98%
	Meghalaya (State growth rate 3.18%)
Greater Mymensingh 1.82%	Eastern Garo Hills 3.84%
Greater Sylhet 1.81%	Western Garo Hills 2.91%
	Jaintia Hills 4.1%
Greater Comilla 1.89%	Tripura 3.36%

Phenomenal growth rates in the following urban conglomerates in West Bengal during the period 1981–91 reinforces the conclusion that massive infiltration from Bangladesh to these areas is underway.

Some Explosive Growth in Urban Areas of West Bengal
National Average 2.35 per cent and State Average 2.45 per cent

Barasat (North 24 Parganas)	5.43%	English Bazar (Malda)	78.98%
Khardah	9.50%	Islampur (West Dinajpur)	7.15%
Madhyagram	4.45%	Raiganj (West Dinajpur)	13.93%
Gabardanga	8.64%	Kaliganj (West Dinajpur)	4.10%
Habra	5.15%	Alipurduar (Jalpaiguri)	4.46%
Ashokenagar (Kalyannagar)	7.45%	Tufanganj (Cooch Behar)	22.45%
Ramghat (Nadia)	5.11%	Meghliganj (Cooch Behar)	7.98%
Santipur (Nadia)	3.24%	Haldibari (Cooch Behar)	5.38%
Murshidabad	4.26%		

A. Growth Rates in Hindu-concentrated Districts of Bangladesh

16. The fact that Hindus are clandestinely migrating to India at an alarming scale is borne out by the much lower growth rates than the national average growth rate in Hindu-concentrated districts of Bangladesh. The following statistics make the point evident:

Barisal	1.2%	Khulna	1.6%
Gopalganj	0.9%	Faridpur	1.2%
Shariatpur	1.2%	Madanpur	1.3%
Manikganj	1.0%	Munshiganj	1.1%
Moulavi Bazar	1.6%	Sunamganj	1.7%
Lakhipur	1.7%	Chandpur	1.2%

Bihari Muslims

17. Among the Muslim infiltrators from Bangladesh are a good number of Bihari Muslims who migrated from Bihar after the partition but who or whose children opted for Pakistan after the liberation of Bangladesh. There were 7.5 lakh Bihari Muslims in this category in the special camps set up by the Red Cross pending their repatriation to Pakistan while approximately only 33,000 have been shifted to Pakistan, the population in the camps has declined to 2.5 lakhs. In other words, 7.5 lakh Bihari Muslims and at least another 5 lakh have found their way into Calcutta, Katihar—Purnea-Samastipur belt of Bihar, and eastern districts of UP. Against the average annual State growth rate of 2.34 per cent in Bihar, Katihar, Purnea and Samastipur districts recorded 2.75 per cent, 2.35 per cent and 2.82 per cent increase in population respectively during 1981–91 decade.

B. Growth Rate of Population and Households in Chittagong Hill Tracts (CHTS)

18. The demographic picture in the three districts of the CHTs is different from the national spectrum. The following statistics from the 1991 census of Bangladesh throw significant light:

National Growth of Population 2.02 per cent
National Growth of Households 2.09 per cent

District	*Growth in*	
	Population	*Households*
Khagrachari	2.2%	4.5%
Rangamati	4.1%	5.3%
Banderban	3.6%	4.3%

19. The higher growth rates of both population and households in Rangamati and Banderban districts are due to settlement of Bengali Muslims from the plain districts. The lower growth rate in Khagrachari district is due to presence of nearly 56,000 Chakma refugees in Tripura since 1986. The higher growth of households in this district only underscores settlement of Muslims from outside which is fast reducing the majority of the non-Muslim tribals in the CHTs. This has heightened the insecurity of the tribals and fuelled Chakma insurgency over the years.

20. The rate of growth of population in many border districts during the decade 1981–91 was lower than the growth rate in the previous decade. This does not denote a decline in the infiltration but only dispersal of the immigrants to one further a field. The fact is that the border districts of West Bengal and Assam as also greater Calcutta metropolitan complex have crossed the saturation point in absorbing the immigrants. Employment potential in these areas has become extremely low due to high level of over-population. As a result, an ever-increasing number of infiltrators, therefore, after crossing the border move to distant places, i.e., interior districts of West Bengal, Bihar, New Delhi, Bombay, Ahmedabad, Jaipur etc.

21. Figures showing comparative growth rates during 1971–81 and 1981–91 in some border districts:

Place	*1971–81*	*1981–91*
Naihati	39.63	15.20
Halisahar	44.21	17.89
Titagarh	18.50	8.89
Kancharpara	25.45	12.81
Barasat	63.19	54.29
Budge Budge	37.95	10.76
Malda	51.49	44.59
Komnagar	48.77	21.49
Kalyani	114.40	48.06
Batanagar	97.76	52.12
Makhla	54.79	24.15
Bhadrakalu	58.36	23.18
Siliguri	58.36	46.83
Habra	44.79	34.54
Nabadrpur	37.79	20.28
Ranaghat	75.19	51.19
Cooch Behar	27.83	15.64
Phulia	469.72	49.18
Taherpur	99.36	25.44
Bangaon	38.28	26.09

22. Interesting confirmation of this dispersal effect was available during interviews with a large number of immigrants in New Delhi. Many of these people stated that they had earlier migrated to Assam and thence after some years moved to New Delhi when the anti-foreigners agitation posed a threat to their security.

Bangladesh

23. The vast majority of the migrants are from the rural areas of Bangladesh. Agricultural surplus is almost entirely appropriated by the rich peasants through share-cropping, money-lending, land mortgage and control of marketing of agricultural produce. The following figures underscore the pathetic conditions of the rural population in Bangladesh and explain the influx:

1. Nearly three-fifths of the total workforce (60%) are engaged in agriculture and fishery. Agriculture is the source of income for 80 per cent of the rural population.
2. 48 per cent of the GDP is derived from agriculture. 80 per cent of the country's exports are from agriculture and agro-based industrial sector, 50 per cent being derived from jute, tea, hides.
3. Of the 15.4 million-hectares total land in Bangladesh, 15 per cent are covered by forest and 20 per cent by rivers, canals etc.
4. Total cultivable land in the country is 90,00,000 hectares, presently under cultivation is 87,00,000 hectares. Under pressure of high growth of population total cultivable land was marginally increased from 8.29 million hectares (1950–57) to 8.70 million hectares (1969–70). Since then there has been no addition to cultivable land. In 1985–86, 3 per cent of the total cultivable land remained follow.

There is excessive concentration of land among a limited number of people:

(i) 28 per cent people have no agricultural land.
(ii) 52 per cent own land less than ½ acre and are practically landless.
(iii) Between 1983–84 and 1989–90, the number of the landless went up by 5 per cent.

(iv) 40 per cent of the people at the bottom of the rural demographic own barely 3 per cent of the total cultivable land whereas the top 5 per cent own 30 per cent.

Factors Encouraging Immigration

There are combinations of factors on both sides which are responsible for continuous influx of illegal migration from Bangladesh. The important push factors on the Bangladesh side include:

(a) Steep and continuous increase in population.
(b) Population density in excess of 800 per square km.
(c) Sharp deterioration in land-man ratio with large increase in landless labour.
(d) Low rates of economic growth particularly performance in agriculture.
(e) Persecution of Hindus and Buddhist tribals.
(f) Islmaic interests encouraging expansion of territory—Formation Greater Muslim Bengal propounded by late Maulana Abdul Hamid Khan Bhasani, Espousal of Lebensraum by Muslim Intellectuals of Bangladesh.
(g) Little, if any, efforts on the part of Bangladesh to prevent efflux.

The pull factors on the Indian side include:

(i) Porous and easily negotiable border with Bangladesh.
(ii) Better economic opportunities.
(iii) Interested religious elements encouraging immigration.
(iv) Patronage extended by the vested political groups.
(v) Organised immigration by touts and anti-socials.

Change in Demographic Landscape

24. Demographic changes have produced sharply adverse Hindu-Muslim ratio in the population in several border districts in the States adjoining Bangladesh. The influx of illegal migrants who have

settled in the border districts in West Bengal, North-eastern States and Bihar has transformed these districts into overwhelmingly immigrant population districts. The change in the religious composition of population has created socio-economic and religious problems. In as many as 56 constituencies they have a major electoral voice. There has been a phenomenal increase in such crimes as boot-legging, drug peddling, prostitution and smuggling in the border districts of West Bengal. The presence of a large population of illegal immigrants constitutes a serious threat to national security. Intellectuals and press in Bangladesh have already launched a campaign for Lebensraum for their excess population in the Eastern and North-eastern States of India.

Review of State Machinery in Tackling the Problem of Infiltration

West Bengal

25. Length of the border with Bangladesh—2230 kms (9 districts are located on Indo-Bangladesh border).

26. West Bengal State is faced with not only legal immigration but transborder smuggling in a big way. There are 160 routes which are reported to be used by illegal immigrants. The specific difficulties faced by the State Government are:

(i) It is difficult to detect B.D. infiltrators because of ethnic similarity.
(ii) Indifferent attitude of the local inhabitants towards the problem of infiltration.
(iii) Non-cooperation of local people and the political parties in detection of BD infiltrators.
(iv) Meagre strength of Mobile Task Force and lack of transport facilities for them.

27. The BSF is primarily responsible for the detection of Bangladesh infiltrators crossing over the Indo-Bangladesh border. In addition, the State Police and Mobile Task Force (MTF) have been detecting BD infiltrators by organising raids in different vulnerable

points of entry on the Indo-Bangladesh border regularly since 1972. The detection figures of Bangladesh infiltrators by the State Police including M.T.F. since 1972 to November 1991 are as follows:

Hindus	62,762
Muslims	1,76,808
Others	876
Total	2,40,446

Assam

28. There are 159 Watch Posts, 15 Patrol Posts, 6 PPCPs and Field Staff in each district of Assam for detection of infiltrators from Bangladesh. The number of infiltrators detected from 26-3-1971 to 1991 is as follows:

Detected	1,35,656

Since the introduction of Illegal Migrants (Determination by Tribunal) Act, 1983 a total of 2,87,096 illegal migrants (Determination) Tribunal cases and 5,09,808 Foreigners Tribunal cases have been taken up. Out of these 24,368 cases were referred to the Illegal Migrants (Determination) Tribunals for determining illegal migrants. 8,181 persons have been declared illegal migrants. 4,658 expulsion orders have been served. 1,101 illegal migrants have been expelled from the State. Out of 33,167 Foreigners Tribunal cases 17,712 cases were disposed of declaring 16,426 persons as Foreigners of 1966–71 stream, 4,252 declared Foreigners have registered their names with FRROs and 3030 Quit India notices have been issued against declared Foreigners for not registering their names within the stipulated time. Names of 16,426 Foreigners were sent to the Election Department for deletion of their names from the voters' list. 1,57,650 inquiries were also initiated against persons enumerated but omitted from the voters' list prepared in 1989. 13,670 fresh/re-infiltrators were detected since 1986 upto 31-01-1992.

29. Progress of detection of Bangladeshi nationals in Assam is very slow. One of the reasons mentioned is the provisions contained in the IMDT Act. This Act has taken away the powers vested in the

State authorities under the Foreigners Act, 1946, for issue of quit notice etc. Moreover under the IMDT Act, the burden of proof lies with the police unlike in the case of the Foreigners Act where the burden of proof lies with the individual concerned. There was a demand for restoration of Foreigners Act for dealing with infiltrators.

Bihar

30. For the purpose of detecting Bangladeshi infiltrators, the district police administration and the S.B. Field Staff keep vigil on the movement of those who arouse suspicion. The method and the machinery used so far is the traditional one which is felt to be grossly inadequate in tackling the problem of such magnitude. A comprehensive proposal was sent to the Ministry of Home Affairs, Government of India for sanction and creation of checkposts in vulnerable areas prone to Bangladesh infiltration and also for creation of Task Force earmarked for the purpose of detecting BD infiltration and also for initiating legal action, investigation of such cases and ultimately for deporting such infiltrators. No information is available regarding infiltrators detected during the period 26th March, 1971 to 31st December 1991.

Meghalaya

31. Machinery to detect those persons who have come to India without visas as infiltrators:

(a) 10 Patrol Posts
(b) 4 Watch Posts
(c) 12 Additional Infiltration Checkposts
(d) 6 Infiltration Checkposts.

There is full-fledged Special Superintendent of Police to check infiltration. Further there is Foreigners Tribunal under the membership of a Senior IAS Officer. Besides, there are members of registered and unregistered village Defence Parties in the bordering villages to detect infiltrators. The number of infiltrators detected within Meghalaya since 26th March, 1971 till 31st December, 1991 is as follows:

No. of persons detected 14,268

Maharashtra

32. In Bombay city, the Special Branch (I) deals with Pakistani and Bangladeshi nationals. It has a strength of 102 officers and men. For Bangladeshi nationals 1 P.I and 3 S.Is and 8 men have been earmarked. For the districts special cells have been carved out depending upon the need of each district. They are keeping a watch on the Bangladesh infiltrators and are arranging round-up to detect them especially at construction sites where they are getting shelter.

Tripura

33. International Border is policed by BSF and interception of infiltrators is mainly being done by the BSF. Mobile Tak Force (MTF) has the strength consisting of 1 SP, 1 DSP, 6 Inspectors, 35 SIs, 69 H.Cs and 76 Constables (in all 188 Police personnel) for detection of Bangladesh nationals who managed to infiltrate into Tripura without valid documents. The figure since March 1971 to December 1982 is not readily available. However, the number of infiltrators detected at the border during the period from 1983 to 1991 is 29,382.

34. The infiltration in Tripura is also taking place because of following factors:

(a) Border is inadequately policed. There are only 11 Battalions of BSF sanctioned for Tripura sectors of Indo-Bangladesh border which is highly inadequate considering the length and nature of the border. However, 5 Battalions out of them have been redeployed elsewhere and at present Tripura has only 6 Battalions of BSF including one auxiliary Battalion. As a result not only the average distance between two posts is very large, the strength available in the posts too is inadequate for effective patrolling.

(b) MTF is understaffed and lacks vehicles for acquiring necessary mobility. Because of these limitations, MTF generally remains confined to a few urban areas only and cannot cover the rural areas effectively.

Mizoram

35. There is no PIF scheme in respect of the work of checking infiltration and is being done by the normal staff of police stations in border areas (ranging from 9 to 12 under Sub-Inspectors). These Police Officers are engaged in checking influx of Bangladeshi nationals. State police force detected and pushed back Bangladeshi nationals coming to Mizoram without proper permits. During Bangladesh War of 1971 about 3 lakh refugees of Bangladesh entered Mizoram and all of them were pushed back. 18,731 Bangladeshi nationals mostly Chakma refugees were detected from 1972 to December 1991 by State Police. 3,18,731 Bangladeshi nationals were detected during the period from 26-03-71 to 31-12-91. State police, BSF and District Deputy Commissioners are entrusted to monitor arrival/departure and overstay of Bangladeshi nationals.

Delhi

36. No dedicated machinery exists for this purpose. However, FRRO, Delhi has been entrusted with necessary powers to deport Bangladesh nationals.

Nagaland

37. No details are available.

Half-hearted Action

38. The administrative efforts in controlling the problem of massive illegal immigration from Bangladesh have been characterised by half-hearted, routine and adhoc approach. The seriousness of the

threat from unstemmed influx of BD immigrants has not permeated at all levels in the administrative machinery in the States. In some cases, the political forces and certain vested interests have made the task of checking infiltration by the State administrative machinery inconsequential and ineffective. Some of the important issues which have merged are:

(a) True dimensions of the problem of illegal immigration are not fully appreciated by the political and administrative systems in the State. The influence and indifference of political system has prevented concrete policy/initiatives being taken in the form of effective administrative measures to deal with this problem. The immigrants are treated as captive vote banks of political parties.
(b) The figures of detection of infiltrators on the borders of BSF and other agencies do not even remotely come anywhere near making a dent on the problem. At best, the miniscule percentage of detection only highlights the magnitude of the problem of illegal immigration.
(c) Detection of illegal immigrants is not being done in a systematic manner with well-defined goals and objectives.
(d) No proper records for documenting are being maintained in the States to prevent reinfiltration.
(e) Local police have paid little attention to check cases of overstay, detection of forged documents including birth certificates, false medical certificates by private physicians etc.
(f) The open border in certain pockets in Assam, Tripura and West Bengal indicates that there are porous sectors from where it is not difficult to enter into India. A short-term strategy in "sealing off" vulnerable sectors needs priority attention.

Measures Taken so far for Detection and Deportation of Illegal Bangladesh Immigrants

Functioning of the Central Schemes of Mobile Task Force and Prevention of Infiltration of Foreigners in West Bengal, North-eastern States and Bihar.

39. To check illegal immigration, administrative measures taken by the Government include:

(a) Strengthening of Border Security Force.
(b) Setting up of Prevention of Infiltration of Foreigners (PIF) scheme in North-eastern States.

Strengthening of Border Security Force

40. The Government of India have sanctioned a 5-year expansion programme in January, 1986 for strengthening the BSF on Indo-Bangladesh border. Under this programme the deployment pattern of the BSF would be redesigned so as to reduce distance between OPs, setting up more observation posts, powers for effective surveillance, providing BSF with additional vehicles for effective mobility and equipping the BSF with sophisticated equipments.

41. At present 40 Battalions of BSF have been employed on Indo-Bangladesh border. The following are the figures of detection by BSF of the illegal entrants during the last three years:

Year	*Hindu*	*Muslims*	*Total*
1989	5,449	15,821	21,270
1990	12,954	27,015	39,969
1991	11,446	36,276	47,772

Prevention of Infiltration of Foreigners Scheme

42. The Prevention of Infiltration of Foreigners (PIF) scheme is operating in the States of Assam, West Bengal, Tripura and Meghalaya with a view to assist the State Government in detection and deportation of illegal immigrants. Under this scheme the following number of posts have been authorised.

Assam	3153 posts
West Bengal	165 posts
Tripura	144 posts
Meghalaya	194 posts

43. In 1988, a special group was set up by the Ministry of Home Affairs to review the implementation of the PIF Scheme, recommend steps for improving portions of the scheme, and suggest measures for effective enforcement of instructions on the issue of RAPs to Nepalese in the North-eastern States. The Group submitted its report on 25-9-1989.

44. The main recommendations of the Group are sanction of additional posts under the PIF Scheme for the States of West Bengal (389 posts), Tripura (390 posts) and Meghalaya (40 posts). Six jeeps and six light vehicles (12 drivers) for West Bengal, and three jeeps and three light vehicles (and 6 drivers) for Tripura have also been recommended for Assam, because the State Govt.'s performance in the field of detection of foreigners had not been commensurate with the strength sanctioned, and there were reports about frequent diversion of PIF staff to law and order duties more than in any other State.

45. The Mobile Task Force in West Bengal and Tripura are part of the PIF scheme.

46. At present there is no central scheme for detection of infiltrants in Bihar. A State Government scheme envisages staff not only for identification and deportation of foreigners but also for prevention of their further infiltration in future. For this the State Government require 13 check posts manned by 13 Inspectors, 39 Sub-Inspectors, 26 Havildars and 117 guards. This part of the proposal is estimated to cost Rs. 31.11 lakhs.

47. State Governments propose to strengthen their Special Branch to get intelligence about infiltration. This part of the proposal involves expenditure of Rs. 11.30 lakhs.

48. Mobile Task Force are required for the Districts of Katihar and Purnia (since bifurcated into four districts). These will act promptly on the information given by the Special Branch. These will work under the direct control of DM and SP of their respective district.

APPENDIX 'A'

District-wise Strength of Bangladeshi Immigrants (Hindu) in South-West Bengal

(1) North 24 Parganas: 10,26,000; (2) South 24 Parganas: 3,05,000; (3) Nadia: 12,92,000; (4) Hoogly: 1,37,000; (5) Burdwan: 1,68,000; (6) Howrah: 25,000; (7) Maldah: 70,000; (8) Badkura: 36,000; (9) Murshidabad: 1,41,000; (10) West Dinajpur: 92,000; *Total 32,92,000.*

Location of Bangladeshi Immigrants (Hindu)

North 24 Parganas

(1) Durganagar: 10,000; (2) Birati: 5,000; (3) New Barackpur: 25,000; (4) Sajirhat-Bor Ghar: 25,000; (5) Madhyam Gram: 5,000; (6) Hridaypur: 10,000; (7) Barasat; 25,000; (8) Ganganagar, Doltala: 20,000; (9) Kanchra Para: 15,000; (10) Naihati: 10,000; (11) Bagda, Helencha, Asharu: 40,000; (12) Bhwanipur, Baneshwarpur, Ranaghat, Chuyatiya: 10,000; (13) Angrail: 10,000; (14) Rajarhat, Jagatpur, Kestapur, Jatragachhi, Ghurni: 1,20,000; (15) Dattapukur, Bamangachhi: 25,000; (16) Kovla Kadamgahhi: 50,000; (17) Bira, Guma, Ashoknagar: 50,000; (18) Habra: 60,000; (19) Maslandapur: 20,000; (20) Gobardanga: 10,000; (21) Thakur Nagar Area: 60,000; (22) Chandpara: 60,000; (23) Bongaon: 60,000; (24) Basirhat, Hasnabad: 50,000; (25) Dattabad, Saltlake: 12,000; (26) Dum Dum Cantonment, Dum Dum Junction: 30,000; (27) Bidhan Nagar: 30,000; (28) Palta: 20,000; (29) Jhilmil, Beleghata: 30,000; (30) Ichhapur: 5,000; (31) Shyam Nagar: 40,000; (32) Kharda: 24,000; (33) Belgharia, Agarpara, Sodpur: 30,000; *Total 10,26,000.*

South 24 Parganas

(1) Thakurpukur: 20,000; (2) Parnasree: 15,000; (3) Baghajatin, Santoshpur, Mukundapur: 20,000; (4) Ghutiasharif: 25,000; (5) Taldi: 15,000; (6) Canning and Adjacent Area: 25,000; (7) Basanti Sonakhali: 20,000; (8) Jharkhali Pakhankhali: 30,000;

(9) Gosaba: 25,000; (10) Sandeskhali: 15,000; (11) Sonarpur: 10,000; (12) Baruipur, Subhashgram: 10,000; (13) Tollyganj: 10,000; (14) Garia: 10,000; (15) Kakdwip: 20,000; (16) Namkhana: 20,000; (17) Frejarganj: 15,000; *Total 3,05,000.*

District—Nadia

(1) Fulia: 30,000; (2) Kalyani: 1,00,000; (3) Shantipur, Nabinpalli, Haripur, Bagdia, Gabar Char, Baghasra Proboddh Nagar: 2,00,000; (4) Betai: 70,000; (5) Betnua Dahari Thana: 50,000; (6) Rangaghat: 50,000; (7) Chakdah: 70,000; (8) Birnagar, Radha Nagar: 70,000; (9) Dhubulia: 50,000; (10) Jhikra-Harin Ghata: 2,000; (11) Krisnanagar, Depara, Rueypukur, Thakurtala, Sebagram, Simultala, Ambagan, Amghata, Maniktala, Patkathi Colony: 1,00,000; (12) Habibpur, Pulin Nagar, Kalai Ghata: 25,000; (13) Dhantala Thana: 1,00,000; (14) Batkulla: 10,000; (15) Kestoganj, Mazdia, Bimpur, Khalboalia, Asanagar, Banpur Gede: 1,60,000; (16) Gayeshpur: 60,000; (17) Mahisbatan: 40,000; (18) Chapra: 50,000; (19) Tehatta: 50,000; (20) Aishtala: 5,000; *Total 12,92,000.*

Hooghly

(1) Hindmotar, Konnagar, Dankuni, Uttarpara: 10,000; (2) Bhadreshwar: 5,000; (3) Chandan Nagar: 7,000; (4) Hooghly Station and Adjacent Area: 25,000; (5) Bandel: 30,000; (6) Guptipara, Charkrishnabati, Charsultanpur, Fultala, Rathhtala, Balagar: 25,000; (7) Tribeni, Magra: 25,000; (8) Kuntighat: 10,000; *Total 1,37,000.*

Bardwan

(1) Nibhuji, Dhatri Gram: 3,000; (2) Kalikatala, Samudra Gar: 10,000; (3) Bishwramba: 5,000; (4) Goyara: 5,000; (5) Chachai, Habaspur: 30,000; (6) Jourgram, Pal Para: 35,000; (7) Masa Gram: 10,000; (8) Sultanpur, Debipur: 5,000; (9) Durgapur, Majher Mana, Ashish Nagar: 30,000; (10) Budbud Panagar: 15,000; (11) Mankar: 5,000; (12) Kalna, Taltala, Sawaspur, Dighirpar, Aramtala, Sahapur: 15,000; *Total 1,68,000.*

Howrah

(1) Ulubaria: 15,000; (2) Belepul, Satragachhi: 10,000; *Total 25,000.*

Maldah

(1) Gajal: 20,000; (2) Pakua: 30,000; (3) Mangal Bari: 10,000; (4) Nala Gola: 10,000; *Total 70,000.*

Bakura

(1) Bakura: 10,000; (2) Rasul Pur: 5,000; (3) Salkar Char: 10,000; (4) Sonamukhi: 5,000; (5) Rangamati: 4,000; (6) Kakardanga: 2,000; *Total 36,000.*

Murshidabad

(1) Kandi: 7,000; (2) Berhampore: 10,000; (3) Jiaganj: 17,000; (4) Bhagwangola: 9,000; (5) Lalgola: 22,000; (6) Sagarpara: 26,000; (7) Jalangi: 38,000; (8) Banjetia: 12,000; *Total 1,41,000.*

West Dinajpur

(1) Gangarampur: 25,000; (2) Shibpur: 7,000; (3) Rajibpur: 5,000; (4) Balurghat: 30,000; (5) Trimohini: 15,000; (6) Hili: 10,000; *Total 92,000.*

This enumeration is only illustrative and not exhaustive at all. It covers only the visible concentration and does not include the immigrants who have merged with the population nor the very large number of immigrants who have settled down in North-West Bengal districts and other states.

APPENDIX 'B'

District-wise Presence of Bangladeshi Infiltrators (Muslims) in South-West Bengal and Bihar

(1) Calcutta: 1,04,500; (2) North 24 Parganas: 1,35,000; (3) South 24 Parganas: 28,000; (4) Nadia: 16,500; (5) Midnapore: 10,000; (6) Malda: 10,000; (7) Howrah: 47,000; (8) Hooghly: 6,000; (9) Burdwan: 8,000; (10) Mursidabad: 34,000; (11) Bihar: 35,000; *Total 4,54,000.*

Calcutta

(1) Bej Bridge: 2,000; (2) Tapshia: 8,000; (3) Park Circus: 6,000; (4) Cossipore: 8,000; (5) Tangra: 10,000; (6) Entally: 12,000; (7) Tiljala: 10,000; (8) Beleghata, Phulbagan: 5,000; (9) Narkedanga, Rajabazar: 12,000; (10) Burra Bazar: 5,000; (11) Ballyganj: 5,000; (12) Kiddepore: 10,000; (13) Garden Reach: 5,000; (14) Jaydevpur: 3,000; (15) Alipore: 2,000; (16) Putairi: 1,500; *Total 1,04,500.*

North 24 Parganas District

(1) Dum Dum: 10,000; (2) Dakhindari: 5,000; (3) Ultadangra: 5,000; (4) Dattabad: 3,000; (5) Matijhil: 5,000; (6) Dhupialala: 4,500; (7) Dhafanmath: 2,000; (8) Salt Lake: 3,000; (9) Jagatpur-Kestopur: 8,000; (10) Kakurgachi, Luthal, Jhilmil: 5,000; (11) Finga: 8,000; (12) Goharia-Majhpara, Chandugarh: 5,000; (13) Sarat Colony (Near Dum Dum): 3,000; (14) Guma-Namta: 5,000; (15) Dum Dum (Cantt): 5,000; (16) Air Port-Nayanpur—Ghughudanga: 5,000; (17) Barasat: 6,000; (18) Bakra; 4,000; (19) Dattapukur: 500; (20) Bamungachi: 2,000; (21) Maslandpur: 6,000; (22) Gaighata: 3,000; (23) Bira: 500; (24) Sajirhat: 1,000; (25) Shyamnagar-Kanchra, Para-Palta: 8,000; (26) Titagarh: 500; (27) Barrackpore: 5,000; (28) Doliala-Rajbari: 1,500; (29) Bashrihat-Hashnabad: 8,000; (30) Haroa Road (on both sides): 2,000; (31) Koira-Kadamgachi: 2,000 (There is a large concentration of Hindu immigrants also in this area. This leads to frequent communal

tension. The Muslim League MLA and the Panchayat Pradhan of the area support the Muslim Infiltrators and this has made them aggressive); (32) Bantala-Milan Nagar-Tubrighata: 5,000; *Total 1,35,000.*

South 24 Parganas District

(1) Chaubagau-Ghatak Pukur: 5,000; (2) Ghutia Shariff: 10,000; (3) Piali-Dhakuria: 5,000; (4) Taldi-Canning: 3,000; (5) Tiljala: 1,000; (6) Kidderpore Dock: 4,000; *Total 28,000.*

Nadia District

(1) Kalyani: 4,000; (2) Madanpur: 2,000; (3) Alpara-Chakdah: 2,000; (4) Ranaghat: 5,000; (5) Krishnagar: 1,500; (6) Barak Pur: 2,000; *Total 16,500.*

Midnapore District

(1) Nandakumar (By the sides of National Highway-6): 10,000; (2) Kazipara-Mullikpara: 5,000; *Total 15,000.*

Malda District

(1) Durgapur: 5,000; (2) Triholi: 5,000; *Total 10,000.*

Howrah District

(1) Kashiari-Amta: 10,000; (2) Shibpore: 3,000; (3) Andul: 5,000; (4) Sultanpur: 7,000; (5) Mullickpara: 3,000; (6) German Road: 3,000; (7) Das Nagar: 8,000; (8) Bolti Gate-Mohwri Station: 8,000; *Total 47,000.*

Hooghly District

(1) Bandel: 3,000; (2) Tribeni-Mongra-Bansbaria: 3,000; *Total 6,000.*

Burdwan District

(1) Samudragarh: 2,000; (2) Debipuri: 3,000; (3) Rasulpur: 3,000; *Total 8,000.*

(Muslim Panchayat Chairman of Rasulpur is helping Muslim infiltrators to settle down).

Nadia

(1) Chakdah and adjacent area: 2,000; (2) Madanpur: 2,000; (3) Kalyani: 4,000; (4) Ranaghat: 5,000; (5) Kirtnagore: 1,500; (6) Barak Pur: 2,000; *Total 16,500.*

Murshidabad

(1) Milan Nagar: 1,600; (2) Nawabganj: 5,000; (3) Madanpur Shehala: 2,000; (4) Bharatpur: 5,000; (5) Beldanga: 1,400; (6) Hazra: 1,000; (7) Baduria: 1,500; (8) Sirajdaulla Road (Murshidabad): 3,000; (9) Alinagar (Murshidabad): 2,000; (10) Belgachia: 1,000; (11) Kazipara: 1,500; (12) Sirajnagar: 5,000; (13) Barua: 4,000; *Total 34,000.*

(*Caution*: This enumeration is not to be considered exhaustive at all. This was an extremely modest effort carried out by way of sampling only in some limited areas in each district and was confined to visible concentrations of infiltrators. Does not include those who have merged with the population.)

Bihar

(1) Muzaffarpur adjacent area: 8,000; (2) Patna and adjacent area: 8,000; (3) Hazaribag adjacent area: 5,000; (4) Dhanbad adjacent area: 6,000; (5) Bubri Road Rangabad (Gaya): 3,000; *Total 35,000.*

(This is only a limited enumeration and does not cover Katihar—Kishanganj-Purnea-Samastipur belt which is the main concentration of Muslim immigrants in Bihar, particularly Bihari Muslims.)

Annexure XI

COPY OF EXPRESS LETTER NO. 26011/16/71—IC, DATED 29-11-1971 OF THE UNDER SECRETARY TO THE GOVERNMENT OF INDIA ADDRESSED TO THE CHIEF SECRETARIES TO ALL STATE GOVERNMENTS AND UNDER TERRITORY ADMINISTRATION

Sub: Grant of Indian citizenship to refugees from East-Bengal, who have crossed over to India after 25th March, 1971. Instructions that applications from such refugees for Indian Citizenship should not be entertained.

Refugees who have crossed over to India from East-Bengal since the 25th March 1971 on account of the situation in that area cannot be treated a ordinarily resident in India. They are expected to return to their native places when the conditions permit. They should not be considered for registration as Indian citizens under Section 5(I)(a) of the Citizenship Act, 1955, read with the Citizenship Rules, 1956. If such refugees make applications to the Collectors who are the prescribed authority for purposes of registration as Indian citizens under Section 5(I)(a) of the Citizenship Act, such applications should be rejected. Enquires on applications for registration under Sections 5(I)(a) of the Act should be made carefully to ensure that no refugees who has come after the 25th March, 1971 from East-Bengal gets registered as Indian citizen by giving any false declarations claiming to be resident in India for long and from a date prior to 25th March, 1971. Suitable instructions may kindly be issued in the matter to all Registering Authorities under your control immediately.

Annexure XII

GOVERNMENT OF ASSAM POLITICAL (B) DEPARTMENT DISPUR, GUWAHATI 781006 NO. PLB. 41/96/243, DATED DISPUR THE 12th OCTOBER, 1998

To

Shri Ambuj Sharma,
Director to the Govt. of India
Ministry of Home Affairs
(Foreigners Division), North Block,
New Delhi 110001

Subject: Repeal of Illegal Migrants (Determination by Tribunals Act, 1983.

Reference: Your letter No. 14011/28/96—FVI, dated 25-8-98.

Sir,

Kindly refer to your letter cited above regarding State Government's comments and no objection to winding up of the Foreigners Tribunals under Foreigners (Tribunals) Order, 1964 in the context of repeal of IMDT Act, 1983.

2. Under Foreigners (Tribunals) Order, 1964, Foreigners Tribunals were set up in Assam (presently 16 tribunals) to adjudicate upon as to whether a person is or is not a foreigner based on the grounds furnished by the registering authority i.e., district superintendents of police. These tribunals were set up in Assam in a situation of peculiar problem faced by it as a consequence of influx of Bangladeshi national into Assam. Directives then received from Govt. of India required that Bangladeshi (erstwhile East-Pakistan) nationals who had entered Assam prior to March, 1971 could not be sent back whereas migrants who entered Assam thereafter would have to be identified and deported. The purpose of these tribunals, therefore, was to determine the nationality of the migrants who

entered into the State prior to 25-3-71. These tribunals were not to deal with migrants entering Assam after 25-3-71. Post-25th March, 1971 migrants could be deported directly for which powers were delegated to the district superintendents of police and deputy commissioners under the Foreigners Act, 1946.

3. After the enactment of IMDT Act, 1983, a new set of procedures were laid down for detection and deportation of post-25-3-71 migrants which nullified provisions of Foreigners Act with respect to direct deportation. IMDT Act, 1983 also required setting up of tribunals to determine the nationality of the migrants who entered Assam after 25-3-71, through elaborate procedure of detection, verification, screening and reference to the IMDT tribunals. Working through the IMDT Tribunals and experience of the State administration brought into focus various lacunae in the Act which created practical constraints and impediments in achieving the objectives of identification and deportation of illegal migrants.

4. The Assam Accord was signed on 15th August, 1985 which specified another classification of Bangladeshi migrants, i.e., foreigners who came to Assam between 1-1-66 and 24-3-71. The Assam Accord provided for detection of this category of migants and deletion of their names from the electoral rolls for a period of ten years (from the date of detection) following which their names would be restored in the electoral rolls. The Assam Accord also provided that detection of this category of migrants would be done in accordance with the provisions of the Foreigners Act, 1946 and Foreigners' (Tribunal) Order 1964.

5. As long as the Assam (Accord) remains in operation the State Administration will have to carry on the work of detection, categorisation, disenfranchisement (for ten years from the date of detection) and subsequent restoration in the electoral rolls of 1966–71 stream migrants in terms of the provisions of Foreigners Act, 1946 and Foreigners (Tribunals) Order, 1964. This will be a continuing task for quite some time till each case falling within the first stream, i.e., 1-1-66 to 24-3-71, is dealt with under Foreigners Act, 1946 and Foreigners (Tribunal) Order, 1964.

6. Continuance of Foreigners Tribunals is also necessary in the context of the Citizenship (Amendment) Act, 1985. Under this amended Act (Sec 6 AO) detection of a foreigner has to be done as

per the provision of the Foreigners Act, 1946 and the Foreigners (Tribunals) Order, 1964 by a Foreigners Tribunal.

7. Therefore, in view of what has been stated above and having regard to the Assam Accord and the citizenship (Amendment) Act, 1985, Foreigners Tribunals set up under Foreigners (Tribunals) Order, 1964 will be required to function. Accordingly State Government feel that the existing Foreigners Tribunals should not be wound up at this stage.

Yours faithfully,
Sd/-
(M.S. Pangtey)
Addl. Chief Secretary

Additional Chief Secretary
And Principal Secretary to the
Government of Assam
Commissioner & Secretary, IAA Department
(Border), Assam, Guwahati 22.

Annexure XIII

IN THE SUPREME COURT OF INDIA
CIVIL ORIGINAL JURISDICTION

Write Petition (Civil) No. 125 of 1998
(Under Article 32 of the Constitution of India)

In the matter of:

All India Lawyers Forum for Civil Liberties (AIFCL) & Another.

... Petitioners.

Versus

Union of India and Others.

... Respondents.

COUNTER AFFIDAVIT on behalf of the Respondent No. 3.

State of West Bengal

I, Saralindu Sekhar Rakshit, aged about 57 years, son of Late Sudhangshu Sekhar Rakshit, by faith Hindu, by occupation service holder, personally working for gain at the Writers Buildings, Calcutta, do hereby solemnly affirm and say as follows:

1. I am the Joint Secreatary, Home (Political) Department Government of West Bengal. I have been authorised by the Respondent No. 3 to affirm this affidavit on its behalf.

2. I am acquainted with the facts and circumstances of the case and having access to the relevant records stated in this affidavit I am competent to affirm this affidavit.

3. I have read a copy of the writ petition upon which notice has been issued and have understood the contents and purports thereof.

4. With reference to Paragraphs 1 to 6 of the Writ Petition in so far as the State of West Bengal is concerned, I may state the

following:

(A) The State of West Bengal has a very long land border with Bangladesh. Out of about 2203 long border, about 643.59 km is riverine. Most of the border is long flat terrain without any natural demarcation.

(B) There is no fencing, wall or any other kind of physical demarcation or barring. The arrangement for interception of infiltrators is not adequate for keeping continuous uninterrupted vigil along the entire length of the border.

(C) The task of effective sealing and closing the border is mainly done by deploying personnel of the Border Security Force which is a Government of India Organisation. The sanctioned strength of the Border Security Force is inadequate to match with the problem of keeping continuous uninterrupted vigil along the entire length of the long border stretching over 2,203 kilometers. As of now, at the border, the deployment of Border Security Force has been much below the sanctioned limit provided for such deployment. In addition to Border Security Force, the Mobile Task Force of the State Government also, in co-ordination with the Border Security Force Personnel, carry out the task of sealing and closing the border. It is necessary to augment Mobile Task Force. At the meeting convened by the Union Home Ministry on 24th August, 1998 which was presided over by the Union Home Secretary, these issues were highlighted. But as on date, there has not been any perceptible improvement in regard to the deployment of Border Security Force personnel or any augmentation of Mobile Task Force.

(D) It appears that between 1972 and 1997 a total number 9,91,031 Bangladeshi nationals entered into Indian territory with valid travel documents but they did not return to Bangladesh and have overstayed.

It may be noted that under First proviso to Section 2 of the Registration of Foreigners (Bangladesh) Rules, 1973, it is not necessary for a Bangladeshi national to obtain a registration certificate unless he intends to stay for more than 180 days. There is a donsequent difficulty in ascertaining the place of residence of such overstaying Bangladeshi nationals. Sometimes, it is found that the local addresses furnished by such persons are fictitious and it becomes extremely difficult to trace them out. In some cases, they change their address quite quickly and renders it difficult to take necessary steps for their deportation. Strict enforcement of the requirement of registration of foreigners in the case of Bangladeshi Nationals and also introduction of the practice of a rigorous scrutiny and verification of Indian sponsors of Bangladeshi nationals before visa is granted to them, may be considered by the Government of India.

(E) There has been substantial improvement in the situation and it will appear that between 1990 and 1997 a total number of 2,35,762 infiltrators who had entered into India through clandestine routes, have been detected and pushed back to Bangladesh. Such pushing back had been authorised and advised by the Government of India from time to time. This figure excludes the persons pushed back by other State Governments.

(F) The Government of West Bengal has all along been making every effort possible to stop infiltration and has been taking every possible step to push back or deport the infiltrators whenever detected. The idea of engaging Central Bureau of Investigation in such work is wholly misconceived and unwarranted. The nature of investigation CBI has the resources to undertake is not at all commensurate with the type of huge task of stopping infiltration of Bangladeshis and when detected deporting such Bangladeshis. Delhi Special Police Establishment Act which has established the CBI, provide for investigation of particular offences by the Officers of the Central Bureau treating such Officers as Officers-in-Charge of the particular area which is coterminous with the local police station. As such Central Bureau is eminently unsuited to perform the job.

(G) Recently with a view to preventing acquisition of documents for the purpose of establishing falsely that a

Bangladeshi is an Indian citizen, West Bengal Government issued a notice in the matter of issue of new ration cards and has widely publicised the same through various newspapers. It has specifically been mentioned there that the certificates issued by any government officials, office bearers of Gram Panchayat, Panchayat Samity, Municipal Commissioners Zilla Parishad Members, MPs, MLAs, may simply be corroborative evidence but such certificates will not be conclusive proof. At the same time, absence of such certificates will not be deterrent to obtaining a ration card if on proper inquiry the applicant is found to be duly entitled. It has specifically been mentioned in that notice that if it appears in course of investigation that the applicant had entered into Indian from Bangladesh after 25 March, 1971, Certificate of Citizenship must be insisted before issue of such ration card.

A copy of the notice is annexed hereto and marked as Annexure.

(H) The Government of West Bengal has consistently been trying to have the Mobile Task Force augmented and the strength of Border Security Force increased. The efforts have not met with much success. On 18 June, 1996, in response to a Fax Message from the Ministry of Home Affairs, Government of India, a Fax Message was sent by the Joint Secretary, Home (Police) Department, Government of West Bengal, giving the details of financial implications of the proposal for augmentation of Mobile Task Force staff in West Bengal in the first phase.

A Copy of the said Fax Message is annexed hereto and marked with letter R-3/2.

(I) It may be worthwhile to mention that the proposal for erecting barbed wire fences has also not progressed satisfactorily. There has been a proposal to erect barbed wire fences along 507 kilometers of land border. But this task has also not yet been completed. Moreover, erecting the barbed wire fencing at a distance of 150 yards from the zero line has resulted in leaving some of the Indian families in between the border and barbed wire fencing. In a letter dated 15 May, 1998, written by the Principal Secretary, Home Department, Government of West Bengal to the Secretary, Ministry of Home Affairs, Government of India, this problem was highlighted and it was pointed out that unless the fencing is carried out at zero line, serious dissatisfaction and despair among the people living between the zero line and the border will render ultimately the attempt of fencing infrustuous. Besides, such erection of fences would have removed the grievances of the local people and would have quickened the process of completion of the task.

A copy of the said letter is annexed hereto and marked with letter R-3/3.

(J) It may also be pointed out that Bangladesh Government has not so far shown any willingness to formally accept those who are sought to be deported in exercise of powers under Section 3(2)(c) of the Foreigners Act, 1946. In fact Bangladesh Government has not shown even willingness to accept those who are sought to be deported on the basis of court orders. Consequently, all actions for pushing back infiltrators are turning out to be infructuous. Many of those who were pushed back re-entered into Indian Territory through clandestine routes.

Annexure XIV

EXCERPTS FROM SUPPLEMENTARY AFFIDAVIT ON BEHALF OF THE GOVERNMENT OF WEST BENGAL

6. (a) Passenger traffice along the border is regulated through International Check Posts. These International Check Posts keep a record of Bangladeshis entering into India with valid documents and submit periodical reports in respect of persons overstaying their visas. Between 1972 and November 1998, a total number of 10,24,322 Bangladeshis (Hindus 6,67,500, Muslims 3,49,738, others 7,084) who entered into Indian territory with bonafide travel documents, have overstayed.

Enquiries held at the addresses of their Indian referees have revealed that in a majority of cases such addresses are either fictitious or that the Bangladeshi has never visited his referee after coming to India.

(b) A year-wise statement of Bangladeshis who have overstayed their visas is enclosed marked 'AA'.

(c) Rigorous search for tracing them out have mostly failed. Until recently there was no local resistance, nor even co-operation of the local people in identifying Bangladeshis who have settled amongst residents of West Bengal.

7. (a) The number of Bangladeshi nationals who have entered India clandestinely without valid documents is likely to be much higher.

During 1972 to November 1998—5,73,334 Bangladeshi Nationals (1,61,077 Hindus, 4,08,349 Muslims and 3908 others) had been detected to have clandestinely entered into India and they had been pushed back across the border.

(b) A year-wise statement of Bangladeshi Nationals who have been pushed back across the border is enclosed and marked 'BB'.

8. The responsibility of checking infiltration across the border rests primarily with the Border Security Force (hereinafter referred to as BSF). For operational convenience the border falling in West Bengal has been divided into two sectors: (i) South Bengal Frontier headed by an Inspector General with Headquarters at Calcutta, is in-charge of the border in the districts of South 24-Parganas, North 24-Parganas, Nadia, Murshidabad, Malda and Dakshin Dinajpur, (ii) North-Bengal Frontier headed by an Inspector General with Headquarters at Siliguri, is in-charge of the border in the districts of Uttar Dinajpur, Darjeeling, Jalpaiguri and Cooch Bihar.

The South Bengal Frontier stretches over 1150 kms including 150 kms of reverine border and the North Bengal Frontier stretches over 1053 kms including 109 kms of riverine border. The sanctioned strength of the BSF for the entire border is 34 Battalions including two Reserve Battalions. At present only 20 Battalions are physically deployed at the border. The rest of the force has been withdrawn for duties elsewhere in the country. In all the BSF mans 405 border outposts along the West Bengal portion of the Indo-Bangladesh border. 226 of such border outposts are located in the Southern Frontier and 179 in the Northern Frontier. The average strength of these border outposts range from two sections to one platoon of force and between themselves they have to patrol and prevent infiltration over five to six kms of the border. Taking into consideration the nature of the border, the BSF presently deployed at the border is absolutely inadequate to prevent infiltration.

9. (a) The Government of India had sanctioned the construction of 1597 kms border roads and 507 kms of barbed wire fence along the Indo-Bangladesh border, covering the vulnerable stretches. Till November 1998; construction of 1232.82 kms of road and 455.14 kms of fence had been completed.

(b) A district-wise chart is enclosed marked 'CC'.

10. There are in all 11 International Check Posts along the Indo-Bangladesh border to regulate passenger traffic across the border. Except for the Check Post at Haridaspur, all others lack elementary infrastructure like accommodation, communication facilities etc. The State Government has initiated steps to upgrade these International Check Posts with financial assistance from the Government of India. These International Check Posts keep a record

of Bangladeshi Nationals entering into India with valid documents and submit periodical reports in respect of persons overstaying their visas. Enquiries held at the addressees of their Indian referees have revealed that in a majority of cases such addresses are either fictitious or such Bangladeshis had actually not come there at any time during their visit to India. Unless pre-verification of the referees is held before the issue of visas keeping track of such foreigners will continue to be difficult.

11. To detect and push back Bangladeshi Nationals who have succeeded in crossing the border unauthorisedly, the Government of India had sanctioned the creation of a Mobile Task Force for West Bengal. The present strength of this force is 1 Superintendent of Police, 2 Deputy Superintendents of Police, 11 Inspectors, 51 Sub-Inspectors and 100 Head Constables totalling to 165 members of the force. It need not be emphasised that the strength of this force is too merge to deal with the problem of infiltration emanating from more than two thousand km long border. In neighbouring Assam the sanctioned strength of the Mobile Task Force is 3,153 officers and men. Government of West Bengal has repeatedly been entreating Government of India to augment this force, in keeping with the nature and volume of the task with which it has been entrusted. These entreaties are yet to find favour with the Government of India.

12. Till 1997 Bangladeshis intercepted in the bordering areas were being summarily pushed back in keeping with the instructions issued by the Government of India in their Circular No. 14011/8/96-F. VI dated 16-9-97. Thereafter the Bangladeshi authorities having resisted such summary push back, instructions have now been issued that such Bangladeshi Nationals, irrespective of the places of their interception, have to be prosecuted under the Foreigners Act and pushed back-deported only after an appropriate order from a competent court.

13. While it is relatively easy to detect, prosecute and push back Bangladeshis intercepted during transit, it is quite difficult to identify those who have already settled in the districts due to the following reasons:

(i) Their features, dress and langauge are largely similar to the residents of West Bengal;

(ii) Many of them have acquired ration cards and have been enlisted in the electoral rolls with the help of local touts and unscrupulous officials and politicians;

(iii) Many sections of the local people, including political leaders of all hues, harbour a sympathy for them and are reluctant to cooperate in their identification and deportation; and

(iv) The sheer number of such Bangladeshis believed to have entered into India after 1971, makes it humanly impossible to prosecute all of them under the Foreigners Act, get a conviction and a court order in respect of each one of them and thereafter push them back to Bangladesh.

Annexure XV

EXCERPTS FROM AFFIDAVIT ON BEHALF OF THE STATE OF ASSAM

14. That in the year 1983, the Parliament enacted Illegal Migrants (Determination by Tribunals) Act, 1983 [hereinafter referred to as the IM(DT) Act] to deal with the problem of influx of illegal migrants to Assam. Though this Act extends to the whole of India, it was applicable to the State of Assam only. The Act provides for the establishment of Tribunals for the determination of the question whether a person is illegal migrant or not to enable the Government to expel illegal migrants from India. The Act was made applicable to those illegal migrants who entered into India on or after the 25th March, 1971.

14.1. That Section 4 of the Illegal Migrants (Determination by Tribunals) Act, gives overriding effect to the provisions of this Act over other enactments on the subject including the Foreigners Act, 1946. Under Section 5 of the Act, Tribunals were constituted for the purpose of detection of foreigners and the member of the Tribunals could be only those person who is or has been a District Judge or an Additional District Judge in any State. Under Section 8 of the Act, detailed provisions have been made for reference to the Tribunal for deciding as to whether any person is or is not an illegal migrant. It is pertinent to note that application can be made by a person to the Tribunal only if he resides within the jurisdiction of the same Police Station where the suspect resides. Further, the application is required to be accompanied by affidavit of two persons and application fee of not less than Rs. 10 and not more than Rs. 100. Under Section 8A, a person can make application to the Central Government for making a reference to the Tribunal. Such application can also be made only by a person residing within the jurisdiction of the same Revenue Sub-Division as that of the suspect. Under Section 14, an Appellate tribunals is constituted for hearing appeals against the orders of the Tribunals. The Appellate tribunals is constituted by a person who is or has been a Judge of a High Court. Under Section 20, the Central Government is required to serve on the illegal migrant so determined by the tribunal to remove himself from India. Under Section 20(2), only an officer not below the rank of Superintendent of Police has the power to ensure compliance of the order of removal passed by the Central Government. Under Section 21, the Central Government may delegate its powers to the State Government. Under Section 28, the Central Government can make rules to carry out its provisions.

14.2. That under Section 21 of the Act, Central Govt. By notification delegated its powers under Sections 5, 6, 7, 8, 8A, 14, 15 and 20 to the State Government.

14.3 That the Central Government in exercise of powers under Section 28 of the IM (DT) Act framed rules, namely Illegal Migrants (determination by Tribunals) Rules, 1984 [hereinafter referred to as the IM (DT) Rules]. These Rules stipulate enquiries at various levels before a reference can be made to the Tribunal. Under Rule 4, a Superintendent of Police or a Sub-Inspector of Police can call upon a person suspected to be illegal migrant to give particulars in Form-I. It is however, pertinent to note that such police officer has no power to compel the person to give information sought for in Form-I. Under Rule 7, the Inquiry Officer is required to submit his report in Form-II to Screening Committee constituted under Rule 8 which consists of the Sub-Divisional Officer and a Police Officer not below the rank of Deputy Superintendent of Police. Under Rule 8(2), the Screening Committee scrutinises the information received from the Inquiry Officer and after considering the relevant materials makes its recommendation to the Superintendent of Police as to whether the person mentioned in the report is or is not an illegal migrant. It is only if the Screening Committee makes its recommendation that the suspected person is an illegal migrant that a reference can be made to the Tribunal Under Rule 9.

15. That under the IM (DT) Act, 16 Tribunals were constituted to cover 23 Districts of Assam. As per provisions of the IM (DT) Act, only the person who is or has been a District Judge or an Additional District Judge can be appointed as member of the Tribunal. However, under the Foreigners (Tribunal) Order, 1964 any person

having judicial experience can be appointed as a member of the Tribunal. The State Government despite repeated advertisements have not been able to get qualified persons for appointment in some vacant posts as members of the Tribunal. The State Government has written to all the Deputy Commissioners to personally contact the retired District Judges or Additional District Judges of their respective areas who are not more than 63 years of age and obtain their willingness to join as Chairman/Member of the Illegal Migrants Determination Tribunal. The State Government has also written a letter to the Registrar of the High Court to funish the list of District Judges/Additional District Judges (serving or retired) who can be appointed as Chairman/Member of the Illegal Migrants Determination Tribunal/Foreigners Tribunal.

16. That the status as on 31-5-99 with regard to number of inquiries made by the Inquiry Officer and the Screening Committee and the cases referred and decided by the Illegal Migrants Determination Tribunals is as here under:

01	Total number of enquiries initiate	3,02,554
02	Total number of enquiries completed	3,00,165
03	Total number of enquiries referred to Screening Committee	2,96,564
04	Total number of enquiries made by Screening Committee	2,93,636
05	Total number of enquiries referred to the IM(DTs)	31,264
06	Total number of enquiries disposed of by the IM(DTs)	15,142
07	Total number of persons declared as Illegal Migrants	9,625
08	Total number of Illegal Migrants physically expelled	1,461
09	Total number of 1Ms to whom Expulsion orders served	5,667
10	Total number of enquiries pending with Screening Committee	2,920
11	Total number of enquiries pending with the Tribunals	16,122

It is submitted that the Screening Committee under the IM(DT) Rules have rejected the cases for reference to IM(DT) Tribunals due to lack of positive evidence since under the IM(DT) Act it is the Government or the Complainant with payment of fees and affidavit who is required to establish by positive evidence that the suspect is an illegal migrant. However, to the contrary under the Foreigners Act, under Section 9, the onus is on the suspect to prove that he is not a foreigner. Section 9 of the Foreigners Act reads as under:

"9. Burden of Proof: If in any case not falling under Section 8 any question arise with reference to this Act or any order made

or direction given thereunder, whether any person is or is not a foreigner or is not a foreigner of a particular class or description the onus of proving that such person is not a foreigner or is not a foreigner of such particular class or description, as the case may be, shall, notwithstanding anything contained in the Indian Evidence Act, 1872 (1 to 1872) lie upon such person."

17. That the IMDT Act is a discriminatory piece of Legislation, because it has made impermissible geographical classification for its application in a particular State only without justification/reason. The object of Legislation is to detect 'Illegal migrants' which is species of foreign national, in order to deport such foreigners. There cannot be any geographical differentiation with the manner of defection and deportation as has been Practiced in the IMDT Act. As such differentia not pertinent to the object of the Legislation and the object to the achieved has no nexus to the classification.

Further, the IMDT Act, within its area of operation, introduced a new 'cut off date,' namely 25-3-1971, for the purpose of defining 'illegal Migrants' who is inter alia, is a foreigner. But for determination of such foreigner the Constitution of India under Article 5 has already laid down such 'cut of date.' So without amending the Constitution, in respect of 'cut of date' as prescribed by the Constitution introduction of new 'cut of date' is wholly illegal and is not sustainable. As the provisions of IMDT Act are much more strict than provisions of the Foreigners Act, State of Assam found many difficulties and impediments in the implimentation of the IM (DT) Act. Even the Hon'ble Governor of Assam submitted a report to the Hon'ble President of India in November, 1998 on illegal migrants and the impediments in the implimentation of IM (DT) Act.

The Government of India in the tripartite meeting with the State of Assam and All Assam Students Union held at New Delhi on 1-7-1999 assured that the repeal of IM (DT) Act is under active consideration of the Government of India. In this meeting various other issues relating to illegal migration were discussed and decisions were taken. Some of the decision taken in the meeting are as under:

(i) The proposal submitted by Government of Assam for creation of additional posts for PIF/MTF was discussed. It was informed that additional posts cannot be considered.

(ii) It was noted that 1000 personnel of PIF/MTF have not been stationed as second line of defence so far. It was decided that 500 personnel would be stationed by July 31, 1999 and another personnel by September 30, 1999.

(iii) Government of Assam informed that 1000 posts are vacant in PIF/MTF. They requested that they may be allowed to fill up these positions not from ex-servicemen but from general category. It was agreed that atleast 500 of the vacant positions should be filed up as per existing norms so that delay is avoided.

Meanwhile, the request of Government of Assam would be considered and decision communicated.

(iv) It was agreed that Rs. 171 crores proposal of Government of Assam additional roads and fencing is recommended for sanction.

(v) AASU urged that an Ordinance be issued for repeal of IM(DT) Act, 1983. Government of Assam representatives supported for issuance of ordinance in this regard. The repeal of IM(DT) Act, 1983 is under active consideration of Government of India. This has also been stated in the address of Hon'ble President of India to the Parliament in February 1999.

State Government has written to the Central Government on a number of occasions for either to repeal the IM (DT) Act or to make necessary amendments in the said Act in order to facilitate the State to detect and deport the illegal migrants.

18. That the major impediments faced by the State of Assam in the effective implementation of the IM (DT) Act are as here under:

(i) The onus of proof is on the prosecution under IM (DT) Act as opposed to the provisions of Foreigners Act, 1946 under which the onus is on the suspected foreigner.

(ii) There is no provision in IM (DT) Act for compelling the suspects to furnish the particulars required in Form No. 1 of IM (DT) Rules of 1984 and penal provision to deal with such suspects in case of their refusal to furnish information as required in Rule 5.

(iii) There is no provision for compelling suspects/witnesses to furnish information or statement to Police Officers making Enquiry and as such, taking recourse to action under Section 176 IPC is difficult in case of refusal.

(iv) The Enquiry Officer is not empowered to search homes/ premises of the suspects nor can they compel the suspects to produce documents or give the necessary information.

(v) Prosecution witnesses do not appear before the Tribunals for want of necessary allowances.

(vi) Once Tribunals declare a person as an illegal migrant he/she becomes un-traced either before the notice is served or during the grace period of 30 days.

(vii) The notice/summons issued by the Tribunals cannot be served due to change of residence by the illegal migrants to some unknown destinations.

(viii) Expulsion orders cannot be served as the illegal migrants change their places of residence very frequently and merge with people of similar ethnic origin.

(ix) It is provided in the Act for filing a complaint against a person to determine as to whether the person is an illegal migrant, two persons living within the same police station are required and an amount of Rs. 10,000 has to be deposited with the application/complaint. This provision of the Act, puts a severe restriction in the matter of filing any complaint against any illegal migrant.

(x) The Tribunals after observing a long drawn procedure declare a person as illegal migrant who is to be deported from India. But very often, the persons declared as illegal migrants change their residence and shift to some other areas.

(xi) There are instances of strong resistance to enquiry officer conducting enquiries against the illegal migrants in Char Areas (Riverine areas) and other areas where there is a heavy concentration of immigrant population. The SPs Police who are otherwise busy dealing with law and order problems have virtually little force to spare for assisting the enquiry officers.

19. It is further submitted that even after detection of foreigners under the Foreigners Act/IM (DT) Act, the physical deportation of such illegal migrants has not been possible in most of the cases.

The Quit India notice is served on the Bangladesh nationals under Section 3 of the Foreigners Act, 1946 and under Section 20 of the IM (DT) Act, 1983 by the Foreigner Registration Officer for two categories of foreigners viz. (i) Bangladesh Nationals who have entered India on or after 25th March, 1971 (ii) and persons who are declared as foreign nationals and deported and later on re-infiltrated as per provisions laid down under the laws. Under the present dispensation Quit India/Expulsion is dependent on the verification report from Bangladesh Government as Bangladesh Rifles does not accept Bangladesh nationals unless nationality is again investigated by the Bangladesh Government. The Foreigner Registration Officers issue the Quit India notice or push back orders as per provisions laid down in the Foreigner Act and IM (DT) Act as mentioned above. But due to the insistence of compulsory verification of the nationality of the Bangladesh nationals by a Bangladesh Agency the desired result is not achieved. Besides this the State Government Authority (concerned SP) cannot keep a person (IM) in police custody for more than 24 hours under Section 57 Cr. PC, 1973. Further there is no provisions for meeting expenses resulting from keeping such foreigners/IMS until their deportation.

20. That the State Government has taken various steps to prevent future illegal migration into the Indian territory from Bangladesh. Some of the steps taken are as hereunder:

(i) Night curfew is promulgated which is in force at Border Districts of Assam and as a measure of deterrent to infiltration at night. In addition the works done by PIF Officers in identification, detection and deportation of foreign national are being quarterly reviewed and suitable instructions are issued to the staff of PIF Schemes for improving the performance.

(ii) Some illegal migrants are using Tripura and West Bengal as corridor for entering in Assam. After detection these illegal migrants claimed to be the residents of Tripura. Inter State Check Post under the PIF Scheme have been set up one at

Srirampur on West Bengal Assam Border and another at Churaibari on Assam Tripura Border.

(iii) In service training for the field officers are arranged at regular interval to improve their field efficiency by imparting lessons on essential acts.

(iv) Speedy completion of border roads and fencing.

21. The State Government respectfully submits that this Hon'ble Court may be pleased to give directions in the following regard to the Government of India both for the purpose of deportation of illegal migrants and for the purpose of preventing further illegal infiltration into the Indian territory:

(i) Repeal/substantial amendment in the Illegal Migrants (Determination by Tribunals) Act, 1983 in view of the impediments in detection and deportation of illegal migrants under the provisions of the said Act as pointed out aforesaid;

(ii) Reduce the distance between two BSF posts on the borders from 6-8 kms to 2-3 kms;

(iii) Creation of dedicated BSF exclusively for Assam and involving the local youth in the said Force;

(iv) Watch the borders with high-tech facilities like satellite surveillance, improving communication facilities, ensuring mobility on the roads as well as on rivers;

(v) Co-ordination with Bangladesh Government to accept the illegal migrants once they are determined as foreigners/ illegal migrants by the Courts/Tribunals of our country;

(vi) Proposal of multi-purpose photo identity cards should be implemented forthwith particularly in the border villages. This work should be done in a time frame. Issue of Photo Identity Cards to the genuine Indian Citizen will go a long way in checking the illegal migration. The Election Commission of India's move to issue Photo Identity Cards to the Indian voters appears to be a step in right direction for checking the illegal migration from the neighbouring countries.

While issuing the Photo Identity Cards as above, a suitable process will have to be evolved to ensure that no illegal migrant retain his name in the Voters List and the names of such illegal migrants are completely deleted from the Voters List immediately after detection.

Photo Identity Cards as an when issued could also be used for grant of work permits to by duly authenticated by competent authority for engagement in non-governmental job, like contractors, labour, vendors, menials etc.

22. It is pertinent to mention here that in the recent past there appears to be a close nexus between the illegal Migrants and the Fundamentalist organisation on the one hand and between the Fundamentalist organisations and Pak ISI (Pakistan Inter-Services Intelligence) on the other. The Pakistan ISI has increased their nefarious activities in India whose action plan inter alia includes subverting the Border Areas by utilising the Fundamentalist Organisations in carrying out Anti-India activities. The recent arrests of 4 (four) Pakistani Inter-Services Intelligence (ISI) Agents at Guwahati Assam, has amply proved the sinister activities of the ISI and its well-laid plans in league with Muslim Fundamentalist Organisation as well as ULFA and other Militants Outfits for destabilisation of the State by indulging in large-scale subversive activities which is a cause of serious concern for the safety, security and integrity of the Nation.

The State of Assam assures this Hon'ble Court that it is taking the issue of detection and deportation of illegal migrants and prevention of further illegal migrants into Assam with all seriousness and sincerity.

Ganesh Kumar Kalita
Joint Secretary, Political Government of Assam
DEPONENT

VERIFICATION

I, the above named deponent, do hereby verify that the contents of above affidavit are true and correct, no part of it is false and nothing material has been concealed there from.

Verified at Guwahati on this 1st the day of Sept., 1999.

The Contributors

Bezboruah, D.N., Editor, Sentinel, Guwahati.

Bhuyan, J.C., Former Deputy Director, Census, Assam.

Chandra, Naresh, IAS (Retd.) former Cabinet Secretary, Government of India; former Indian Ambassador to the USA.

Changkakoti, N., IPS (Retd.), former Director General of Police, Assam; former Vigilance Commissioner, Assam.

Das, H.N., IAS (Retd.), former Chief Secretary, Assam.

Gill, K.P.S., IPS (Retd.), former Director General of Police, Punjab; President, Institute for Conflict Management; Editor, Faultlines, New Delhi.

Gopalkrishnan, R., Dr. Professor, Department of Geography, North-Eastern Hill University, Shillong.

Hazarika, Sanjoy, Senior journalist/columnist and author; formerly Senior Fellow, Centre for Policy Research, New Delhi; Managing Trustee-Settlor, Centre for North-East Studies and Policy Research, New Delhi.

Kumar, B.B., Dr. Secretary, Astha Bharati, Delhi; Editor, Dialogue and Chintan Srijan.

Madhab, Jayanta, Dr. Development Economist, former Director, Asian Development Bank; former Chairman, NEDFI; President, Astha Bharati, New Delhi.

Mishra, Udayan, Dr. Professor, Department of English, Dibrugarh University.

Pandey, Onkareshwar, Journalist with Sahara TV.

Pramanik, Bimal, Director, Centre for Research in Indo-Bangladesh Relations, Kolkata.

Ray, Jayanta Kumar, Dr. Formerly Centenary Professor of International Relations, Calcutta University; former Vice-chairman, Maulana Abul Kalam Azad Institute of Asian Studies, Kolkata.

Roy, J.N., IPS (Retd.), formerly Commissioner, Civil Aviation Securities, former Joint Director, IB; Treasurer, Astha Bharati, Delhi.

Saha, Arunodaya, Dr., Professor, Department of Economics, Tripura University, Agartala.

Saikia, Anup, Dr., Reader, Department of Geography, Guwahati University.

Sarma, Arun K., Dr., M.P. (Lok Sabha), formerly, Member, Rajya Sabha.

Singh, Prakash, IPS (Retd.), Padmashri, formerly Director General of Border Security Force; former DGP, Assam; former DGP, UP; has written books/papers on Nagaland, Naxalite Movement, Disaster Response and on Terrorism.

Thomas, C. Joshua, Deputy Director, ICSSR, NERC, Shillong

Vohra, N.N., IAS (Retd.), former Home Secretary, Government of India.

Index